Cleethorpes

The Creation
of a Seaside Resort

Cleethorpes in 2000, after more than two centuries as a resort. This photograph illustrates the growth of the town from the three ancient hamlets of Oole, Itterby and Thrunscoe and also shows how the town merges into Grimsby to the north and west. The latter's docks and dock tower are at the top of the picture. Opposite the Boating Lake, in the lower left-hand quadrant, is the vacant land currently under development as the Meridian Point Leisure and Retail Park.

Cleethorpes

The Creation
of a Seaside Resort

Alan Dowling

Phillimore

2005

Published by
PHILLIMORE & CO. LTD
Shopwyke Manor Barn, Chichester, West Sussex, England

ISBN 1 86077 343 5

Printed and bound in Great Britain by
THE CROMWELL PRESS
Trowbridge, Wiltshire

*Dedicated to my two Dorothys and
Sheila and Anne for making me so welcome*

Contents

List of Illustrations

Frontispiece: Cleethorpes, 2000

Illustrations are included by courtesy of the North East Lincolnshire Libraries and Museums (4, 6-10, 14-31, 33-4, 36, 41-54, 65-9, 73-4 76, 78, 82, 84, 86, 91-6, 98, 101-2), the *Grimsby Telegraph*, www.thisisgrimsby.co.uk (frontispiece, 38, 88-9, 97, 100, 104, 106, 109, 110), the North East Lincolnshire Archives (56, 64) and the Trustees of the Manchester Regiment Archive (58). Several generous private collectors have also been most helpful (32, 35, 55, 60, 62, 70-72, 75, 79, 81, 90, 99). The remaining illustrations were provided by the author.

Maps are reproduced with the kind permission of the Ordnance Survey (3, 40, 57, 87, 103), Rex Russell (5, 11) and the North East Lincolnshire Archives (12, 13). Illustration 1 is taken from C. W. Foster and T. Longley, *The Lincolnshire Domesday and the Lindsey Survey* (1924) and 39 has been drawn by the author.

Foreword and
Acknowledgements

This book tells the story of the creation of a seaside resort: Cleethorpes, which evolved from a collection of hamlets into a select 18th-century bathing place, then into a bustling Victorian resort, and subsequently into a lively modern seaside holiday venue. But how did this transformation come about? Was it merely by chance or deliberately planned, or somewhere in between? And was its development different from that of any other similar resort? Certainly, seaside resorts such as Cleethorpes do share standard physical characteristics such as beaches, promenades, piers, gardens, amusement arcades, seaside rock, candy floss and saucy postcards. But despite general similarities each resort has a distinctive history which has been shaped by a variety of factors. Is the resort like Scarborough or Whitby in having an attractive or dramatic setting? Was it favoured with royal patronage as were Weymouth and Brighton? Is it similar to Blackpool or Southend in being within reach of a heavily-populated catchment area? Was it akin to Eastbourne or Skegness where an aristocratic landowner played a dominant role in shaping the resort? Factors such as these have influenced how resorts have grown in their own particular way. Which begs the question, what elements were particularly important in influencing the creation and development of Cleethorpes? It is hoped that this book will go some way towards answering that question.

During the course of writing the book, I have been helped by many people. These include the staff of the Grimsby Central Library's Reference Library (in particular Jennie Mooney and Simon Balderson), the North East Lincolnshire Archives (John Wilson) and North East Lincolnshire Council's National Fishing Heritage Centre (Andrew Tulloch). The staff of the National Archives at Kew have also been very helpful as have David Moss of the *Grimsby Telegraph*, Nicholas Rogers of Sidney Sussex College and Michael Keane of Tameside Local Studies and Archives. Janet Wilmott has given helpful advice on the draft text and Colin Newton took time to read through some of the more recent additions. Annie, John and Roannah Smyth have helped in a variety of ways. Rex Russell kindly allowed me to use some of his excellent maps, and the staff of the Grimsby Print and Copy Centre have been very helpful. I apologise to anyone whom I may have inadvertently omitted to thank here.

Finally, I am very grateful to my wife Dorothy, without whose encouragement, support and practical help this book would never have been written.

Abbreviations

BC	Borough Council	GT	*Grimsby Telegraph*
CBC	Cleethorpes Borough Council	LA	Lincolnshire Archives
CLB	Cleethorpes Local Board of Health	LNER	London and North Eastern Railway
CWF	Commissioners of Woods and Forests	LRSM	Lincoln, Rutland and Stamford Mercury
ELR	East Lincolnshire Railway	MS&LR	Manchester, Sheffield and Lincolnshire Railway
GCL	Grimsby Central Library		
GCR	Great Central Railway	NA	National Archives
GET	*Grimsby Evening Telegraph*	NELA	North East Lincolnshire Archives
GFP	*Grimsby Free Press*	SMR	Sidney Sussex College Muniment Room
GGG	*Great Grimsby Gazette*		
GG&SJR	Great Grimsby and Sheffield Junction Railway	UDC	Cleethorpes Urban District Council
GI	*Grimsby Independent*	VAD	Voluntary Aid Detachment
GN	*Grimsby News*	WVS	Women's Voluntary Service
GNR	Great Northern Railway		
GO	*Grimsby Observer*		

I

Cleethorpes Before the Resort

In the 1950s Cleethorpes boasted that it was 'Planned for Pleasure' and provided 'A Tonic Holiday for All the Family'. Justification for such expressions of confidence may be found in photographs of the time, which show the thousands of holidaymakers who thronged the resort, presumably finding there both pleasure and a tonic. This was certainly a far cry from the farming and fishing community which had once occupied the same spot. So how did this particular resort come into being and why has it developed in the way it did? Well, that's our story—but before we begin, just a few words to set the scene ...

Cleethorpes lies on the Lincolnshire coast where the Humber estuary meets the North Sea. Historically, the resort formed part of the parish of Clee in the ancient administrative area of the county known as the Bradley Wapentake. The parish included the inland parent village of Clee and four separate hamlets. One of these, Weelsby, lay inland, but the other three, Oole (or Hoole/Hole), Itterby and Thrunscoe, were on the coast. The hamlets were known as 'thorpes' of Clee, signifying that they were outlying settlements. By the 16th century the name 'Cleethorpes' was being used as a composite name for Oole and Itterby. During the 19th century, Thrunscoe was absorbed into Cleethorpes and became part of the resort. The parent village, Clee, and a significant portion of Weelsby, were absorbed into the neighbouring borough of Grimsby in the 19th century. The proximity of Grimsby is significant to the story of Cleethorpes. It will be seen that the two towns were interdependent and shared some common interests, but found it difficult at times to reconcile their respective aspirations and ambitions.

* * *

Our earliest, if incomplete, picture of the area is from the year 1086 and is given in Domesday Book. This was not designed to be a guidebook for the benefit of latter-day historians so we have to assess the information which it contains and make certain conjectures. Clee, Weelsby, Itterby and Thrunscoe are listed and shown to be farming communities concentrating on arable cultivation with the aid of ploughs pulled by teams of oxen. Prior to the Norman Conquest of 1066, the Anglo-Saxon local landowners were Elaf, Grinchel, Algar and Grimbold. After the Conquest, they were dispossessed and the land was divided among five Norman lords. These were the Bishop of Bayeux (Odo, who was also the half-brother of William the Conqueror), the Archbishop of York, Ivo

Taillebois, Drew De Beurere and the interestingly named Waldin the Engineer. Some of the land was farmed directly on behalf of these lords but most of it was divided into holdings for cultivation by local farmers. There may have been in the region of sixty households in the four communities, which would give a total population of between two and three hundred. The hamlet of Oole is not referred to in Domesday Book, but is mentioned about thirty years later in the Lindsey Survey of 1115-18.[1]

Grimsby is also mentioned in Domesday Book and had a population of less than 400 in 1086. The town flourished and 200 years later had a population of about two thousand. It had become established as a borough by 1194, giving it a measure of control over its internal affairs that parishes such as Clee did not have. This higher status was subsequently confirmed and reinforced by several royal charters, the first being in 1201. Domesday Book demonstrates an early connection between Grimsby and Clee and its thorpes in showing that some of the land in Grimsby, Clee, Itterby and Thrunscoe was in the same manor and the same soke. A soke was a wider grouping of land. Tenants of this land, some of which later formed part of Cleethorpes, paid rents to the borough of Grimsby. These rents were part of the annual payment which the borough made to the king in exchange for the granting of its borough liberties. In addition, the Mayor and Burgesses of Grimsby were Lord of the Manor of Clee, and a manorial court held in Grimsby dealt with matters relating to this land and its tenants.[2] This early involvement of Grimsby in the affairs of what eventually became Cleethorpes presaged the conflicts which would arise between the towns in the 19th and 20th centuries.

In addition to the farming that sustained the communities in what is now Cleethorpes, fishing was almost certainly also taking place. There is ample evidence from the 14th and 15th centuries that men from Clee and its thorpes were fishing in the Humber and as

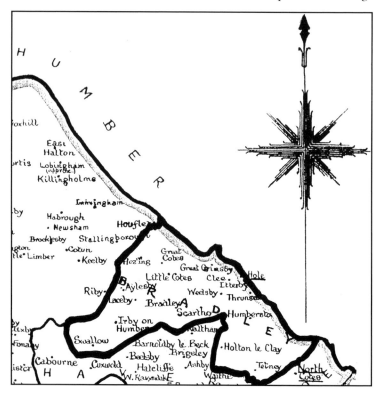

1 *Bradley Wapentake (within the bold line) at the time of Domesday Book.*

far afield as Iceland. The various dangers of seafaring were brought home to Brian Curtis of Clee and the crew of his ship in 1432 when they were captured by enemies at sea, although they were freed later on payment of a ransom. Trading in fish and other goods was also taking place. In 1332, this led to a complaint from the burgesses of Grimsby that markets were being held illegally in Clee, Itterby, Oole, Thrunscoe and neighbouring Humberston. These markets were attracting trade and merchants away from Grimsby. It was subsequently ruled that no markets should be held which were to the disadvantage of the borough. Three years later, the burgesses complained of fish and other goods being landed at Oole, again leading to a loss of trade at Grimsby. In this case, it was ruled that fish had always been landed at Oole and that other goods were not loaded or unloaded there. The importance of markets as sources of income was demonstrated in 1362, when the Earl of Lancaster and Richmond, the king's son, was granted the right to hold a weekly market and annual Michaelmas fair at Thrunscoe.[3]

The comparative prosperity of the parish of Clee was shown in 1334, when a national tax was levied on the value of movable goods in communities at the rate of one-fifteenth for parishes and one-tenth for boroughs. The Clee parish's one-fifteenth payment of £6 13s. 11d. was the highest amount of those paid by the 13 parishes in the Bradley Wapentake. Grimsby borough's one-tenth payment was £9 14s. 5½d., revealing that the populations of Clee and Grimsby had comparable taxation values approaching £100. Thus Clee was more prosperous than other local parishes and comparable with Grimsby in wealth. The latter certainly suffered a long-term decline in trade and population and by 1563 its population had fallen to about 650 persons. In contrast, the Clee parish maintained, if not increased, its population. In 1563, there were 22 households in the village of Clee, 14 in Oole, 18 in Itterby, 16 in Thrunscoe and six in Weelsby, giving a total of 76 households or an estimated population in excess of 300 people for the parish. Of this total about 200 would be living in Oole, Itterby and Thrunscoe, the area of the future resort.[4]

A window into life and work in the parish of Clee during the ensuing two centuries is provided by an analysis of probate inventories for the parish dated between 1536 and 1742. These list the goods and chattels of the deceased. For those leaving few possessions, an inventory may not have been deemed necessary, so our view will be of the better-off residents. Within these limitations, the inventories show that Clee was essentially a farming community, practising a mix of arable and pastoral farming. Beans and barley are listed in the inventory of John Mason; William Colby had agricultural implements such as a cart, wain, ploughs and harrows; Robert Curtis, who died in December 1557, left a crop of autumn-sown wheat. The inventories give indications of whether particular residents were craftsmen or dealers and traders, but they show that such people were likely to be involved in farming as well. There is other evidence of a network of informal credit in the parish, which would facilitate trade and assist residents whilst, for example, they were awaiting income from the sale of goods, crops or livestock. Also shown is a continued participation in the fishing trade. Some men were involved in both agriculture and fishing. One of these was Wiilliam Stables, whose inventory of 1536-7 showed that he possessed half a share in a cog boat, plus nets, hawsers and lines; all this was in addition to his horses, a mare, pigs, sheep and cows. References to fishing occur mainly in the 16th century, with emphasis on having shares in boats. Later inventories show a change, with emphasis on the use of traps and fixed nets near the shore, and it was reported in 1628 that, although there were five fishermen in Cleethorpes, none of them was a boat owner.[5]

Although life in the farming community would be relatively undisturbed during this period, the year 1616 saw a major event for the future development of Cleethorpes. In that year Sidney Sussex College, one of the colleges of the University of Cambridge, became a major local landowner. The College had been founded in 1596 with a bequest left by Lady Frances Sidney, Countess of Sussex. Its main purpose was the training of men for the ministry of the established Protestant Church. The founder's bequest of £5,000 turned out to be insufficient to provide the necessary buildings and an income for the support of the original foundation (a master, 10 fellows and 20 scholars). Consequently, from its early days the College had financial problems and became dependent on other benefactors. These included Peter Blundell of Tiverton in Devon. Blundell died in 1601 and left £40,000 in various benefactions, the most important of which was the endowment of Blundell's School at Tiverton, which was founded in 1604. He also left £2,000 to found six scholarships at Oxford and Cambridge for pupils of the school. Four scholarships were assigned to Sidney Sussex College and in 1616 land comprising the Manor of Itterby in the parish of Clee, Lincolnshire, was purchased for £1,400 to provide rental income for their support. There were 20 College tenants in 1618, renting property in Clee, Itterby, Thrunscoe and Oole. The largest of the College's farms in 1662 had 50 acres of arable land, 20 acres of meadow and 10 acres of pasture, as well as the right of grazing cows and oxen in the West Field. This arrangement reflected the overall balance of local agriculture. The College's estate also included houses and cottages without land. The College tenants usually had their holdings on 21–year leases. The first half-year's rent from the estate was £41 7s. 11½d. and remained at this level until 1773 when it increased to £64 0s. 7½d. The rent was a significant factor in the College's finances and as a proportion of its total annual income ranged between 20 per cent and 12½ per cent at this time.[6]

An examination of the parish register for this period confirms the continued importance of agriculture in the community. Of the 163 adult males buried at Clee church during 1609-40, over 50 per cent (85), were described as labourers, followed by 24 husbandmen (occupiers and workers of land), six yeomen (larger farmers), six tradesmen and five gentlemen. No occupations were given for another 37 men. Half of the 174 adult females buried in the same period were described as wives, followed by 53 widows, 13 spinsters and six paupers or vagrants. A further 15 were not described.[7]

A major, long-standing problem in the area had been the action of the sea on the coast, causing flooding, erosion and silting. Grimsby experienced persistent problems with silting and in 1280 had proposed scouring its haven of silt, but there is no indication that any action was taken. In 1492, the burgesses complained that the town was 'decayed and wasted', and gave the silting of the haven as one of the causes. A major flood in 1571 drowned more than 1,000 sheep on land between Grimsby and Humberston. Sidney Sussex College's estate was affected: at least 18½ acres of its arable land and about three acres of pasture were said to have been 'wasted by the sea' in the course of the 17th century. These problems were brought home to clergyman Abraham de la Pryme when he visited the area in 1697. He was told that, during the reign of Queen Elizabeth, the sea had begun to destroy the cliff at Cleethorpes, carrying away pieces as big as churches at every high tide. He was also told that 'there has been several miles' length of land wash'd away, and people have been forced to pull down their houses and build them together again furder [sic] off'. Pryme suggested that the silting of the Grimsby haven was being caused by the clay from the Cleethorpes cliff being carried upriver and settling in the haven. There was talk of dredging and improving the haven, but Pryme remarked that

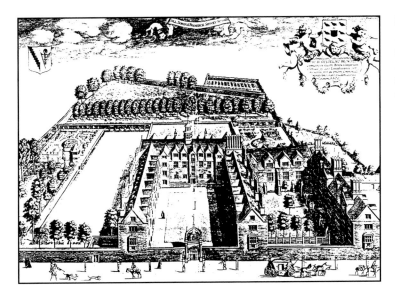

2 *Sidney Sussex College, 1688. The College purchased its local estate in 1616, which made it the largest landowner in Cleethorpes.*

the improvements would never succeed unless they also made a 'staithe' at the foot of the Cleethorpes cliff to check further erosion. The advent of the 18th century saw Grimsby still in a state of decline, with a population of only 400 or so. In contrast, Clee and its thorpes had maintained a fairly stable populace of approximately 300 inhabitants.[8]

In 1697, Pryme also commented on the decline in the Grimsby fishing trade, which tallies with the evidence we have seen in the probate inventories of changes in fishing practices from Cleethorpes during this period. However, information from the succeeding century shows the existence of a local oyster fishery. This involved cultivating oyster beds on the Cleethorpes seashore, but also fishing for oysters in distant waters. The inventory of Thomas Manby of Cleethorpes lists oysters and two boats in 1728. Cleethorpes resident Amos Appleyard was engaged in the oyster fishery in the late 18th century, travelling as far as Scotland to buy cargoes and fishing for oysters on grounds 20 or 30 miles distant. He built up trading contacts in various places including Hull, York and Selby.[9]

The 18th century also saw the emergence of a new influence that would have a significant part to play in the history of Cleethorpes: Methodism made its appearance locally in 1743. In October of that year, John Wesley made the first of his several visits to Grimsby. However, he had been preceded in February by another well-known preacher and pioneer of Methodism, John Nelson, who recorded in his diary that 'some friends from Tetney and Cleathorpe [sic] prevailed with me to go to a shepherd's house near the sea-coast'. A meeting-place for prayer was established in a farmhouse in Thrunscoe. Meeting-places were subsequently set up in houses in Itterby and Oole. With the establishment of a local Methodist society, a farmhouse in Oole was formally registered as a Methodist place of worship in 1759, but the local pioneers struggled to attract and hold members in the early years. In 1769 there were 15 members; the number had risen to 40 by 1780.[10] The following year saw a visit by John Wesley. He travelled from Grimsby in order to preach at Cleethorpes and recorded in his journal:

> I preached at Claythorp [sic], three miles from Grimsby: here likewise there has been an outpouring of the Spirit … I could not go into any of the little houses, but presently it was filled with people; and I was constrained to pray with them in every

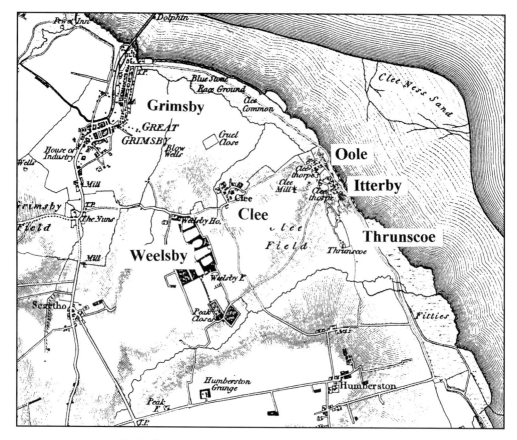

3 *North-eastern Lincolnshire in 1824, with added place-names.*

house, or they would not be satisfied … And there is scarce a house in the village
wherein there is not one or more earnestly athirst for salvation.[11]

Notwithstanding this enthusiastic account, membership of the society had fallen to
26 by 1791 and, despite a revival in the 1790s, was still only 37 by 1800.[12] These figures
belie the eventual growth and importance of Methodism in Cleethorpes.

As the 18th century drew to a close, another important factor in Cleethorpes' story
appeared. This was the Thorold family, which was an ancient family of country gentry.
The Thorolds' main presence was in south Lincolnshire, but there were also long-standing
connections with north-east Lincolnshire. Some members of the family were freemen
of Grimsby and served as aldermen and mayors of the borough. The family also owned
about 2,000 acres in the nearby Wolds parishes of Cuxwold and East Ravendale, where
they were lords of the respective manors and patrons of the church living at Cuxwold.
The Rev. William Thorold, mayor of Grimsby in 1787 and rector of Cuxwold, forged
the family's connection with Clee and Cleethorpes. He leased land in Clee in 1787
and 1796, and by 1798 he was living in the parish at Weelsby House. In 1801 William
purchased the house and land and became a local resident landowner. On his death in
1814 he was succeeded by his son Richard, who continued to live in the parish and
who will feature later in this book.[13]

II

The Bathing Place
1700s–1840s

The economy of early Cleethorpes was based on agriculture and fishing. However, in the late 18th century we see the first indications of the place joining the growing band of coastal health resorts which were termed 'watering places' or 'bathing places'. These grew in number as sea bathing, and the drinking of sea water, became fashionable. Although they stressed their basic function as health resorts, they also increasingly provided diversions for visitors. There is little doubt that the Lincolnshire coast participated in this new form of recreation. Cleethorpes' first guidebook, published in 1850, refers to the resort's early days with the (unsubstantiated) statement:

> It appears that Cleethorpes was a favourite place for the residence of country gentlemen, and members of Parliament during the vacations; and no doubt was one of the pleasantest places for health and amusement of any in the county of Lincoln.[1]

Certainly, the Lincolnshire coast was attracting visitors and in 1772 the *Vine Hotel* at nearby Skegness advertised accommodation for 'gentlemen, ladies, and others … [and] as clean a shore as any in England'.[2] Cleethorpes had its own traditional attraction that brought in visitors from the neighbourhood, although it is unlikely that many 'gentlemen and ladies' would have attended. An annual feast had for long been held at Clee, commencing on Trinity Sunday. This led to the holding of 'Fortnight Sundays' which were held every alternate Sunday on the seafront at Cleethorpes during the summer:

> The crowds of people who attended from the neighbouring towns and villages—and the excesses committed—were enormous: pugilists, wrestlers, and football players were in request. A great number of candidates for these so-called amusements attended from the now civilised and enlightened villages of Humberstone, Tetney, Fulstow, North Thoresby, Holton, Waltham, Scartho, Bradley, Laceby, and other places, some more than 20 miles distant. Stalls were erected in front of the *Dolphin Hotel* … and also near the cliffs, and on the sands, for the sale of goods and wares, gingerbread, etc.[3]

The event became known as the 'Folly Feast' and an undated description of early daytrippers to Cleethorpes runs:

> Farmers on cart horses, on the then dirty lanes,
> Going to Cleethorpes fearless of the rains;

4 *Cambridge Street with the tower of St Peter's Church in the background, post-1866. The buildings on the left were typical of others in the town before the rebuilding and development that followed the coming of the railway.*

> Their wives upon pillions well seated behind,
> No veil on their bonnets, nothing of that kind.
> And agriculturalists from the plough tails,
> With thrashers, who commonly used their flails,
> And tradesmen and others were wending their way
> Unto Folly Feast, for to spend that good day.[4]

We are also informed that, after arrival at Cleethorpes, the men partook of a good supply of 'threepenny tankard, October brewed' ale.[5] However, not everyone found the event to their liking:

> This was continued until the thinking part of the population began to see it wrong thus to desecrate the Sabbath, and called it 'Folly Feast' ... The scenes of riot and drunkenness practised on these days became so notorious that the magistrates determined to put them down; this they finally accomplished in the year 1786. The site where these scenes of iniquity were practised on Fortnight Sundays, is still known by the name of 'Folly'.[6]

The Folly Feast was held in the area of what is now Sea Road and some local residents still refer to that road as the Folly Hole.

Whether the small band of local Methodists had any influence on the magistrates' decision is unknown. However, it is perhaps symbolic of their later involvement in the resort that it was a Methodist member of the county gentry who figures as our earliest named visitor to the infant bathing place. He was Robert Carr Brackenbury, of Raithby Hall near Spilsby, a well-known Lincolnshire landowner and Methodist preacher who came to Cleethorpes in 1782 to recuperate after a long illness. This was in line with the accepted view of the time: that the basic purpose of watering and bathing places was to act as purveyors of health and well-being.[7] Brackenbury was followed nine years later by the town's best known early visitor. This was John Byng, later Lord Torrington, who visited the Lincolnshire coast in July 1791 during a tour of the county. After visiting the bathing places of Skegness and Saltfleet he arrived at Cleethorpes and called it 'a bathing place of a better complexion than the two others we have seen upon this coast'.[8]

Early in the following century, Cleethorpes was described in a book on Lincolnshire as:

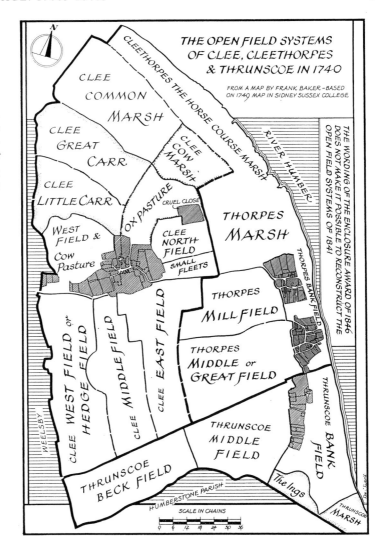

THE OPEN FIELD SYSTEMS
OF CLEE, CLEETHORPES
& THRUNSCOE IN 1740

FROM A MAP BY FRANK BAKER – BASED
ON 1749 MAP IN SIDNEY SUSSEX COLLEGE

5 *Open field systems in the parish of Clee in the 1740s. The shaded areas show the old enclosures of Clee village and the ancient hamlets of Oole, Itterby and Thrunscoe.*

… a little fishing hamlet called Cleathorpe [*sic*] where there is a large and commodious hotel, erected of late years, with stables and other conveniences … It is now become, during the summer, the resort of much genteel company, it being universally allowed to be the most eligible and agreeable bathing place on the Lincolnshire coast.[9]

By 1819 the bathing place was being mentioned in national directories as 'a small township of great resort in the bathing season. Here is an excellent inn for the accommodation of strangers'. In 1826, the first Lincolnshire county directory described it as 'formerly only a fishing hamlet, but it is now resorted to as a bathing place'.[10] The vicar of Clee, the Rev. George Oliver, possibly with a degree of local bias, described the place in favourable terms in 1829, and emphasised its health-giving properties:

Modern Cleethorpes … is now frequented as a place for sea bathing. Many new lodging houses have been recently erected, and the general accommodations much improved; and the salubrity of the air … will always render it a desirable summer retreat for the valetudinarian or the invalid.[11]

6 *A reminder of the resort's rural past. Cleethorpes had two windmills, one high up on Mill Road (pictured) and one near the seafront in Mill Place.*

Certainly, Cleethorpes was attracting members of the county landed gentry such as Sir Charles Anderson, Sir William and Lady Ingilby, and members of the Tennyson family.[12]

Getting There

Despite all this favourable comment, Cleethorpes, like most resorts, was not an easy place to get to. The prospective visitor had a choice of two forms of transport: by road or by water. Two journeys made to Cleethorpes in the early years of the 19th century by the Archdeacon of Nottingham, the Venerable John Eyre, illustrate both. In August 1817, the Archdeacon and a companion made an 'expedition' by horse-drawn gig from Babworth in Nottinghamshire to Cleethorpes. The distance by road was about sixty miles. Setting off at 7.30 a.m. they stopped for meals at the towns of Gainsborough and Brigg and arrived at the village of Great Limber by 7.00 p.m., where they passed the night at the *New Inn*, having travelled 44 miles. The following morning they travelled a further 16 miles to Cleethorpes and spent the day at the resort, returning to Great Limber in the evening. The next day saw their return journey, departing Great Limber at 8.00 a.m. and getting home by 7.00 p.m. The Archdeacon wrote that it had been a rainy drive and parts of the road were bad.

On his stop at Gainsborough he had taken great interest in the steam packet service to Hull which had begun operating in 1815. This regular service reduced the journey between Gainsborough and Hull to five hours instead of the three to seven days it could take by sail.[13] Consequently, when he made a further 'expedition' with three companions to Cleethorpes in August 1818, they caught the 9.15 a.m. *British Queen* steam packet at Gainsborough, the fare being 6s. 0d. for a 'best cabin'. The boat made a speed of about ten miles an hour over the 52 miles of the voyage, but ran aground on a sandbank near Hull at about 2.00 p.m. and the travellers were not able to disembark there until 4.00 p.m. The following morning they set off at 8.00 a.m. in another steam packet for the 18-mile trip to Grimsby, for which the fare was 1s. 6d., and walked from there to Cleethorpes, a distance of approximately three miles. After time in the resort, they took a chaise back to Grimsby and set off in the Hull packet about 4.00 p.m. At Hull they boarded the *Albion* packet and arrived at Gainsborough by 10.00 p.m. Taking a chaise from Gainsborough they arrived at Babworth at 11.30 p.m.[14]

Despite the possibility of set-backs such as those encountered by the Archdeacon, travelling by water became popular, and in 1832 the county newspaper waxed eloquently on the improvements in local river travel brought about by the new steam packets:

> There are many days in every month in which the tide will suit so as that a voyager leaving Gainsborough after breakfast for Hull, shall be in time to be forwarded thence to Grimsby (only a short hour's walk for Cleethorpes) the same afternoon, and all for about a day's wages of an ordinary mechanic.[15]

Special day excursions took advantage of the region's lesser waterways, such as the River Ancholme which flowed into the Humber:

> Many of the inhabitants of Market Rasen and its neighbourhood are looking forward with much glee to a pleasant excursion on Monday next. Mr Darlby's pretty little packet the *Expedition* will leave Bishopbridge for Ferriby Sluice early in the morning, and thence the party will be forwarded in that fine vessel the *Dart* to Grimsby and Cleethorpes returning the same evening.[16]

Onward transport from Grimsby to Cleethorpes was available for those who did not relish an hour's walk to the resort. Cleethorpes grocer and draper E. Turner announced that he 'attends at Grimsby Lock, the Sailing and Arrival of the Steam Packet plying between Grimsby and Hull, every day during the Bathing Season (Sundays excepted) with a neat and convenient conveyance for passengers and goods to and from Cleathorpes [sic]'. Similarly, George Burgess of the *Crown and Anchor Inn* at Cleethorpes had 'a light Cart, which attends on the Hull and Grimsby Steam Packets, daily, at tide time, for the conveyance of Passengers and Luggage, Cleethorpes being distant from Grimsby about three miles'.[17]

For those who travelled by road, and did not have their own transport, a coach ran from Lincoln during the season:

> Many citizens with their families are seizing the opportunity afforded by the regular conveyance which has been established between Lincoln and Cleethorpes of visiting the sea-side to recruit their health.[18]

Such was the competition between road carriers in 1845 that the county newspaper reported fares being so reduced that 'people can get to this watering place for next to nothing'. This was an exaggeration, because the advertised fare at the time from Lincoln to Cleethorpes was 3s. 6d.—no small amount to a working man. Coaches left Lincoln at 12.30 p.m. and arrived at Cleethorpes at 6.00 p.m. The return journey left the resort at 7.30 a.m. and arrived in Lincoln at 12.00 noon. Onward transport was available at Lincoln for such places as Nottingham, Derby, Newark and south Lincolnshire.[19]

The difficulties of travelling were exemplified in 1839 by what turned out to be an abortive proposal that the novelist Charlotte Brontë should take a holiday in Cleethorpes. Her friend Ellen Nussey made the suggestion in June of that year. Charlotte's enthusiastic response was that an excursion with Ellen 'whether to Cleethorpes or Canada ... would be to me most delightful'. Her reply continued:

> ... when do you wish to go?—could I meet you at Leeds? to take a gig from Haworth to Birstal would be to me a serious increase of expense—and I happen to be very low in cash—O Ellen rich people seem to have so many pleasures—at their command which we are debarred from—however no repining—if I could take the coach from Keighley to Bradford & from Bradford to Leeds and you could meet me at the Inn where the coach stops [in Leeds]—on your way to Cleethorpes for I presume you go by the Leeds & Selby Rail-road—it would be the most convenient plan for me ... [20]

To summarise Charlotte's travelling arrangements: she would have to get to Keighley from Haworth, then take coaches to get to Leeds, where she would meet Ellen and they would take the train from Leeds to Selby. They would then have to get from Selby to Cleethorpes by road or river transport. Despite this planning, and because of other factors, they took a holiday at Bridlington instead.

Somewhere to Stay

Having got to Cleethorpes, the quality of local accommodation was important. Although John Byng may have commented favourably on the bathing place in 1791, he was critical of his accommodation:

> *Cleathorps Inn*, a bathing place of a better complexion than the two others we have seen upon this coast; for here are [a] large dining room, and a card room. But why

come we here? A place to be avoided by tourists, as in no place are you so much neglected! There to lodge in a cock-loft! The company shirk you; and conversation were thrown away. We desired privacy, and procured a dirty little parlour, with a fire, for it was dismally cold; our room was fill'd with smoke; at last we did get some tolerable victuals to eat, and we sat muddling over the fire … [The following morning] our breakfast was hast'ned as much as possible, and we felt happy to get away; tho' from the best of the Lincolnshire bathing shops; where the people were civil, and the bill reasonable.[21]

Had Byng returned in August 1803, he could have stayed at Benjamin Chapman's lodging house where the charge on 3 August was 1s. 6d. per night for 'two Gentlemen' sharing a bed plus a total of 1s. 6d. for their breakfast and the same charge for their tea. The following week saw Mr Oliver of Manchester having the sole occupancy of a bed on 12 August for a charge of 1s. 0d. a night. Chapman's visitors stayed for periods ranging from one night to three weeks. They came not only from Lincolnshire towns such as Barton, Brigg, Gainsborough, Grantham and Market Rasen, but also from much farther afield, including Rotherham, Derby and Manchester. For the most part they seem to have been leisured 'ladies and gentlemen', including the Rev. Mr Hoyle, Lieutenant Smith and 'Capt. Wood and Wife and Servt'. During the year Chapman's takings were £4 0s. 9d.[22]

When John Eyre made his trips to Cleethorpes in 1817 and 1818 he did not stay overnight but remarked that 'the Hotel on a rising ground on the beach, with a fine view of the sea' had two excellent rooms for dining and a drawing room but the bedrooms were small. A charge of 5s. 0d. per day included all meals except liquor. Of the boarding houses, he noted that Chapman's had three bedrooms and one ground-floor bedroom but he considered that one he referred to as 'Taylor's' was the best. The charge there was two guineas a week and it had one sitting room and two bedrooms, one being over the kitchen. He also noted, in 1818, that the Bishop of Lincoln and family were at 'the Hotel' and had a private sitting room.[23]

Another clergyman, however, thought it too costly to stay in Cleethorpes. George Tennyson, the father of the future Poet Laureate, Lord Alfred Tennyson, was rector of Somersby in Lincolnshire, and also absentee vicar of Grimsby during 1815-31. Although he and his brother Charles did not have a close relationship, their respective families liked to meet for seaside holidays. However, whilst Charles preferred Cleethorpes, George wrote to him in 1813 that it was too expensive for 'a poor parson who could not be supposed to have spare rhino [money] to sport away in extravagant expeditions'. He preferred the Mablethorpe area, which in any case was considerably nearer to Somersby.[24]

Twenty years later the *Crown and Anchor Inn* in Cleethorpes was charging 3s. 6d. per day for board and lodging for adults with 'children in proportion'. Warm baths were 2s. 6d. and a shower bath 1s. 6d. The inn also had 'Superior Quality' wines and spirits and 'Good Stabling, Corn and Hay at moderate charges'. Residents' letters and parcels could be conveyed to and from the Grimsby post office and steam packets. The range of services also included breakfast, dinner, tea, supper, tobacco, ginger beer, ale, porter, oysters, shrimps and sea baths.[25]

The 1820s and 1830s saw increasing numbers of visitors and more local residents providing lodgings for them. Fourteen 'lodging houses' were listed in 1826, mostly provided by residents who also had occupations. July 1834 saw 357 visitors staying in 61 lodging houses, plus others staying in the inns. By July 1838, this had increased to 712 visitors staying in 71 lodging houses and the inns, but 'notwithstanding this great influx of company there are several respectable houses to let'.[26]

Passing the Time

John Byng found few attractions on his visit in 1791 and complained of the lack of a good garden and bowling green. However, acting on the basis that bathing places were seen essentially as health resorts, the owner of the *Cleethorpes Hotel*, John Maltby, summed up the attractions of the place when, in 1834, he advertised that 'The delightful situation of the Hotel, commanding an extensive view of the Sea and Humber, together with the salubrity of the air, cannot fail to impart those pleasures and benefits to health so much sought after'. Common pursuits included taking the air, strolling on the cliff and sands, bathing and boating. On John Eyre's visit in 1817 he spent a couple of hours 'on the water'. In 1818 he found the common between Grimsby and Cleethorpes to be 'fine clean turf. Airy, excellent for Children to walk etc.'[27]

Bathers could hire bathing machines in which to change for bathing. These changing huts on wheels were drawn into the sea by horses, whereupon the bather would discreetly descend steps into the sea, usually assisted by one or more female attendants or 'dippers'. In 1826, the *Cleethorpes Hotel* advertised its rates for bathing machines, which included 'Ladies Baths when drawn into the sea 10d. ... Two Women in attendance at Tide-time, whose charge is included in the above'. For those who needed resuscitation after experiencing the chilly North Sea, it also offered 'Warm Baths'.[28] In 1833, the owner of the *Crown and Anchor Inn* proclaimed that his facilities for bathing included:

Vocal Concert.

BALL AND CARD ASSEMBLY,

At Cleethorpes Hotel,

On Wednesday Evening Aug. 4th.

The Stewards being desirous of promoting as much as possible the gratification of those Ladies and Gentlemen who may attend the Ball, heretofore announced; take this opportunity of apprising them, that they have engaged a Professional VOCALIST, of great Celebrity, from London, who (with the assistance of several amateur Gentlemen) will in the course of the evening, give RECITATIONS, and Sing a variety of SONGS, DUETTS and GLEES, &c.

E. C HOLGATE, Esq. }Stewards.
LIEUT. THOMAS, R. N.}

SKELTON, PRINTER, GRIMSBY.

7 *Vocal Concert, Ball and Card Assembly at the Cleethorpes Hotel, 4 August 1824.*

CLEETHORPES RACES.

ON MONDAY, JUNE 11th, 1827,

A SADDLE

Will be run for by Horses of all ages, not thorough bred.

ON THE SAME DAY,

A   BRIDLE

Will be run for by Ponies.

JINGLING MATCHES, JUMPING in SACKS, &c. as usual.

The Horses to be entered at the Hotel, and to pay on Entrance for the Saddle, 5s.

[SKELTON, PRINTER, GRIMSBY]

8 *Cleethorpes Races, 11 June 1827.*

> New Machines for Sea Bathing, and also a new commodious Warm Bath, which he has erected at considerable expense, contiguous to his Inn, containing a neat Dressing-room, and Dutch Tile Bath ... It being well known that this Shore, for Sea Bathing, is preferable to any other on the Lincolnshire coast.[29]

Special events were organised at intervals, such as a 'Vocal Concert. Ball and Card Assembly' that was held at the *Cleethorpes Hotel*, on Wednesday evening, 4 August 1824. It featured 'a Professional Vocalist, of great Celebrity, from London, who (with the assistance of several amateur Gentlemen) will in the course of the evening, give Recitations, and sing a variety of Songs, Duetts [*sic*] and Glees.' At a similar event in 1826, tickets cost 5s. 6d. but only 4s. 6d. for ladies; dancing commenced at 9.00 p.m.[30]

9 *Excursion of the Steam Packet* Pelham, *30 August 1832.*

10 Cleethorpes Hotel, *June 1834.*

Advertised attractions in the 1820s and 1830s included horse races held on what was referred to as the 'Horse Course Marsh' along the Humber bank. The races varied from year to year. The main race was usually for 'horses of all ages, not thorough bred'. The prize for the winner was usually a saddle. Other races were run for donkeys and ponies, prizes being whips or bridles. There was also a variety of other events such as a 'jingling match' (a pound of tobacco was awarded to the winner), a foot race (prize, a bottle of gin) and 'jumping in sacks and various other sports'.[31]

For the adventurous visitor, boatmen provided trips on the Humber. The very adventurous could be taken a few miles across the river to Spurn Point in Yorkshire. The trip could be made in more comfort aboard a steamboat. In August 1832, the steam packet *Kingston* left Hull at 7.00 a.m. and called at Grimsby at 9.00 a.m. on its way to Spurn. Alternatively, on 30 July the *Pelham* left Hull at 7.15 a.m. and Grimsby at 10.00 a.m. for 'an Excursion to Sea, Calling at Spurn'. The owners of the latter boat had altered it 'at considerable expense, by which more accommodation and greater dispatch is obtained ... no expense shall prevent them from making their Packet equal, if not superior, to any in the Humber'. Fares on either boat were 'Best Cabin, 1s. 6d. Fore Cabin, 1s. 0d.'.[32]

Place and People

Throughout this period the town was growing slowly. In 1801, the area which now comprises Cleethorpes (i.e. Oole, Itterby and Thrunscoe) had 284 residents and 60 houses. Over the ensuing 50 years there was steady growth until 1851, when there were 839 residents and 198 houses. Even at mid-century, the three communities remained quite distinct and separated by fields and closes. The houses of Oole were clustered mainly in the area of the present Market Place, Market Street and Short Street. Those at Itterby were located between Humber Street and Sea View Street, whilst Thrunscoe consisted of two farms, one farmhouse being on the site of the present Signhills Schools and the other one near the junction of Oxford Street and Bradford Avenue.

Fishing, particularly the oyster fishery, had become an important part of the local economy. About twenty boats and fifty men sailed to oyster fisheries on the Yorkshire and

Lincolnshire coasts, in the English Channel, and round the Isle of Wight. On their return the immature oysters were deposited in tidal beds or pits on the foreshore to fatten. These beds were rented from the Earl of Yarborough. Large quantities of mature oysters were sent weekly to markets in Hull, York, Leeds and Sheffield. The 1826 directory listed 12 residents who were fishermen and oyster merchants plus one who was a net-maker. The next largest group were farmers, of whom there were 10, followed by four grocers and drapers, three shoemakers, three tailors and drapers, two blacksmiths, two corn millers, a coal merchant, a customs riding officer, the master of the National School (also described as a linen manufacturer), and three 'gentlemen'. Three inns were also listed.[33]

The growing population did not yet have its own Anglican church. Residents and visitors who wished to attend church services had to make their way to the parish church, which was over a mile away in the village of Clee (nowadays known as Old Clee). It was not until 1835 that the National School in Cleethorpes was used for Anglican Sunday worship and even then it was used 'more particularly for the accommodation of Visitors'.[34] The local Methodists made better provision: despite their small number, the first Wesleyan Methodist chapel opened in Chapel Yard (off High Street) in 1803. Membership of the society was growing, but there were still only 60 members when, in 1821, they replaced the chapel with a larger building in High Street. In 1848 this was itself superseded by an even larger building in Oole Road (now St Peter's Avenue). The same year saw the opening of a Primitive Methodist chapel in Cambridge Street.[35] Primitive Methodism, based on a return to the basic ideals of the Methodist revival, had come to the bathing place, with its enthusiasm and evangelism, in 1819. With regard to local Primitive Methodism, it has been asserted that:

> The vigour and spiritual zeal of the non-Wesleyans in Cleethorpes was a very important factor in keeping the Wesleyans 'on their toes', so that the Nonconformist Conscience was very much alive. For good or ill the Methodist witness as a whole was generally recognised at this time as the most important ingredient in forming the character and policy of the village. Even compilers of guide books pointed out that 'Cleethorpes is regarded as a village where religious feeling predominates'.[36]

To what extent the Methodists influenced the ethos of the bathing place during this early period is difficult to say. The influence which they may have exerted could have been out of proportion to their actual numbers. With regard to the provision of amusement for visitors, a local Methodist minister and historian has argued that:

> On the whole, life was fairly quiet in Cleethorpes … There were occasional balls and concerts, however, to add a touch of gaiety. The Anglicans utilised the National School Room for concerts … It seems fairly certain that the Methodist preponderance in Cleethorpes was mainly responsible for delaying the introduction of even more secular amusements. Good Methodists would not dream of entering the theatre … Even the concert in the National School Room, with amateur musical talent 'assisted by Miss Wilson, the Celebrated Blind Vocalist' would be suspect for our somewhat strait-laced grand-parents.[37]

The Cleethorpes of these earlier years has been described by the same writer as a Methodist village in an Anglican parish,[38] but, whatever their doctrinal differences may have been, all sects agreed on observing Sunday as a day of worship and rest. We have seen that Edward Turner, a Methodist, did not run his carriage service to Grimsby on Sundays. The Anglican church also helped to exert parochial discipline, as a public notice of 1834 emphasised:

Sabbath Breaking. Whereas it hath been represented that certain individuals are in the habit of attending their fishing business on the Sabbath. NOTICE is hereby given, That whoever may be found netting Oysters or attending their fish Nets, on the Sabbath, will be dealt with as the Law directs. John Anderson, Constable. John Mackrill, Edward Dobson, Churchwardens. Cleethorpes, Feb. 1st, 1834.[39]

The first recognised school, a National School, was opened in 1815 on a site by the Cuttleby footpath, midway betwen Oole and Itterby. Although it was a Church of England school, attendance was open to all Cleethorpes children. In 1823 the Matthew Humberstone Free School was established in the adjacent parish of Humberston. This school was open to boys living in Cleethorpes. In 1828 an attempt was made to open a school for girls in Cleethorpes, of which it was announced that 'the Object of this Infantine Establishment is to bring the Scholars up in the principles of the Christian Religion, and if any object can be more desirable than that, it is to instruct the infant mind to reverence the Sabbath'. A 'Seminary' for day pupils was opened in 1836. The terms were 12s. 0d. per quarter for children under the age of 12 and £1 1s. 0d. for those over that age. Subjects taught were 'English Language, History, Geography, Writing and Arithmetic, Plain and Ornamental Needle Work, etc.'[40]

Land and Landowners

We shall see that the ownership of land had an important effect on how the resort grew. Although Cleethorpes was developing as a summer resort, agriculture was still the pervasive local activity. Most of the land was farmed in very large open fields. There were three separate open-field systems in the parish. Clee had its open fields and commons, Oole and Itterby shared a system and Thrunscoe had its own system.[41] Under the open-field system, farming took place on a communal basis and an owner's land could be scattered in many small plots across a large area. This fragmentation and communal control was unfavourable to improved land use, whether for agriculture or building. Consequently, the larger landowners wished to obtain an Act of Parliament to enable a process known as parliamentary enclosure to begin. Under this procedure an owner's fragmented land holdings were consolidated and enclosed with hedges. The resulting enclosed fields, now with sole and independent owners, would be more adaptable for improved farming practices or other uses.

In 1770 an early attempt to initiate enclosure came to nothing. Subsequent attempts in 1811, 1814 and 1821 met with opposition from the Grimsby Corporation and the Grimsby Enrolled Freemen.[42] The Corporation was anxious to maintain its rights as Lord of the Manor of Clee and the Freemen were fearful that enclosure might endanger their rights of common grazing. There was disagreement over the boundary line between Grimsby and Clee where it ran over common grazing land. This led to disputes between the men of Grimsby and Clee, with each side taking action on the livestock of the other. In 1822 a Cleethorpes shepherd removed stock of the Freemen from the disputed common. Two years later the Grimsby Corporation had to pay damages after losing a court case over its impounding of horses belonging to Clee men.[43] A court case in 1828 decided the boundary issue in favour of Cleethorpes, but, as a local solicitor and Freeman later wrote:

This not satisfying the Freemen of Grimsby, they continued stocking the Commons, but the Cleethorpes Commoners impounded the cattle of the Freemen, and one Sunday about one hundred Freemen armed with hammers and clubs, marched in

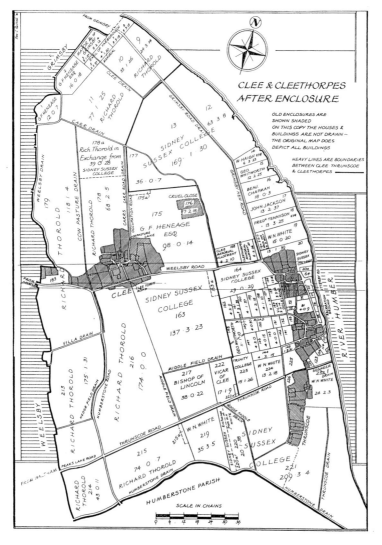

11 *Land ownership in Clee and Cleethorpes after the enclosure of 1846. The shaded areas show the old enclosures of Clee village and the ancient hamlets of Oole, Itterby and Thrunscoe.*

battle array to the Cleethorpes pound, stormed it, released the cattle, and drove them away with triumphant huzzas.[44]

At an ensuing trial, nine of the Freemen were sentenced to a month's imprisonment but were looked upon as local heroes in Grimsby and were each allowed 10 shillings a week by the Corporation during their confinement. The land in dispute covered about 69 acres and a civil action took place at the Lincoln assizes in 1830 to decide whether the land, which had been gradually left by the sea in Clee, belonged to the Corporation as Lord of the Manor or to landowner Richard Thorold. The verdict went against the Corporation and a state of comparative peace ensued. The Corporation agreed to proposals from Richard Thorold in 1838 for the enclosure of Clee, which would include compensation for the loss of its manorial rights.

Accordingly, the larger Clee landowners obtained an enclosure act in 1842 and set in motion the process of parliamentary enclosure. The enclosure was under the control of

12 *Cleethorpes central seafront area in the 1840s showing land ownership and acreages. The built-up areas of the hamlets of Oole and Itterby are shown to the right and left respectively. Oole Road later became St Peter's Avenue and Itterby Road became Alexandra Road.*

an enclosure commissioner, John Higgins of Alford in Lincolnshire. He was a well-known country land agent who acted for the Thorold estate at Clee and also carried out work for Sidney Sussex College. The process of enclosure was completed in 1846 and showed that the parish contained about 2,240 acres, of which 1,054 acres lay in Cleethorpes. Richard Thorold was the largest landowner with 889 acres in the parish, followed closely by the College, which held 756 acres. More relevant to Cleethorpes' future development, however, was the fact that only 130 acres of Thorold's land lay in the resort, whereas 603 acres of the College's land were in Cleethorpes itself. The College therefore owned more than half the land in Cleethorpes and was by far its largest landowner. Its land was mainly in large blocks in the north, west and south of Cleethorpes and Thrunscoe, with a very limited holding near the seafront. The next largest owner in the parish was G.F. Heneage who owned 152 acres, none of which, however, was in Cleethorpes. The only other landowner to hold an appreciable amount of land in Cleethorpes was W.N. White, who held 115 acres. As Lord of the Manor of Clee, the Grimsby Corporation was placated with the award of 10 acres in lieu of its rights and interests in the land of the parish. Similarly, the Earl of Yarborough was awarded four acres as Lord of the Manor of Scartho-cum-Cleethorpes, and the College's holding included an award of 16 acres as Lord of the Manor of Itterby. The remaining 200 or so acres were shared among 49 other owners, many of whom held very small areas. For example, 10½ acres on the seafront were divided among 36 owners.[45]

The Enclosure Act included an instruction that at least two acres should be awarded to the churchwardens and overseers of the parish 'in the most appropriate situation, as a Place of Exercise and Recreation for the Inhabitants of the said Parish and Neighbourhood'.

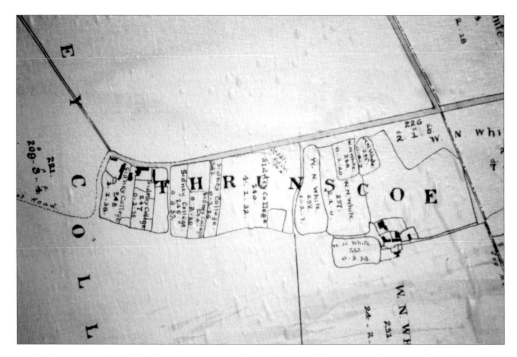

13 *Thrunscoe in the 1840s, showing land ownership and acreages. The road running across from right to left is now Hardy's Road and the farm buildings to the extreme left now form the site of the Signhills Schools. The road to the right running vertically is now Taylor's Avenue. The buildings of White's Farm are shown in the lower right-hand quadrant and would be located in the vicinity of the junction of Oxford Street and Bradford Avenue.*

Although the instruction did not mention visitors as such, the county newspaper subsequently made a relevant comment on the needs of Cleethorpes as a resort:

> The inclosure ... is progressing ... and it is hoped that the comforts of the visitors will not be lost sight of ... but that the frontage to the sea will be laid out so as to present those attractions of which it is highly capable, and which, by causing an additional influx of company in future seasons, will amply repay any additional outlay that may be occasioned.[46]

To comply with the Act, the churchwardens and overseers were awarded just over two and a quarter acres on the cliff top as an area of public recreation.[47] The completion of enclosure, its legal apportionment of land and the ratification of ownership meant that it was now much easier for land to be bought, sold and leased, and thereby made available for housing and other uses.

III

The Coming of the Railway

1840s–1860s

The picture of Cleethorpes so far is of a largely self-supporting community which was growing slowly and had a mixed economy based on farming, fishing and seasonal services for visitors. It was not an easy place to get to, provided little in the way of visitor attractions and served a small clientele of largely middle-class visitors. As a bathing place, it had largely pulled itself up by its own bootstraps with little in the way of outside help. This was to change in consequence of the most important single event in the resort's life—the coming of the railway.

By Rail to Grimsby

The initial interest of railway promoters was in a trading link between the manufacturing districts of Lancashire, Yorkshire and the Midlands, and a port on the east coast. As early as 1831 consideration was given to a railway between Manchester and the east coast; the Grimsby Corporation agreed to 'render every facility to such an Undertaking'. Their support is not surprising, because at this time trade and commerce were at a low point in the port.[1] Even so, it was not until the following decade that the idea became a reality. In 1844 Lincolnshire landowners, the Grimsby Corporation and entrepreneurs in Sheffield and elsewhere, enthusiastically supported a railway that would connect Sheffield with Grimsby via Gainsborough. The Great Grimsby and Sheffield Junction Railway Company (GG&SJR), as they became known, was in 1845 granted powers to run a line from Gainsborough to Grimsby.[2]

The GG&SJR was envisaged as the eastern section of a railway which would run across the country from the Mersey to the Humber 'through the most populous and fertile portions of the Kingdom'.[3] Accordingly, in 1846, it was amalgamated with other railways and the Grimsby Docks Company to form the Manchester, Sheffield and Lincolnshire Railway Company (MS&LR). Their proposed line would run from Manchester, through Sheffield and Gainsborough to Grimsby. Here it would connect to a large new dock constructed under the scheme. This dock was completed in 1852 and named the Royal Dock. Prior to amalgamation, the GG&SJR had decided to construct a branch line to Cleethorpes.[4] However, Cleethorpes had to take a back seat for the time being, because the MS&LR's interest was in the great things which could be achieved at Grimsby, which it saw as a port 'which it is hardly possible at present adequately to appreciate;

14 *Cleethorpes cliff looking south to High Cliff, pre-1873, viewed from the approximate location of the present railway station. Note the stalls and bathing machines on the beach.*

but which must in a few years become the scene of extensive commerce, and in times, whether of peace or war, of great national importance'.[5]

The East Lincolnshire Railway Company (ELR), formed in 1846, were also interested in running into Grimsby, and constructed a line from Grimsby to Boston. The line was leased to the Great Northern Railway (GNR) in 1847 and was soon linked, via Peterborough, to London.[6] Both the MS&LR and the ELR lines into Grimsby were opened during 1848-9, providing the port with important connections to northern and midland industrial areas and London.

Despite the fact that trains only ran as far as Grimsby, the new service led to a rapid increase in the number of visitors to Cleethorpes. Trains from Nottingham and elsewhere led to an influx of 5,000 visitors on Wednesday, 19 June 1850. It was said of this time that 'the cheap trains begin to pour their shoals of bipeds to enjoy a ramble along the extensive sands of Cleethorpes'.[7] By 1854, visitors were coming from Sheffield, Bradford, Hull, Glossop, Derby, Wakefield, Retford, Huntingdon, Nottingham, Newark, Dewsbury, Leicester, London, Worcester, Worksop, Rotherham, Doncaster, Manchester, and places in Lincolnshire.[8] On arrival at Grimsby, passengers could either walk to the resort or travel in one of the horse-drawn conveyances still provided by local hoteliers and entrepreneurs. However, such conveyances were not ideal:

> The clumsy and rotten omnibus which takes passengers from Grimsby station to Cleethorpes has broken down twice within a month ... the inhabitants of Cleethorpes as they are the parties benefiting from the number of visitors there, in letting lodgings etc., should club together to procure a proper carriage. The railway proprietors also ought to see that a safe conveyance is used for the purpose. Delicate females are often squeezed up in a single omnibus with a dozen or more.[9]

By August 1852, the MS&LR was running its own regular service of omnibuses.[10]

The growing popularity of the resort was indicated by the publication of its first handbook in 1850, which commented on the changes that had taken place:

> About twenty-five years ago, two or three bathing machines were sufficient for the accommodation of visitors; but so rapidly has this place sprung up to popularity, that there are now 19 machines for bathing, and three warm Bath Houses, for the convenience of those who, from any cause, dare not bathe in the open sea. So late

as the year 1800, there were no lodging houses in the place … but in this, as in other matters, demand creates supply, and at the present time there are 106 lodging houses, and three inns, fit for the reception of visitors in all classes of society.[11]

Eight years later, the guide was revised in view of 'the many changes and alterations which have taken place'. It noted that 'visitors who have been in the habit of attending this watering place in former seasons will find great improvements, both natural and artificial.' To cater for the increasing number of visitors, the resort now had 35 bathing machines and 170 lodging houses.[12] Most of the latter were homes of local residents, who supplemented their incomes by providing seasonal accommodation.

Steamers, too, continued to bring visitors to the resort, via Grimsby:

> Two steamers conveyed some hundreds of people from Hull for Cleethorpes on Sunday last and landed them at the Royal Dock, at the low price of 6d. each person for the voyage to Grimsby and back to Hull, a distance of 40 miles. Surely this is the age of 'cheap travelling'. The visitors returned to Hull about 4.00 p.m., seemingly delighted with their excursion. Some of the male portion appeared to have become rather elevated during the stay on shore.[13]

But it was the railway which enabled so many people from towns in the Midlands and Yorkshire to catch an early morning train to the resort, spend time by the sea and return home in the evening, frequently by cheap day excursions. For example, August 1855 saw a 40-carriage excursion train running from Derby to Grimsby, from which most of the passengers 'made all haste to Cleethorpes, the only place of attraction in the neighbourhood … many took the opportunity of having a trip to Spurn'. Societies and organisations planned their own trips. In July 1858, for instance, the Cleethorpes

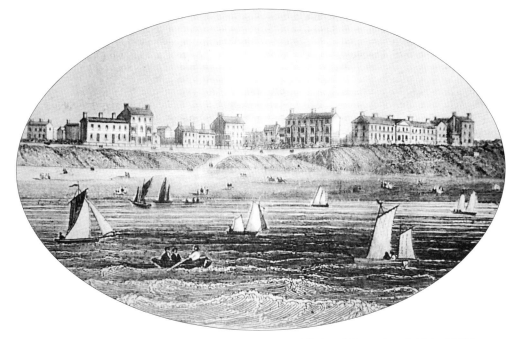

15 *Cleethorpes from the sea, 1860. To the right is High Cliff, the Cliff Hotel and High Cliff Terrace, leading down to the then Fisherman's Road and thence to the beach in the vicinity of the present Brighton Street slipway.*

16 *Cleethorpes cliff looking north from High Cliff, 1861. Bathing machines are shown on the beach. The beacon (of Beaconthorpe) is on the right in the distance, the Grimsby Dock Tower is in the centre distance and the sails of the Mill Place windmill can be seen to the left.*

Primitive Methodists made arrangements for special cheap outings from Sheffield, Retford, Gainsborough, Scotter, Brigg, Lincoln, Market Rasen, Hull and Barton, which brought 2,000 passengers to the resort for a 'monster gathering' in aid of a chapel building fund.[14]

Onward to Cleethorpes

Despite the resort's increasing development, the fact that the railway line proceeded no further than Grimsby was unsatisfactory. Although the primary objective of the MS&LR had been to develop trade through Grimsby, there was interest in extending the line to Cleethorpes, as the GG&SJR had envisaged. Such a line would have to cross several landowners' property, and this proved a major obstacle to agreeing a route.[15] Sidney Sussex College offered to lease land for the line, and during the years 1849-55 the railway company made several unsuccessful attempts to procure agreements with the Grimsby Enrolled Freemen and Richard Thorold.[16]

   However, the potential financial benefits to the railway company of being able to carry passengers directly into Cleethorpes could not be ignored and in 1860 it was reported that the MS&LR were determined to carry a branchline forward to Cleethorpes: 'It is to pass by the shores of the Humber, free from all obstructions hitherto preventing its progress.'[17] The company board received a report on the projected line that gave an estimated cost of £10,000 for a single line and station, or £18,000 for a double line, larger station and refreshment room. It went on to say that the line would bring 'a large amount of Traffic to this watering place, which now finds its way to other Districts, or does not exist at all', and that it would be a very remunerative investment. It also emphasised that:

> We do not suppose that any traffic such as that of Scarborough will spring up at Cleethorpes but such is the want of an outlet for the manufacturing Districts of Sheffield and Nottingham, and even so far as Manchester, that we think with this branch made, Cleethorpes would soon supply such a want. The Agricultural Districts too want access to some watering place, and there are the precedents of Blackpool, Southport, etc., etc., and other places on the West Coast promoted by the Lancashire and Yorkshire [Railway] Company, which show that beauty of scenery is not essential to the prosperity of a watering place.[18]

Parliamentary approval was given for the line in the summer of 1861, and work began in April 1862.[19] The single track line ran for about two and a quarter miles, and was opened on Easter Monday, 6 April 1863, when 'very large excursion trains' ran from Hull, Manchester and Sheffield among others. Meanwhile, another line of importance to Grimsby and Cleethorpes was being planned; the Trent, Ancholme and Grimsby Railway was completed in 1866, and gave additional access, via Doncaster, to freight and passenger traffic from heavily industrialised and populated South Yorkshire.[20]

17 *The first MS&LR train at Grimsby, 1848. The coming of the railway, and the extension of the line to Cleethorpes in 1863, led to the rapid growth of the resort.*

Beach Conflict

The beach was of intrinsic importance to the resort. As the number of visitors using the foreshore increased, the number of traders there also grew. Consequently, the question of the ownership and control of the foreshore, which first arose in the 1860s, became a persistent issue during Cleethorpes' development.

Local people, such as fisherman Joseph Grant, were keen to take advantage of the opportunity to enhance their incomes by catering for the needs of summer visitors. Grant expanded his business by going into partnership in 1851 and providing bathing machines:

> SEA BATHING, Cleethorpes. Joseph Grant and Edward Moody respectfully inform the visitors to Cleethorpes that they have SIX bathing Machines on the shore in front of the Oyster Booths: they hope by prompt attention and great care in conducting of the business to obtain a share of public patronage. Joseph Grant returns his thanks to his kind friends who have favoured him with their visits at his Oyster Booth for the last twelve years, and hopes by strict attention to secure a continuance of their favours.[21]

The venture was successful and the number of machines was increased to eight in the following year. As the number of visitors increased, others set up booths on the beach, and in 1858 the situation was described in the local guide:

> From the highest part of the Cliff is a sloping road of artificial steps leading to the oyster booths of Mr Levi Stephenson and Mr William Rowston and also to the bathing machines and pleasure boats ... There are other booths on the sands, particularly those of Joseph Grant, Joseph Sleight, and Amos Appleyard; the two former keep donkeys to let out to visitors, which are often in great request, and the latter is master of a pleasure boat. In the booths are sold oysters, biscuits and temperance drinks; tea is also prepared on short notice.[22]

This scene was disturbed in 1860 when landowner Richard Thorold objected to a new booth that had been sited without permission on the foreshore in front of his land. The Crown owned the foreshore (that part of the shore between high and low water marks). Crown land was administered by the Commissioners of Woods and Forests, to whom Thorold complained:

> I possess property in the Parish of Cleethorpes, on the Banks of the Humber abutting on the Foreshore and I am annoyed by an irresponsible person having erected a Wooden Booth for the purposes of drinking and other disorderly purposes over

18 *The first Cleethorpes Railway Station, of 1863, at the end of Princes Road, now used as a public house. The present station was built a short distance away as part of the MS&LR improvements of 1885, giving immediate access to the seafront.*

which I have no personal control. May I take the liberty of asking in what way I
am to proceed in order to abate the nuisance.[23]

Extensive correspondence over the ensuing year revealed that there were eight booths
trading on the foreshore 'to the annoyance of the more respectable inhabitants and visitors
of Cleethorpes'. The booths were sizeable structures and one was described as a timber
shed 80 feet long. The eight booth holders were local residents, at least four of whom
gave their occupation as fisherman. They dealt in such items as oysters, ginger beer, tea,
coffee, hot water, tobacco, cigars and toys. The Commissioners' response to the complaint
was that whilst they wanted to give protection to the property of landowners who fronted
the foreshore ('frontagers'), they were 'not disposed to adopt hard measures against a
number of poor persons who are endeavouring to obtain a livelihood upon the beach
at Cleethorpes'. As it was difficult to exercise control from a distance the Commissioners
suggested that the frontagers lease the foreshore from the Crown, at moderate rents. This
would 'empower the frontagers to protect their property'.[24]

The booths provided a popular service for visitors but residents complained of Sunday
trading, the sale of intoxicating liquor and the poor appearance of the structures. There
were also complaints of unfair competition with local hotels, public houses and shopkeepers.
Thorold's main object was to ensure

> that a control should be exercised over these parties to prevent some of the annoyances
> which are now experienced by the Inhabitants by the total absence of control at
> present and I have no doubt that the complaints of irregularity are well founded. It
> is admitted by Mr Thorold and his agent that some of these erections under proper
> control would be an accommodation to the public and he by no means desires them
> to be all removed—he only desires to exercise a proper control over them.[25]

The situation was resolved by allowing the booth holders to remain and leasing the
foreshore in question to the two largest landowners whose property fronted it: Richard
Thorold and Sidney Sussex College. From 10 October 1860 the owners could exercise
control under 21-year leases.[26] Richard Thorold died childless four years later and his
estate in Clee and Cleethorpes passed to his nephew Alexander William Thorold Grant
(1820–1908), who adopted the surname Grant-Thorold and took up residence in the
parish at Weelsby Hall.

A Growing Place

Landowners who were able to turn their land over from agriculture to building now had
new prospects for financial gain. Sidney Sussex College, although the largest landowner in
the area, was one of the poorest colleges in Cambridge, and welcomed the possibility of
an increased income. Even though the railway did not initially reach as far as Cleethorpes
the College anticipated a demand for its land in two areas: the resort area, where it held
about 40 acres, and north-west Cleethorpes, where it held a block of over 300 acres
lying less than a mile from Grimsby's large new dock. In the latter area it expected a
demand for land for industrial, commercial and residential purposes.

However, as a corporate body the College could not ordinarily sell its land and could
only grant short-term building leases, which were unattractive to builders. Consequently,
it obtained a parliamentary Act in 1853 giving it sanction to issue 99-year building leases
that would produce annual ground rents, although it still had no general powers to sell
land.[27] In the event, none of its northern land adjacent to Grimsby was taken up at this
stage, since other owners, beyond the Cleethorpes boundary, had large tracts of cheap

building land on the market that were even nearer to the docks. These owners included the Grimsby Enrolled Freemen and Richard Thorold.

There was an increase in building in the seafront area and plots of land were built over. In resorts such as Skegness, landowners holding large blocks of land in central areas played a major role in resort development, but no single owner dominated the Cleethorpes seafront. Richard Thorold held only about 10 acres in the central resort area and the College's 40 acres were dispersed in several blocks. In addition, any influence which the College could have exerted on the seafront was weakened when it sold over eight acres of prime seafront land in the 1840s to cover its enclosure expenses. By 1850, buildings which had been built on this land included 'the splendid buildings lately erected by the Rev. E.R. Mantell, Vicar of Louth, which have the Pleasure Ground and the sea in front', and 'the High Cliff Terrace, a splendid pile of buildings, containing seven houses, fit for the reception of large families; they command a full view of the sea, from which they are only a few yards distant'.[28] Both of these building developments provided lodgings for visitors.

The influence of the larger landowners was weakened still further by the many owners of small plots of land in the resort area, who either sold their land for building or leased it out on lower ground rents. Consequently it was more likely to be taken up by builders than College land. A market in land grew up with smaller landowners selling freehold land for building in the New Brighton, Highgate, Crow Hill, Beaconthorpe and Sea View Street areas.[29] The College managed to dispose of a small amount of leasehold land, including a plot on the highest part of the seafront that was leased to the Rev. Dr John Parkinson of Ravendale who had two 'lofty buildings' built there.[30]

The extension of the railway to Cleethorpes in 1863 saw the rate of house building increase. The College leased out more land for building, including sites for five shops in Sea View Street; building also took place on the land of other owners. Between 1851 and 1871 the population of the town more than doubled, rising from 839 to 1,768, and the number of houses rose from 198 to 427. The inter-relationship of Grimsby and Cleethorpes deepened as Cleethorpes began to act as a residential or 'dormitory' suburb of the port. This had been foreseen in 1854, when it was supposed that a link to Cleethorpes would:

> present very favourable opportunities to those gentlemen who transact business at
> the new dock works having their family residences at Cleethorpes, which will then
> be brought within a few minutes run of the town of Grimsby, and by which they
> will be enabled to come in the morning and return in the evening in less time than
> would be requisite for walking from one end of the town to the other.[31]

The extension of the railway to Cleethorpes encouraged commuting and in 1871 it was reported that 'A great many persons who have business occupations in Grimsby now reside at Cleethorpes, and it is calculated that not less than 150 have been going to and fro every day from Grimsby.'[32]

Public Health

As the town, and the number of visitors, grew the potential public health problems increased. Such problems would have to be countered if Cleethorpes were to maintain its attraction as a health resort. The local government of the town was quite inadequate to deal with its rapid growth. The parish came within the area of the Caistor Poor Law Union, which covered a large area and which, in addition to poor law administration, had responsibilities regarding public health. Such local government as Cleethorpes had was carried out by the Clee parish vestry, a body that consisted of local ratepayers. The vestry had both ecclesiastical and civil responsibilities, which included collecting the church, drainage and poor rates, maintaining footpaths and highways drainage, and the prevention of nuisances. The officers of the vestry were elected at an annual meeting and included churchwardens, constables, guardians of the poor, overseers of the poor, assessors of new property, surveyors of the highways, pinders, and dikereeves.[33]

There was little public control over building, sanitation and public health. This inadequacy had serious repercussions when the resort had an outbreak of cholera, in August 1854 at the height of the season, with over a thousand visitors staying in the town. Deaths soon occurred and visitors quickly left, as did those residents who were able to do so. Sixty people had died within three weeks. The outbreak was most severe in Itterby in the area of Wardall Street. Small houses there were closely packed: one had 25 people lodging in it. A Grimsby newspaper commented:

> The cholera has at length broken out in Cleethorpes, in a most virulent form, and what is it to be attributed to? Some say the bad water, others inefficient drainage and the filthy habits of the inhabitants, who keep swine close to their dwellings, and allow all kinds of nuisances to accumulate without any attempt to cleansing and draining, which is admitted on all hands a most necessary precaution against the origin or spread of the Epidemic disease. Our neighbours at Cleethorpes should … get the place effectually drained, and obtain an unlimited supply of good water, and make some pleasure grounds to enable them to redeem their character, as being the most healthy and salubrious watering-place on the Lincolnshire coast.[34]

The vestry used its inadequate powers as best it could, as seen in a public notice of 1860:

> Caution. All Persons found depositing Rubbish of any description, or throwing any other offensive matter into the Streets or Highways in the village of Cleethorpes, or leaving Carts or Barrows in the Public Roads, will, after this Notice, be Prosecuted as the Law directs. By order of the Surveyors of the Highways. June 18th 1860.[35]

The question of improving the drainage of the town led to repeated vestry debates in 1868. The course of the main drain ran along the road to Grimsby and then to an outfall at the Grimsby Docks. It was found that the drain was faulty, but even so the vestry decided unanimously that 'the Parish of Cleethorpes is properly drained as far as circumstances will allow'. Despite the vestry's unwillingness to act, the following year saw a large public meeting to elect a committee to carry out the drainage of the town. A new system was completed in 1871 at a cost of £2,500, by which sewage was discharged into 'Humberstone Beck'.[36]

The lack of effective local government became more apparent as they failed to address other needs of the growing town. In 1865 the vestry attempted, unsuccessfully, to get property owners interested in improving the cliff top by creating a promenade and pleasure ground. It also took steps to control street trading in 1873. However, its wider aim of getting byelaws 'for the better regulation of Cleethorpes' came to nought.[37] As with house building, much of the provision of services was left in the hands of private enterprise, such as the Cleethorpes Gas Company, which was formed in 1863 and began to supply gas in April 1864.

Another service was aided by a friendly society, the Independent Order of Odd Fellows (Manchester Unity), which financed the acquisition of a lifeboat. The craft was named the *Manchester Unity* and was launched on 17 August 1868. It was a day of public rejoicing and over 50,000 people were reported to have come to see the inaugural launching. Charles Day, the proprietor of the *Queen's Hotel* in Itterby, soon opened a *Life Boat Inn* on Sea Bank Road not far from the lifeboat house, which was located near the present Winter Gardens. As well as effecting rescues at sea, the lifeboat provided displays for the entertainment of visitors. However, there were persistent difficulties in launching the boat, including the loss of horses by drowning, and recurring sea damage to the hard standing in front of the lifeboat house. Consequently, the lifeboat was moved to the Grimsby Dock Basin in 1882.[38]

Church and Chapel

Although the predominant religious force in the town was Methodism, the Anglican presence in the parish received an impetus in 1850 with the appointment of the Rev. William Price Jones as vicar of the parish church of Clee. Methodist historian Dr Frank Baker has described Jones as:

> A man of vision and energy, and it was undoubtedly his influence which brought new life to the Anglican church in Cleethorpes, and consolidated the gain made possible by the influx of church people to the village.[39]

He was responsible for building a vicarage in the town in 1852 and a new larger National School in 1856. The latter could take 300 pupils and was built on what is now the site of the Church Hall in St Peter's Avenue. Price Jones was conscious of the need to provide for the growing number of Anglicans in the town and was the driving force behind the building of the town's first Anglican church, St Peter's. The church was consecrated in 1866, whereupon 'a new era dawned for Cleethorpes Anglicans'.[40] The dominant religious influence in the resort was, however, still Methodism. The Primitive Methodists in particular took a leading role in the emerging temperance movement:

> The Cleethorpes teetotallers held a temperance meeting every four weeks, and in 1851 commenced publication of their own 'Speakers' Plan of the Cleethorpes Temperance Society'. Although one of these was Wesleyan ... the majority were Primitive Methodists ... On Monday, 25th August 1851, this group held a Temperance Festival or tea meeting in a Booth erected for the occasion, on the cliff, near the water-side.[41]

The Primitive Methodists also opened a new larger chapel on the corner of Mill Road in 1857. Their annual tea meeting was well organised and advertised and in 1863 had a huge response:

> The private enterprise of the Primitive Methodists combined with facilities offered by the newly opened railways to asssemble by far the largest crowd that Cleethorpes had ever seen, on Monday, 3rd August, 1863. In addition to almost 30,000 carried by train, thousands came on foot, and by means of nearly four hundred vehicles of various kinds. A special packet trip was run from Hull (one of the national centres of Primitive Methodism) to Grimsby.[42]

Methodists of both persuasions played an active part in the commerce of the town and it has been estimated that, of the hundred or so houses that were classed as lodging houses in 1850, at least two-thirds were run by Methodists.[43]

IV

Pier and Cliff
The 1870s

The once quiet bathing place was now much busier, and its genteel middle-class visitors had been joined, or even displaced, by a wider spectrum of society from the manufacturing districts of the Midlands and South Yorkshire. There had also been significant increases in the size and population of the town, giving rise to problems in public health and local administration already touched on. However, the 1850s and 1860s had seen little change in the general picture of visitors still depending very much on the enterprise of residents to cater for their needs. The 1870s were to see the first indications of real change.

A Changed Resort

Writing in July 1870 whilst on a visit to Cleethorpes from Nottingham, the Rev. R.W. Sibthorpe commented on the changes in the resort since the coming of the railway:

> I am here for a few days ... for a little sea air; but which I have not had, the wind blowing off land, and the shore so crowded with shoals of operatives from Yorkshire and Lancashire districts, with their wives and children, that I feel excluded from the hubbub. This was, twenty years since, a nice quiet place: now it is a scene of bustle and distraction. Every day, especially Sunday, excursion trains, three and four a day, with loads. But I am, perhaps, the fretful, complaining old man.[1]

On Good Friday 1872, five excursion trains brought a total of 6,000 passengers. Although many of the visitors were merely high-spirited, others imbibed too freely and the public houses did a roaring trade, as a local newspaper reported:

> Drunkenness stalked the streets. Men and women, boys and girls, aye children even – ragged and forlorn – were drunken and sickened with drink. One striking feature was the greatly prepondering youthful element of which the visitors were composed, many of whom depended upon the walls and fences for support ... Brutalising language and free fights among the youths, bruised features and oaths of intoxicated girls ... the sound proceeding from many of the drinking rooms – this tremendous worship of Bacchus at Cleethorpes on Good Friday – proclaimed the nearest approach to an earthly Pandemonium that I have ever been able to discover. Besides, there were back-room and passage scenes of which delicacy forbids a description, unabashed though were the parties by the presence and entrance of others.[2]

Respectable residents and visitors were offended in August of the same year by people bathing without using the bathing machines, whilst hundreds looked on and seemed to enjoy the 'nude, rude and savage scene'.[3]

On a subsequent visit in 1877, the Rev. Sibthorp chose, wisely, to come in October:

> I came here yesterday for the very fine, invigorating air of this little watering-place
> – now nearly empty of its visitors; who, crowding from Sheffield, etc., have raised
> it up to a population of 7,000. But I find the change from Nottingham very
> delightful.[4]

The impact of visitors on resorts increased with the passing of the Bank Holiday Act of 1871. The first Bank Holiday took place on 4 August 1871 and, encouraged by the provision of numerous excursion trains, the result was an increase in the rush to the seaside on Bank Holidays. Cleethorpes saw an estimated 10,000 visitors on Good Friday 1872. Some came by steam packet to Grimsby Docks and then by rail from the Docks Station to Cleethorpes, but most came by rail, from Hull, Halifax, Bradford, Leeds and Penistone. At the end of the season it was reported that 'The excursionists from Midland and other towns have numbered not less than 270,000 exclusive of home visitors'. On Good Friday the following year, the streets were almost impassable because of the crowds.[5] In order to cope with increased passenger numbers, the single-track rail line was doubled in 1874.

The Pier: A False Start

The increase in visitor numbers heralded another major advance in the resort's evolution: the construction of a promenade pier. Even after the railway was extended to Cleethorpes, visitors continued to make their way to the resort by steam packet to Grimsby and then by road or rail. A pier would provide a convenient landing place at Cleethorpes and also be an attraction for visitors, and a merchant and two 'gentlemen' from Middlesex promoted such a scheme. By 1866 Grimsby solicitors W.H. Daubney and Anderson Bates were involved in an application to the Board of Trade requesting authority to construct a promenade pier at Cleethorpes. The estimated cost was £8,500.[6]

The Cleethorpes Promenade Pier Order was obtained in 1867. This permitted the formation of the Cleethorpes Promenade Pier Company with a share capital of 1,000 £10 shares, with authority to construct a pier at Cleethorpes. The Company could charge tolls to vessels, passengers, freight and promenaders for its use. However, a sharp-eyed Board of Trade official noticed that the Order infringed a legal technicality. Accordingly, it was invalid and the promoters had to get it confirmed by a private Act of Parliament later in 1867. Under the Act the pier had to be constructed by 15 July 1872.[7]

Despite the trouble and expense of obtaining the Act, there was no progress on the formation of the pier company or the construction of the pier. Time was running out when, in 1871, a local directory drew attention to the state of the resort and the need for improvements:

> In some respects Cleethorpes is not made the best of by the inhabitants. This may be
> partly owing to the governing body being merely a sewage authority, and not having
> the powers of a Local Board of Health. Nature has done much for Cleethorpes, but
> the people have added to it but few artificial attractions. The *Dolphin* is the only
> decent Hotel. The cliff is allowed to crumble away without effort to save it. Artificial
> walks with pleasant grottoes in the cliffs are unknown. There are a number of seats

on the cliff, but not a single gas lamp, and the long stretch of gardens between the cliff and the road reminds the visitor of a piece of uncultivated common with a mixture of cabbage gardens, rather that what it should be, an ornamental pleasure ground for visitors.

The writer then stressed the need to proceed with the pier scheme as a matter of urgency, and underlined the commercial benefits it would bring to the resort:

A pier had been projected, but the Act of Parliament empowering a Company to build it will shortly lapse, so that nothing but prompt action can secure this great improvement. Cleethorpes in addition to general salubrity, and advantage of situation, is capable of affording additional attractions at small cost to the inhabitants. No reasonable outlay should be begrudged in securing these, for, as in other places of a similar character, the increased number of visitors will repay a hundred fold the expenditure.[8]

Making a Fresh Start

The following year, 1872, saw the first signs of movement on the pier project when solicitor W.H. Daubney was reported to be forming a company 'to carry out a pier' from the Cleethorpes cliff.[9] The *Grimsby Observer* reported that the intention was to spend some £7,000 on the construction of a pier of 'strength and durability'. It hoped that these attributes would be 'combined with good taste, if not elegance, and that the proposed pier will be a notable ornament on the coast'. The paper went on to emphasise the two functions for the pier, mentioning firstly that the Gainsborough, Hull and Grimsby steamboats that landed hundreds of visitors in Grimsby regularly could in future be taken to the Cleethorpes pier, and that trips to Spurn would probably make the pier a port of call. It then referred to the pleasure role of the pier, suggesting that it could be a place of promenade and refreshment, with tea, coffee and news rooms.

The pier was seen as a superior financial speculation and a means of increasing property values and attracting 'visitors of the better class'. The paper also commented on the 'thoroughly respectable and genuine character of the undertaking', as epitomised in the quality of its provisional directors, A.W.T. Grant-Thorold, who 'headed the landowners', E. Bannister, ex-Mayor of Grimsby, and Colonel G.M. Hutton of Gate Burton Hall near Gainsborough, who represented the MS&LR and 'may be taken to represent the commercial spirit of the enterprise'. Hutton was a director of the railway company and, because of his residence in Lincolnshire, was frequently involved in MS&LR matters relating to Grimsby and Cleethorpes.[10]

On 8 April 1872, London engineers J.E. & A. Dowson sent plans of the proposed pier to the Board of Trade and requested permission to site the pier 528 feet north-east of the location shown on the deposited plan. By May 1872, 530 of the £10 shares had been applied for by members of the public of which 192 were applied for by people with Grimsby addresses and 164 by those with Cleethorpes addresses. Of the latter group, 10 applications came from fish merchants, fish salesmen or smack owners, whose businesses were probably based in Grimsby. This meant a large proportion of the shares on the list were held by people either living in, or with businesses in, Grimsby. Most of the remainder of these 530 shares were bought by people resident in local villages or elsewhere in Lincolnshire. Applications for only 40 shares came from those with 'outside' addresses and with no known connection with the locality: of these, 20 were from Bradford, 15 from Bingley and five from Belfast.[11]

The majority of the 530 shares originally applied for went to comparatively 'small' subscribers. Out of the 58 applicants, 25 wanted 10 shares and 17 only five. The applicants' occupations covered a wide social and economic range. As well as those in professional or business occupations, the list included a police constable, a commercial traveller, a sanitary inspector, a refreshment room keeper, a station master, a bazaar keeper and a watchmaker. Five of the applicants were women, only one of whom gave an occupation, domestic servant.[12]

The legal formalities for setting up the pier company were carried out, belatedly, on 21 June 1872, when the first general meeting of shareholders was held at the *Royal Hotel* in Grimsby. The first elected directors of the company were Colonel G.M. Hutton, A.W.T. Grant-Thorold, E. Bannister, J. Atkinson, J. Anningson, E. Ross and T. Saunby. The board now included two representatives of the MS&LR, the director, Hutton, and the secretary, Edward Ross, which was in line with a report that the railway company had taken 200 of the 1,000 shares. Owing to the lack of progress during the previous five years, a further private Act of Parliament, enacted on 26 May 1873, validated the belated company formation and allowed an extra two years to complete the pier.[13]

Opening the Pier

The pier was constructed by Head Wrightson, of Stockton-on-Tees, to Dowson's designs and 528 feet north-east of the original site. These two firms were experienced pier contractors and had worked together on piers at Eastbourne, Scarborough and Redcar. Head Wrightson went on to become one of the most prolific pier builders, and were responsible for the pier at nearby Skegness. The Cleethorpes pier opened on Bank Holiday Monday, 4 August 1873. A local newspaper reported that:

> Commencing at the cliff, it runs in a straight line into the Humber a distance of 1200 feet. It presents an unusually light and graceful appearance, its designers having evidently had in view the idea of combining ornament and beauty with utility ... On being thrown open to the public, large crowds of people quickly availed themselves of this new attractive and truly enjoyable promenade. The fact of its being high water at the time conduced to the greater enjoyment of the people, who were congregated at Cleethorpes in unprecedented numbers. The almost general adoption of the Bank Holiday throughout the country had undoubtedly tended to swell the numbers of pleasure-seekers, who arrived from all districts by excursion trains, steamboats, and vehicles of every description.

19 *The pier in 1874, the year following its opening. It was described as having 'an unusually light and graceful appearance'—possibly the reason why it had to be strengthened with steel girders in 1897.*

20 *The pier from the cliff, c.1880. The rough surface of the clifftop is evident and bathing machines are lined up on the beach.*

Amusements for visitors on the day included several boat races, including the Cleethorpes Stakes for Ships' 16-oared Jolly-Boats. This was won by *Deerhound*, which beat *Mariner's Friend* to scoop the £5 prize. The Cleethorpes lifeboat crew demonstrated the self-adjusting qualities of their boat, but only at their second attempt, because 'from some mishap the first experiment was not successful, but the second attempt was much more satisfactory'. About three o'clock, a procession consisting of the directors, engineer, contractor, shareholders and members of the public, and preceded by a band, marched down the pier. The chairman, A.W.T. Grant-Thorold, declared the pier open. The contractor stated that, although he had built many piers, this was decidedly the prettiest one he had ever constructed. Afterwards the band played dance music 'which induced the younger people to trip the light fantastic toe on the spacious promenade at the pier head'. Fireworks followed in the evening.[14]

On the opening day, 2,859 people paid 6d. for admission. After this special day, the charge was 1d. By 24 September, admissions totalled 49,229. Sales also included season tickets and the receipts for the seven weeks totalled £321 6s. 11d. Press comment was that:

> At this rate the pier will pay the company a handsome dividend, although the improvement of the place and the provision of an attractive promenade and lounge for visitors was the primary object of the shareholders, most of whom are interested in the prosperity of Cleethorpes. The twofold result of a remunerative speculation and a charming novelty is most gratifying.[15]

In 1875 the transport function of the pier was emphasised by the construction of a landing stage at the pier head to improve the use of the pier for the landing and embarkation of passengers. The popularity of the pier continued. On Good Friday 1878, the opening day of the pier for the season, 7,272 people, in addition to the season ticket holders, paid for admission.[16] Later in the same year, a visiting journalist commented that:

> A few years ago, an excellent pier with a very pretty pavilion at the end was built ... It goes far out to sea and when the tide is up is used as a landing pier for steamers which run occasionally to and from Grimsby, Cleethorpes and Hull, but the pier is mainly used for promenade. During about three months (the season at Cleethorpes) a brass band is engaged and plays for six or seven hours each weekday near the pavilion ... [and] as evening comes on couples pair off for dancing and people come to enjoy themselves. The pier is always free from sand and dust, and being clean and pleasant becomes naturally one of the principal attractions of the place.[17]

An Expanding Place

As the resort grew busier, so its population continued to grow, rising from 1,768 in 1871 to 2,840 in 1881. The pace of house building also accelerated and during the 1870s the number of houses increased from 427 to 655. Many local companies were involved in building, including the Spurn View Building Company, the Great Grimsby Perseverance Building Company, the Great Grimsby Conquest Building Company and the Great Grimsby Advance Building Company. The Beaconthorpe Freehold Building Company was formed to build 35 five-roomed houses at Beaconthorpe 'on a superior scale' for the working classes. Development was widespread, taking place at New Brighton, Suggitts Lane, Hope Street, Cambridge Street, Crow Hill, Mill Road, Beaconthorpe, Sea Bank Road and Thrunscoe Road. 1872 saw the building on Sea Bank Road of the Birmingham Villas, which would be 'six stately villas ... with such houses ... we may look forward to an influx of visitors of a high class'. Increased visitor numbers also led to the rebuilding and enlargement of the *Dolphin Hotel* during 1873-4.[18]

It was becoming ever more apparent that the town could no longer be adequately governed under the old vestry and needed a local government body with more authority. Despite this, a meeting of ratepayers in 1869 rejected a proposal that the town should become a Local Health District, which would have given the resort more control over house building and public health. However, a meeting of ratepayers in May 1873 unanimously agreed that the vicar, the Rev. W.P. Jones, should apply to the Local Government Board requesting that the town should be declared a Local Health District with authority to elect a Local Health Board.[19]

The request was granted and the first election for the 12 seats on the Cleethorpes-with-Thrunscoe Local Board of Health took place in December 1873. Seven of those elected were fish merchants, emphasising once again the close relationship between Grimsby and Cleethorpes. A local newspaper was not impressed with the result:

> This 'codocratic' party are all more or less self-made men and have graduated on the Grimsby Pontoon ... The result, however is anything but a satisfactory one to many. Let us hope that the progress of the place will be not impeded, and that the new Board will show that they are keenly alive to the importance of improving Cleethorpes and making the place a more 'abideable' one to bide in.[20]

This produced a riposte in the form of a letter from 'One of the Twelve' who countered:

> It is to be regretted certainly that the members of the Board are not more generally men of education, but he who would deny that they are men of business would unjustly slander them, for the lowest in learning amongst them are the most substantial of the citizens.[21]

The Board had its first meeting on 24 December 1873 and the Rev. W.P. Jones was elected its first chairman, and designed its coat of arms, with the motto 'Vigilantes'. The Board appointed Yorkshireman Benjamin Greaves as its Clerk and Grimsby borough councillor and general practitioner Dr T.B. Keetley as its part-time Medical Officer of Health. Also appointed were a treasurer, a nuisance inspector (who doubled as the rate collector) and a surveyor. With the exception of the chairman and possibly two other members, the Board's members were all Methodists. After two years as chairman, Jones was succeeded by a Methodist. The Methodist presence in the town continued to grow: in 1872 the Wesleyan Methodist chapel in Oole Road (now St Peter's Avenue) was extended, and four years later the Primitive Methodists built a larger church on their Mill Road site.[22]

The Board attempted to ensure the building of decent housing: for example they served notice on the Advance Building Company, in 1877, requiring it to construct buildings according to the submitted plans; it had been laying flooring over stagnant water without making provision for ventilation or drainage. The Board also expressed concern that houses were being occupied before being certified as fit for human habitation, and considered the local water supply to be poor. At their request, the Grimsby Waterworks Company started laying water mains in 1883.[23]

During 1875, the Board acquired local byelaws that gave them powers to regulate hackney carriages and drivers, boats and boatmen, beach donkeys, bathing and bathing machines. The byelaws also enabled the Board to control the construction of new streets and buildings and to prevent public health nuisances. A local newspaper commented that the byelaws 'cannot fail to improve this favourite seaside resort in many ways. For example by providing a better and sightlier class of houses and the proper drainage of them'. To allow the Board to supervise the beach it was agreed with A.W.T. Grant-Thorold in 1875 that they should control the foreshore from the High Cliff Terrace to the railway station. This was the foreshore Richard Thorold had leased from the Crown and the Board offered to reimburse Grant-Thorold the £8 he paid annually. The Board drew up a plan showing where stalls and the like would be allowed on the sands and fixing rental charges. In 1877 they decided that unauthorised stalls on the sands were to be removed.[24]

A public health question that was not the Board's responsibility was that of burials. The churchyards of both the parish church at Old Clee and St Peter's Church in Cleethorpes were almost full. Later in the decade they were both closed to further burials 'for the protection of the public health'. A Clee Burial Board was elected in 1875 and a cemetery laid out on eight acres purchased for £1,200 from Sidney Sussex College. This was subsequently extended and forms the present town cemetery.[25]

The Crumbling Cliff

Despite the continuing improvement to the resort, the seafront was still dominated by an unsightly and crumbling cliff that attracted criticism from residents and visitors alike. At its highest point, the cliff rose about fifty feet above the beach. Unfortunately, being composed of boulder clay, it was subject to severe erosion by tides, rain, wind and frost. This was not a new phenomenon: by 1697 Abraham de la Pryme had already mentioned the need to construct a 'staithe' at the foot of the cliffs to prevent further erosion.[26]

The two and a quarter acres of land awarded to the parish under the 1842 Enclosure Act as a place of exercise and recreation stretched in a strip along the edge of the central and highest part of the cliff (between what is now Sea Road and Sea View Street) and provided a public area overlooking the beach and sea. It became known as the Recreation Ground and was held by the churchwardens and overseers of the poor on behalf of the parish. It was backed on its landward side by a strip of land belonging to several owners, who used it for various agricultural and trading purposes. Salvage from wrecked ships was auctioned and stalls and circuses were erected in the summer. The Grimsby Observer commented that the cliff top, which 'in other places would have been a pleasure ground for visitors, beautifully placed and laid out with park-like walks, has at Cleethorpes been used for cabbage and potato gardens'.[27]

It proved difficult, however, to get backing for any improvements. The parish vestry's 1865 attempt to interest landowners in creating a promenade and pleasure ground on

21 *Cleethorpes cliff looking north from High Cliff, c.1880. The crumbling and fragile state of the cliff is evident. Bathing machines and the faint outline of the pier may be seen in the distance. To the left is Yarra House on Alexandra Road and just to the left of centre is the Dolphin Hotel.*

the cliff top failed; In 1872 the matter was taken up by Clee churchwarden W. Ayre, who tried to gain local landowners' support for improving the cliff and protecting it from erosion:

> the great necessity ... is for taking active steps for the preservation of the Cliff and improvement of the pleasure ground ... one to two yards of the Cliff is taken away annually so that in a few years there would be little left to protect or improve and it is nearly the only attraction that Cleethorpes possesses to bring visitors to reside awhile.[28]

As visitor satisfaction became increasingly important to the local economy, the condition and appearance of the cliff and Recreation Ground developed into a pressing local concern. In 1873, the MS&LR were approached for help by the churchwardens and overseers, who continued to press the need to protect and improve the Recreation Ground: this, too, was unsuccessful.[29]

When the new Local Board was appointed later that year, it soon took up the question of protecting the cliff, but once more little progress was made. The local press criticised the Board for its lack of action and commented on the continued 'annihilation' of the cliff, which was becoming 'smaller by degrees'.[30] Eventually, in August 1877, the Board asked for a scheme of cliff protection to be prepared. It was submitted by J.E. Fisher, who was the MS&LR's resident engineer at the Grimsby docks, and involved constructing a promenade starting at the pier and running in a southerly direction for 600 yards to New Brighton (this was the line eventually taken by the present Central Promenade). The scheme also included a plan for pleasure gardens on the top of the cliff.[31]

The estimated cost of the scheme was £14,500, a large sum for the infant Board to raise with its very limited income. The part-time Medical Officer of Health, Dr. Keetley, urged them to act, saying 'What you expend now you would reap in the future tenfold'. He also warned of the danger that the resort might be superseded by 'other places with not half your advantages'. Despite such arguments, the Board took no action on the scheme.[32] It subsequently attempted to acquire control of the Recreation Ground so that it could see to its maintenance and management, but the 1870s drew to a close with the churchwardens and overseers still in control of the Recreation Ground on top of the unsightly and eroding cliff.

V

The Railway to the Rescue

The 1880s

The 1870s had seen Cleethorpes continuing to expand, helped by the construction of its first large-scale attraction, the promenade pier. The needs of the growing town had led to the creation of a new local government authority, but the decade ended without it having been able to address the urgent need to protect the rapidly eroding cliff.

The Railway and the Cliff

In January 1880, the Local Board wrote to the railway company asking it to consider protecting the cliff. A member of the Board, I.D. Good, commented that:

> He would admit that the Railway Company had a considerable interest in the matter but so long as Cleethorpes answered their purpose in its present state they would never spend a fortune in making a sea-wall and improving the cliff. Personally he believed that the class of people who came to Cleethorpes now would come if the place was nothing but mud. He thought the owners of house property were more interested in the preservation of the cliff than the landed proprietors.[1]

Despite Good's pessimism, and his low opinion of the resort's visitors, the MS&LR was indeed considering making improvements to Cleethorpes. The company chairman was Sir Edward Watkin, who had an enviable reputation as a railway promoter and became one of the most prominent men in the rail industry during the latter part of the century. He had a forceful personality and has been called 'the stormy petrel in railway politics'.[2] There ensued a period of intense consideration of the cliff problem. In July, the Local Board appointed a committee to meet the MS&LR, and, at the instigation of Board member and overseer F.A. Peck, also wrote to the company describing the continuing damage to the cliff, emphasising its potential importance to both the resort and the railway company as a visitor attraction, and suggesting that the cliff could also be made attractive to visitors in the winter if indoor amusements were provided. In addition, the letter volunteered the Board's support in any moves to improve the cliff.[3]

Watkin and the company's head engineer, C.R. Sacre, subsequently met a deputation from the Board. When Watkin asked what the Board had to offer the company, the reply was 'the cliff or pleasure ground, which was parish property, and which they were pretty sure the parish would be willing to turn over to the railway company, on condition that the latter would undertake to make certain improvements'. Watkin was also concerned to know the attitude of landowners who had land on the cliff, and whether there was likely to be any opposition to a scheme of improvement. If the Board would give their support, he continued, and do their best to prevent opposition, he was sure the railway company would be willing to carry out a scheme of improvement. In order to forestall financial objections, he assured the deputation that the scheme would not require any input from local ratepayers, and stated that it would be best if the improvements eventually became the property of the local authority.[4]

September saw a flurry of activity by both the Board and the MS&LR. J.E. Fisher prepared a plan of improvement for the railway company's consideration, similar to the one he had prepared for the Board in 1877, consisting of a promenade from the railway station to the point where the central cliff ended at Fisherman's Road (now High Cliff Road). He noted that beyond this point lay Sea Bank Road, where the land was owned by 25 freeholders and the shore was already protected. He stressed that 'what was necessary, was to protect the [central] cliff itself, which was the property of the inhabitants of Cleethorpes'.[5]

22 *Sir Edward Watkin, Chairman of the MS&LR for 30 years until his retirement in 1894. He was the prime mover in the MS&LR investment in the resort.*

The Board responded favourably to Fisher's plans, but asked if 'baths and any other indoor recreation for the winter months [could] be inserted in the plan'. Members also asked if the promenade could be extended to the lifeboat station, which was further along the shore, in the region of the present Winter Gardens, believing that the owners along the Sea Bank Road would be agreeable. Such was the Board's enthusiasm for the proposals that this expression of support was quickly followed by a telegram to Watkin pledging their efforts to prevent opposition and secure local support.[6] This in turn was followed by a public meeting[7] called by Peck in his capacity as an overseer. In his opening address he stressed the need for the co-operation of local landowners in the matter:

> Now he wanted to impress upon the owners of land abutting on the shore, and also every inhabitant of Cleethorpes, the importance of assisting the Railway Company in every way posssible. By giving up their frontages the landowners would be doing something for their own pecuniary benefit and also for the benefit of the parish at large.

The chairman of the meeting, the Rev. W.P. Jones, remarked that:

> The pleasure grounds at present belonged to the public, but in a few years there would be no pleasure grounds left. They would lose their right in the cliff, because the sea would take it away. The matter had been talked over many times, but it had always ended in wind.

Dr Keetley continued to argue that the town should undertake the work itself but he received no support and the meeting agreed unanimously 'amid applause' that the inhabitants of Cleethorpes, as far as it lay in their power, should help the railway company in carrying out the projected improvements. In the face of such enthusiastic communal support, Watkin reported back to the railway directors with a proposed scheme, which made no mention of the Board's repeated request that the promenade should extend as far as the lifeboat station but did include the provision of baths and other visitor facilities. The estimated cost was £20,000 and the railway company agreed:

> to apply to Parliament for powers to construct such works of protection as may preserve the Cliff at Cleethorpes and may enable the land saved to be converted into a place of Recreation with Baths and Waiting Rooms ... Provided that the land required shall be given or sold at nominal rates for these purposes and that the Company have power to make a reasonable charge for admission in the usual manner, with powers however for local authorities to become the owners of the improvements within some defined period, paying a moderate rate of interest on their outlay as Rental.[8]

The company then applied for a private Act of Parliament which would grant the necessary powers. As 1881 got under way, Cleethorpes residents were understandably anxious about the progress of the bill in parliament, and in March Peck contacted the MS&LR's secretary, Edward Ross:

> As I am constantly having enquiries as to the Passing of the Cleethorpes Improvement Bill I should take it as a favour if you will kindly Wire me ... as soon as the Bill is passed that I may announce the same to the many enquirers.[9]

The Act was passed later in 1881.[10] The scheme of improvements was now placed in the hands of civil engineers and contractors H.B. and A.F. James of Westminster. The firm had already carried out similar schemes at Dover, New Brighton and Hythe, and undertook much work for the MS&LR in both Cleethorpes and Grimsby. A.F. James stressed the importance of the improvements with regard to the company's passenger traffic:

> The main object of the improvements was the protection of the Company's property at Cleethorpes and the preservation of the shore, which if not taken in hand would lead to the rapid deterioration of Cleethorpes as a watering place, and the Company's traffic would be seriously injured thereby.

The scheme was larger than previously envisaged and was divided into three sections. Section 1 extended for 2,100 feet, from the company's fish dock in Grimsby to what is now the northern end of the North Promenade; Section 2 stretched 1,320 feet along the line of the present North Promenade as far south as the railway station; Section 3 ran for 2,100 feet along the line of the present Central Promenade. The company decided that Section 2 should be carried out forthwith and Section 3 should follow as soon as the arrangements for the purchase of the land on the cliff had been completed.[11]

There were other matters that had to be resolved. For instance, the work would need the approval of the Humber Conservancy Commissioners, whose consent was required for any proposed structures on the shoreline which might affect navigation; this was received in July 1882. In addition land on the cliff for pleasure gardens had to be purchased. The Recreation Ground was purchased from the parish authorities for the nominal sum of £50. The remaining five and a quarter acres were divided among

23 *Constructing the Central Promenade.*

four owners, Grant-Thorold, William Haigh, the Rev. E.R. Mantell and Sidney Sussex College; a total price of £1,200 was agreed by the end of the year. Finally, a stretch of foreshore in front of the cliff face had to be acquired, on which the promenade would be constructed. Part of it was held by the Crown and part by the Humber Conservancy, and £700 was paid in total.[12]

Railway Promenades

Work on the improvements could finally begin. April 1883 saw the signing of the agreement between the company and James for the construction of the sea wall, promenade and so on for the sum of £21,862, plus 2s. 6d. per ton for the carriage of slag from the Frodingham ironworks. The work, which was set to be completed before 30 April 1884, consisted of the Sections 2 and 3 of James' proposals, which comprise the present North and Central Promenades. His Section 1, which would have extended the sea wall to the Grimsby fish docks, was not included in the contract.

In essence, the work would provide a sea wall, an asphalted parade 25 feet wide, a road 40 feet wide, two sets of steps and a slipway to the beach. The sea wall was to be constructed of slag, shingle and sand, laid in fine concrete of the best quality Portland cement, and with all crevices carefully filled to form 'one solid mass'. It was to be faced with concrete blocks made of broken slag and Portland cement. The labour costs were estimated at 6½d. per hour for labourers, 9d. per hour for excavators and 1s. 0d. per hour for masons and bricklayers.[13]

This contract did not include any work on the cliff, but by September 1883 Sacre and James were concerned about the 'shaky condition' of the cliff face south of the pier.

They considered that if left as it was, the construction work would 'start the toe and bring the whole thing down upon us, entirely covering, if not destroying, what is now in progress'. James proposed to 'shape and slope, or ramp down the Cliff ... and provide an extensive set of steps ... [which] will make a complete job of the place and be a great improvement'. The proposal was approved at an estimated cost of £2,274. James also proposed lowering the cliff, and Alexandra Road, by about eight feet at its highest point, opposite Knoll House, depending on the agreement of the owners of the house.[14]

The engineers, too, were concerned about the effect of the pier on the new works. The promenade would run under the pier and it was commented that 'Unless it [the pier] is raised to meet the altered circumstances it will have a most unsightly appearance.' The headway above the new promenade would be only 6ft. 6in. under the first span and barely eight feet under the centre span. Lifting the pier entrance would give 12 feet and 12ft. 6in. respectively. The work was approved at an estimated cost of £731, subject to the agreement of the pier company.[15]

We have seen that the MS&LR was well represented on the pier company's board and was reported to be a major shareholder. It is therefore not surprising that the pier company agreed to the MS&LR proposal; it also suggested that the railway company might lease or purchase the pier so that all improvements at Cleethorpes could be under railway control. This suggestion was swiftly followed by an application to parliament by the MS&LR for an Act permitting it to take over the pier. Negotiations between the two companies followed. The average annual net earnings of the pier during the period 1876-83 had been £450, which represented a return of four and a half per cent on the share capital of £10,000. After some haggling, the MS&LR agreed to lease the pier at an annual rental of £450; the agreement was validated in the MS&LR Act of 1884, which also allowed for the sale of the pier to the railway company by mutual agreement.[16]

24 *The pier entrance c.1885 and, to the left, work being carried out on the new promenade. Also to the left is the Mill Place windmill. To the right is the* Dolphin Hotel.

James went on to prepare plans for a swimming baths, at an
estimated cost of £2,847, which were approved in January 1884.[17]
However, not all the shareholders were happy with the large outlay
at Cleethorpes. At the half-yearly meeting of shareholders in the
same month Sir Edward Watkin rebutted the complaints:

> The fact is that in 1864 you carried 47,030 passengers from
> Cleethorpes and 70,462 to it; and in 1881 you carried from
> Cleethorpes 184,689 and to it 283,022. I say, gentlemen, that
> a traffic of that kind is really worth a little outlay in order to
> sustain it … There are three reasons why we should make this
> extension. One is to prevent the sea breaking in and damaging
> our property. Another reason is that we should make the place
> more attractive to visitors, and thus get a larger passenger
> traffic. A third reason is we want outlets for our traffic; we
> want watering places of our own for the populations on our
> railway. Therefore, I think that if anybody will seriously consider
> these arguments they will come to the conclusion that the
> proposed outlay at Cleethorpes is a wise one.[18]

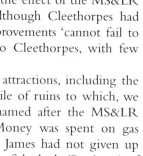

Watkin won the day and more estimates and tenders followed
from James for such work as laying out gardens on the top of the
cliff, turfing the cliff face and constructing a refreshment pavilion
on the approach road to the pier. The company also made up the High Cliff Road and
widened the Fisherman's Road for the Local Board.[19] Such was the effect of the MS&LR
construction work that a local newspaper commented that, although Cleethorpes had
never lacked day and half-day excursionists, the company's improvements 'cannot fail to
draw a fair proportion of that aristocratic patronage which to Cleethorpes, with few
exceptions, has hitherto been unknown'.[20]

1885 saw continuing work on the construction and other attractions, including the
provision of what was termed by a local paper 'the imitation pile of ruins to which, we
believe, the title of Ross Castle has been given'.[21] This was named after the MS&LR
secretary Edward Ross and still overlooks the promenade. Money was spent on gas
lighting for the promenade and also on a photographic studio. James had not given up
on his proposal that the sea wall should continue upriver to the fish dock (Section 1 of
his original scheme) and submitted a revised
tender for £4,778, which was left in abeyance
by the company board of directors.[22]

Royal Opening

The work being carried out by the MS&LR
was a major piece of civil engineering, and
called for an appropriate opening ceremony
and celebration. Royalty, in the person of
Prince Albert Victor, the eldest son of the
Prince of Wales, accepted an MS&LR
invitation to open the improvements. Special
arrangements were made for the running
of trains during the Prince's visit. In all,
10 'specials' were run for the Prince, his

26 *Admittance pass to the royal opening of the
MS&LR promenades, etc., in 1885.*

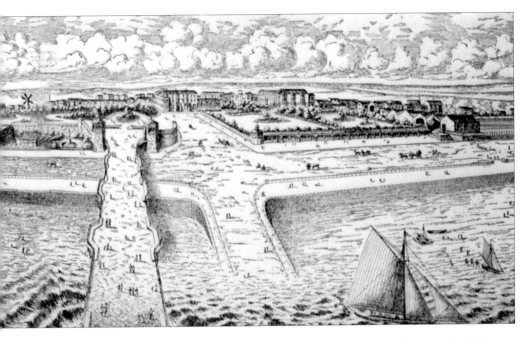

25 *Bird's eye view of the pier and the new sea wall, promenades, pier slipway and Sea Road, 1885.*

entourage, MS&LR directors and others and for transporting the horses and carriages which would be needed by the royal party during their visit. Detailed instructions were given to staff on keeping the lines clear for these trains and some regular services were cancelled or re-timed.[23]

The Prince stayed overnight at Brocklesby Hall as the guest of Lord Yarborough and made his way from there to Grimsby Town Station on 2 July 1885. Here a procession was formed, which made its way first to the *Royal Hotel* to view the statue of the Prince's grandfather, the late Prince Consort (the statue had been paid for by Watkin). It then proceeded to Cleethorpes. Apart from the Prince and his retinue, the procession included Lord and Lady Yarborough, Watkin and other directors of the MS&LR, Edward Heneage and Alexander Grant-Thorold and members of their families, and members and officials of the Grimsby Corporation. At the Cleethorpes boundary they were joined by members of the Cleethorpes Local Board. The procession was accompanied by a police escort, brass bands, fire brigades, friendly societies and other clubs. Guards of honour were provided by the Lincolnshire Rifle Volunteers and the Lincolnshire Artillery Volunteers. After inspecting the gardens and planting a commemorative tree, the Prince declared the gardens and improvements open. Following lunch in the special pavilion, he departed by train from the Cleethorpes railway station, stopped en route to inspect the Royal Dock, and went on to Brocklesby.

Decorations were provided at points along the route, such as the railway stations and the promenade, gardens and pier. A 'Grand Triumphal Arch of Solid Blocks of Ice', consisting of more than 30 tons of ice, was erected on the highest point of the cliff. A firework display was held in the late evening, which included 'a Colossal Portrait of H.R.H. Prince Albert Victor ... and a Grand Triumphal Arch supported by Diamond

Pillars surmounted by the Railway Company's Arms, with a motto "Prosperity to the Trade of Grimsby"'—possibly not the most diplomatic motto to display on Cleethorpes' day of celebration.[24]

The official guide[25] to the day's events described the improvements:

> All along the most frequented part of the foreshore now stretches a magnificent sea-wall, composed of solid concrete ... [which] encloses a width of the old beach varying from seventy to one hundred feet, which has been filled up and solidified level with the wall, making a broad even surface, along the entire length of which is formed an imposing promenade, carriage drive, and inner walk. The promenade, which is beautifully asphalted, occupies twenty-five feet of the outer edge, and is separated from the carriage drive by an ornamental dwarf wall, which may be easily stepped over. The drive has a uniform width of forty feet ... The former rugged brow of the Cliff, euphemistically termed the 'Recreation Ground' is now a smiling garden, artistically laid out ... and planted with shrubs and flowers ... The jagged and dangerous edge of the old Cliff has given place to grassy slopes, with rustic and picturesque paths down to the lower grounds and the promenade: and its highest point opposite Sea View-Street is now marked by a peculiar conical structure built after an ancient fashion, with stones of all shapes and sizes roughly stuck together with cement, designated 'Ross Castle' the pile, appearing at a short distance like some tower or castle of 'ye olden time' ... The superiority of 'Ross Castle' as an 'observatory' is chiefly due to its advantageous position, its height being scarcely above that of the adjacent ground, for the Railway Company in carrying out the improvements have been careful to avoid obstructing the view from the houses which front the beach.

Other improvements were also eulogised:

> Midway between 'Ross Castle' and the Pier, on a lower terrace of ornamental grounds, has been built a handsome bathing establishment ... The interior arrangements are formed on the newest and most approved principles, and comprise ... both salt and fresh water baths, hot or cold, and shower baths, besides a large salt water swimming

27 *The splendid new Sea Road access to the seafront and the pier entrance built by the MS&LR in 1885 in place of the unsatisfactory track known as the Folly Hole. The Refreshment Room in the centre of the picture, and a large part of the pier entrance area, were absorbed into the wider Sea Road in the 1930s.*

28 *An essential part of the MS&LR improvements of 1885 was the Central Promenade, seen here in the early 1900s. The pier can be seen at its original length along with the present Pier Pavilion, which was opened in 1905. Ross Castle, on the left, is a 'folly', also built in 1885. It is named after Edward Ross, secretary of the MS&LR for 42 years, who died in office in 1891.*

29 *Interior of the swimming baths built on the Central Promenade in 1885 as part of the MS&LR improvements.*

30 *The Grotto Café in the Pier Gardens, built by the MS&LR as part of its 1885 improvements and seen here in the 1920s. The site is currently occupied by the waterfall on the Central Promenade.*

bath ... To the west of the Pier the old sandy track from the *Dolphin Hotel* down to the beach, once known as the Folly Hole, and latterly as the Sea-road, is now a road in fact, as well as in name, which, after crossing the sea-wall, is extended by a gentle declivity to the level of the sands, with a paved carriage way and flagged side walks, which form a most convenient landing place for the numerous pleasure boats that ply for hire during the season. Fisherman's-road, at the east end of the sea-wall has also been made a similar path to the beach. From the top of Sea-road, and separated from it by a wall describing a shapely and rising curve, runs a substantial road up to the Pier gates, and in the recess formed on the lower side of the wall, a suite of refreshment rooms has been constructed ... The sea-wall, the carriage drive, and promenade, extend beyond the station to opposite the Gas works, and there is in active progress a further extension which will make the whole length nearly a mile ... and a broad stone staircase ascends from the wall to the high ground at the top of Sea View Street.

Tribute was paid to Watkin:

Sir Edward Watkin, the astute and far-seeing chairman of the Company, had to encounter considerable opposition from shareholders before the heavy expenditure which the enterprise involved was sanctioned, but there is little fear that the diffident shareholders will have any cause to regret the outlay, as the general effect produced, if it has not really exceeded the anticipations of Sir Edward and his colleagues, has certainly so immeasurably enhanced the natural attractiveness of the place that Cleethorpes must now rank as one of the prettiest and most seductive watering places on the east coast, and the number of visitors, both for the day and for the season, is sure to be greatly increased.

Improvements to the railway station and the financial benefits to the railway company were set out:

> Although both Great Northern and Midland excursion trains come to Cleethorpes in the summer season, they have to run over the line of the MS&LR Co., who at present have the monopoly of the railway communication, and it is in the increased traffic that they will find remuneration. Ample provision for this has been made within the last few years, the station accommodation being now most convenient and extensive. The long asphalted platforms will admit of a half a score big excursion trains being loaded at once, whilst the most commodious sidings afford space for as many or more to be shunted, and for the stowing of a large number of reserve carriages.

The royal opening did not see the end of railway company expenditure. Subsequent tenders from James that were accepted included a Grotto in the Pier Gardens and an arcade of stalls at the southern end of the promenade. Timber groynes were constructed, both for the protection of the sea wall and to accumulate sand to make the foreshore more attractive. A return wall was also built at the northern end of the promenade in order to protect back land and prevent flooding from the sea.[26]

In October 1888 a clock tower with four dials was erected at the station. Such was the increase in the number of visitors to the resort, that approval was later given for James to erect 16 additional shops and a colonnade 'in order to avoid the congestion of Traffic' under the existing colonnades. The MS&LR also provided a fish 'Hatchery & Aquarium' in the Pier Gardens, which was opened to the public on Good Friday 1889.[27] The heavy expenditure paid off: increasing passenger numbers were apparent. During the three months from July to September 1887, a total of 211,109 passengers visited the resort. The railway's historian has commented that Cleethorpes was one of the best investments the MS&LR made.[28]

31 *Pier entrance with the Dolphin Hotel to the right, c.1890.*

The Railway and the Pier

After leasing the pier, the railway company used it as a major attraction to encourage more rail passengers to visit the resort. Only three weeks after the opening of the promenade and gardens in 1885, the MS&LR directors were considering a tender from James for the erection of a concert hall on the pier head; this was subsequently accepted and a pavilion with seating for 800 people was opened in 1887. The following year saw alterations and additions to refreshment rooms on the pier.[29] At this time admission to the pier cost 2d., which included the pier gardens.

The new pavilion was referred to as the Grand Concert Hall and 1888 saw the bringing in of theatrical expertise to improve the pier's attractions:

> The M S and L Railway Company intend carrying their enterprise still further by arranging to hold concerts daily in the pier pavilion during the ensuing season. Mr J.H. Curry, the energetic proprietor of the Prince of Wales Theatre, Grimsby, has been intrusted the office of engaging the artistes, etc. and under his direction a suitable stage has been erected and certain structural alterations carried out. Mr Curry's connection with the theatrical and music-hall world, and his experience as a manager, will enable him to put on an entertainment calculated, if possible, to please all classes of pleasure-seekers.[30]

Variety performances became the customary entertainment, held twice daily at 2.00 p.m. and 6.30 p.m., except for Sundays. In addition, a band played music for dancing in the morning, afternoon and evening (before, between and after the variety concerts). July saw the beginning of the music hall style of summer entertainment, which included 'Miss A. Desmore and Spence Bros., with their Wonderful Elephant, The Famous Herr Frikell, with his Mystic Novel Illusions and Capital Fun, Mr Tony Sinclair, the quaintest Negro Comedian, with his American Songs and Dances, and Miss Alice Desmore, Ballad Vocalist and Male Impersonator'. On Sunday no dancing or variety entertainment was provided; instead, 'selections' were played by the band in the afternoon and evening.[31]

Visitors in July 1889 could see 'The Man Fish', Mr Oscar Dubourg. He was billed as the 'Champion Tank Performer of the World!' who 'has travelled all over the world and had the honour to perform before all the Crowned Heads of Europe and Asia'. He was assisted by 'Miss Lolla, The Finest Lady Tank Performer Extant'. Dubourg performed such underwater feats as eating an orange, smoking a cigar, drinking a bottle of wine, dressing, undressing and singing a song with his head in a bucket. Miss Lolla would write on a slate, sew, look for eggs, peel an apple, swim like a fish and do an acrobatic performance with a hoop. The two would come together when Oscar performed his imitation of a drowning man and Miss Lolla came to his rescue.[32]

This blend of music hall variety turns, concerts and dancing continued into the next decade. June 1890 saw entertainment by:

> Snows minstrels, a quartette of the burnt cork fraternity, who sing and dance fairly well, crack one or two new jokes, and a lot of hoary-headed old chestnuts, which despite their age gain a laugh, and in addition to some quick cartoon sketching, introduce other business which serves to provide an agreeable turn.[33]

The same pattern of entertainment could be enjoyed in the new century. In the summer of 1900 the pavilion featured 'Grand Variety Entertainments' daily at 2.30 p.m. and 6.30 p.m., Friday evenings and Sundays excepted. In addition to a comedian and a tenor, artistes included 'Ernest, the Human Orchestra: marvellous vocal and instrumental mimic'. Admission to the pier and gardens was still 2d. plus a further 2d. for admission to the entertainment.

At the beginning of the new century, the resort's guidebook summarised the entertainment provided on the pier:

> The total length of the Pier is 400 yards, the deck is pitch-pine, pleasant to promenade, and very suggestive of an ocean greyhound in fine weather. At the sea end of the Pier is a very pretty Concert Hall, capable of seating 880 people. The popularity of the place proves its inadequacy, it is to be hoped ere long the … [railway company] will see their way clear to enlarge it to quite double its present dimensions. Twice daily a first-class Entertainment is given, at 2.30 p.m. and 6.30 p.m. by artistes of high standing … The Concert Hall is open for Dancing from 11.00 a.m. to 12.30 p.m., 3.30 p.m. to 5.00 p.m., and from 7.45 p.m. to 10.00 p.m., Friday evenings excepted. On Friday a grand Promenade Concert is being given. Sundays: Sacred Concerts are given at 3.00 p.m. and 8.15 p.m.[34]

But piers were subject to extreme weather conditions and the Cleethorpes pier soon began to need remedial attention. In the autumn of 1890, concerns were raised about the need to carry out repairs. About a third of the timber runners under the planking deck were decayed and in need of immediate replacement; the planking and main joists had about three or four years' life remaining; the ironwork was in a very loose state throughout and needed a thorough overhaul: bolts needed to be screwed up tight, a number of tie rods needed to be renewed and some additional ones installed. In addition, the pier and pier buildings needed cleaning down and painting before the next season. The company engineer was instructed to get the work carried out as economically as possible. More crucial work was needed only six years later. In February 1896, a report stressed the urgent necessity of strengthening the pier, without delay, at a probable cost of £2,650. The work was carried out in 1897, when the pier's cast-iron cylindrical columns resting on piles were strengthened by the addition of rolled steel girders.[35]

Temperance and the Pier

Although the railway company was now the major force in the development of the resort, its plans could still be forestalled by residents who were unhappy with the way the resort was evolving. The increasing numbers of visitors to the resort contained a wide spectrum of the population, from the peaceable to the boisterous. There is no doubt that it was the former, the 'respectable' visitors, whom the residents welcomed most, although it was probably the latter that spent more money and benefited local traders. A report on Good Friday 1873 commented:

> Of course there was the usual amount of lawless conduct which is the inevitable concomitant of these universal holidays. Rough, boisterous men and youths, totally disregarding the comfort of the more orderly and peaceable visitors, indulged in uproarious horse-play … Towards night these disorderly scenes became more frequent. The dissipation of sadly too many was followed by the usual consequences—quarrelling and fighting. On all sides, men, women, and youths could be met in one stage or other of intoxication, and on the following day, even in our own town, many a cut forehead with a contused and blackened eye testified to the serious brawls or the strength of the beer.[36]

Public conduct problems caused by the more 'merry' element sometimes led to tension between residents and the resort's commercial interests. This is exemplified in the controversy that arose over the application for a liquor licence for the pier. There was a long-established temperance presence in the town, pioneered largely by the local Methodist congregations, and the Primitive Methodists in particular. The movement had been formally present in the town since 1851, and such was the local involvement that a temperance meeting held in the town in 1872 heard that Cleethorpes was 'becoming famous for its local abstainers'. Specific temperance groups in 1888 included the Cleethorpes Branch of the British Women's Temperance Association and the Cleethorpes Band of Hope, which had over 700 members drawn from Primitive Methodist, Wesleyan and Anglican churches.[37]

On several occasions during the 1870s the pier company applied to the local magistrates sitting as the brewster licensing sessions for a wine or liquor licence for the pier Refreshment Room but on each occasion this was refused. It is likely that the decision was influenced by recurring reports of the drunkenness of trippers visiting the resort. Possibly reports of what was termed 'indecorous' dancing by men on the pier did not help.[38] In 1885, after the railway company leased the pier, it applied for liquor licences for the pier and also for the Refreshment Room situated by the shore end of the pier at the entrance to the promenade. A liquor licence was granted for the Refreshment Room but refused for the pier.[39]

In July 1888 the MS&LR applied for an occasional licence for the Pier Pavilion on those days in the season (July to September) when excursion trains were run, Mondays, Wednesdays and Saturdays. This was seen by the company as an interim measure, because they intended to apply for a full licence at the brewster sessions in the coming September. The application was contested by religious groups, and a petition was presented. It was signed by the vicar of the parish, local nonconformist ministers and between 400 and 500 other people. It was presented by the Primitive Methodist minister, the Rev. R.W. Keightley, who 'sincerely trusted that their Worships would decline to afford facilities for obtaining intoxicating drink on the Pier or in the Gardens; as the petitioners were of opinion that there were quite sufficient facilities for procuring such liquors without granting any further licences'. The petition read:

> We are convinced that the granting of such licence will be injurious to the credit
> of the town by promoting drunkenness amongst excursionists, and thereby greatly
> interfere with the comfort of respectable families and visitors who are now accustomed
> to use the Pier as a pleasure resort. We therefore pray your Worships to decline the
> application for the licence.

The magistrates refused the licence, taking into account the 'very strong' expressed opinion of the inhabitants of Cleethorpes, on the grounds that it would not be 'conducive to the public convenience, comfort, and order'.[40] The refusal produced a rival petition, organised by the railway company, requesting a licence for the Pier Pavilion. A further anti-licence petition was organised for presentation at the annual brewster sessions on 4 September. A local newspaper commented that:

> The Temperance party is very strong here, and, in the hands of such energetic workers
> as the ladies of the Cleethorpes Branch of the British Temperance Society; the Rev.
> R. W. Keightley, and Mr Johnson Brown, it may be safely assumed that every effort
> will be made to make the counter petition as formidable as possible.[41]

At the subsequent sessions on 4 September, the railway company put in an application for a full liquor licence or, in default of that, a wine licence for the Pier Pavilion. The railway company's application was made by Mr Mason, solicitor. He handed in three petitions requesting the grant of a licence and signed by 1,209 excursionists, 276 residents

32 *Crowds on the North Promenade in the early 1900s—ample justification for the MS&LR's heavy investment in Cleethorpes.*

of Grimsby and district and 70 residents of Cleethorpes. The Rev. Keightley then presented a petition signed by nearly 1,000 Cleethorpes inhabitants, requesting that the licence be refused, and threw doubt on the validity of the railway company's petition. He also pointed out that the town already had 11 or 12 'on' licences and three of those were held by the railway company. He went on to say that:

> Of the 1,200-odd persons who had signed the memorial for a licence, a large number probably would never see Cleethorpes again. The petition he presented was signed by persons who had a very great stake in the place. The Railway Company were not the only investors in Cleethorpes; there were many other people who had staked their all there, and who were very much concerned about the respectability of the place, and the comfort and order of those who frequent the Pier. The granting of a liquor licence on the Pier would practically exclude a very large portion of the visitors who came to Cleethorpes, and shut out the children of thousands of respectable families.

The bench retired for 25 minutes and the application for a licence was refused.[42] Although the temperance lobby won on this occasion, the growing popularity of the resort meant that it was becoming increasingly difficult to satisfy the increasing numbers of visitors who were reluctant to put up with what were considered to be outmoded restrictions on their relaxation and entertainment. Indeed, the question of licensing was only one of the changes which its development as a popular resort brought to the town:

Gradually its Methodist puritanism was being watered down, both by the huge numbers of non-Methodist immigrants, and by the changing views of many of the Methodists themselves. Asked what she considered the greatest change in the town during her lifetime, an old Methodist lady … stated that it was the secularisation of Sunday by the trips and the consequent Sunday trading. A Primitive Methodist lady remarked on Cleethorpes that: 'It's getting bigger, but oh! it's getting wicked'.[43]

Railway Domination

The question of liquor licensing was not the only contentious issue in which the railway company became embroiled. Although the Local Board had good reason to be thankful for the high level of investment in the resort by the company, it was concerned when the latter appeared to be trying to exert too much local control. There was conflict in particular over the regulation of the foreshore. We have seen that earlier in the century the indiscriminate use of the beach by traders led to complaints. The Board had fundamental concerns over the ownership, control and regulation of the foreshore. Firstly, the beach was an essential part of the resort: its appearance and the conduct of those using it helped to form the visitor's impression of Cleethorpes. Secondly, local traders felt that only local ratepayers should be allowed to trade on the sands. Consequently, the Board complained in 1886 when the railway company claimed the right to license users of the foreshore in front of its promenade, arguing that this conflicted with its own licensing rights.[44] Eventually, in 1889, the Board complained to the Crown agents, the Commissioners of Woods and Forests, that the MS&LR was letting out portions of the foreshore and collecting tolls:

> for the privilege of erecting stalls, swing boats, Aunt Sallys of various kinds and various other entertainments—which is a great obstruction and an actual damage to the thousands of people who resort to this favourite watering place during the Summer months. The Local Board further respectfully beg to remind you that the people have had the privilege of roaming upon the sand and foreshore at will for a great number of years. And I am further instructed to ask … when and how did such powers reach the hands of the Railway Company.[45]

The Commissioners wrote to the MS&LR, asking for comments on the Board's letter. The response was an indignant reply from Edward Ross that the company's rights on the foreshore came under a lease dated 1883 from the Crown to A.W.T. Grant-Thorold. The company had obtained an assignment of the lease in 1888 in order to control the immense numbers of visitors and providers of amusements who had been attracted as a result of the company's investment. Ross contended that:

> In exercise … of their rights as lessees of the foreshore, the Company have charged these caterers to the public amusement a small toll for the privilege of placing their stands and plying their various businesses upon the sea shore in front of the Company's works and the Company have also appointed police to regulate the positions of the stands and it is altogether untrue to say that there is any obstruction to visitors roaming on the sands.

He continued with strong criticism of the local authority:

> It is with regret that my Directors find that the local authorities should try to thwart their efforts to make Cleethorpes attractive and misconstrue their motives, especially after their neglect of their obvious duty in the past which has made it necessary for the Company very reluctantly to take in hand the preservation of the place, which

but for them would have ceased to exist as a place of resort for visitors from the populous district which it appears naturally to serve, and they can only fear that their action is prompted by merely local jealousy.[46]

The Commissioners wrote to the Board enclosing a copy of Ross's letter and stating that a local inquiry would be held into the dispute if the Board so wished, in which case it would have to provide a deposit of £10 towards the costs. However, the Commissioners saw 'no reason to interfere further in the matter'.[47]

The Board took no further action and the railway company continued to dominate the control and development of the seafront. A further incident, however, shows the continuing tension between the two bodies. The Board complained that MS&LR officials were locking the gates that gave access to the cliff steps down to the promenade, and gave instructions that if need be the Board's surveyor should force them open. In November 1890, Ross wrote to the Board that 'It does seem extraordinary that after the Company have expended nearly £100,000 for the benefit and improvement of Cleethorpes they should be met on every hand by the Local Authorities [sic] in the most hostile spirit'.[48]

* * *

These conflicts between the MS&LR and various local groups illustrate the change in the resort caused by the coming of the railway. We have seen the Rev. Sibthorpe complaining in 1870 that 'This was, twenty years since, a nice quiet place: now it is a scene of bustle and distraction.' The local vestry, and then the fledgling and poorly financed Local Board, had courted the MS&LR as a potential benefactor, but soon began to appreciate that the help came at a price: the domination of the resort by a large entrepreneurial organisation with its own agenda. This was succinctly explained by Watkin in 1884 when he told reluctant shareholders that 'we should make the place more attractive to visitors, and thus get a larger passenger traffic', with the understandable intention of achieving good annual dividends; the Local Board had no quarrel with such intentions. However, conflict began to arise in response to Watkin's view that 'we want watering places of our own'. So what Ross called the local 'hostile spirit' may be seen merely as the representatives of the local community reacting to the realisation that what had once been a locally developed and financed resort was now in the hands of a powerful outsider whose essential motive was profit.[49]

The change is exemplified by the fact that, whereas the pier was largely built with capital provided by local residents, the massive improvements undertaken by the MS&LR were financed by outside capital. This was followed by more investment by outside businessmen: a switchback railway constructed in 1887 was provided by an entrepreneur who had erected similar switchbacks throughout England; another switchback was erected in 1888 by a Manchester contractor working for a Bolton proprietor.[50]

A commentator emphasised the railway domination of the resort in 1895:

> This is rapidly becoming the most crowded watering-place in Lincolnshire … This little town is quite a unique development of railway enterprise, belonging as it does, almost entirely to the Manchester, Sheffield and Lincolnshire Railway … Cleethorpes, owing to its easy railway access, is invaded daily in summer by enormous crowds of excursionists from Yorkshire, Lancashire and the Midland counties.[51]

However, two events in the same year saw changes which led to more robust challenges to the railway's authority. The first was the replacement of the Cleethorpes-with-Thrunscoe Local Board of Health with the more powerful Cleethorpes-with-Thrunscoe Urban

District Council; the second was the entry into the arena of resort development of a group of local businessmen who proposed to build:

> ... a large Public Hall, suitable for Concerts, Balls, Lectures, Stage Plays and Public Meetings, also to provide Reading and Billiard Rooms, Social Club-house and Library. The Hall is intended to meet an urgent public necessity ... It is being erected upon a central and valuable site fronting the Alexandra Road ... The annual increase of the number of summer visitors to Cleethorpes renders the erection of a large public Hall an actual necessity, and in order to meet this and to provide the inhabitants of the town and neighbourhood with a suitable resort during all parts of the year, the Directors have great confidence in asking the public to take shares in the company.

The estimated cost of construction was £4,000, and of the initial 5,000 one pound shares, 1,700 had already been applied for by 1 October 1895. The building opened on Whit Monday 25 May 1896, and was named the Alexandra Hall. About four years later it was altered and re-named the Empire Theatre. The promoters and initial directors were four 'Steam Fishing Vessel Owners' (George E. Moody, Henry Sleight, William Grant and William Mudd), the Secretary of the Coal, Salt and Tanning Company (Charles F. Carter), the Chairman of the new Cleethorpes-with-Thrunscoe Urban District Council (Frederick W. Mackrill), a Brick Manufacturer (Walwyn T. Chapman) and a Fish Merchant (Arthur Brown).[52] They represented an imposing cross-section of local interests and were characteristic of a new breed of local entrepreneurs who had successfully survived the rough and tumble of local industry. In time, they and their ilk might provide a suitable counter to the railway company's domination of the resort.

VI

New and Old Cleethorpes

The 1880s and 1890s

The improvements carried out by the railway company had made the resort much more attractive and had propelled it into the mainstream of resort development, leaving it open to influences such as outside capital, shareholders' interests and competition between railway companies and 'their' resorts. The company's large-scale local investment created the conditions for it to become the dominant figure in the resort, but although this was to the resort's great benefit, it is not surprising that the 1880s had seen conflicts with local institutions as the company's domination of the resort began to be questioned. Whilst the railway company was concentrating on improving the seafront and taking control of it, however, another body, Sidney Sussex College, was using its authority as a landowner to take control of another part of Cleethorpes.

New Cleethorpes

House building was continuing at a good rate in the town: 313 houses were built during the 1880s, a good proportion of which were in or near the resort area, including on Yarra Road, Albert Road, Prince's Road, George Street and Charles Street. However, it was the 1890s that saw the greatest growth. Between 1891 and 1901, the population of Cleethorpes increased dramatically, rising from 4,306 to 12,578 inhabitants; houses went from 968 to 2,926 in number. The reason for these dramatic increases lay with neighbouring Grimsby. We have seen that the coming of the railway to Grimsby in 1848, and the completion of a new dock in 1852, had led the College to expect that its land in north-western Cleethorpes, less than a mile from the new dock, would soon be in demand for building development. Unfortunately for the College, other cheap building land was readily available even nearer to the dockland industrial area, some of which was in the parish of Clee between the borders of Grimsby and Cleethorpes. Such was the rapid growth of Grimsby in the 1860s that house building spilled over the borough's border on to this land, which in 1873 was constituted the Clee-with-Weelsby local health district. Its heavily-built up northern area became known as New Clee. In 1889, Clee-with-Weelsby was absorbed into Grimsby, which meant that from that year north-western Cleethorpes had shared a common boundary with Grimsby.

As Grimsby's New Clee became built up, housing began to spread into Cleethorpes and on to College land in and near Park Street. This started in 1886, 33 years after the

33 *Horse-drawn tram on Alexandra Road. The service began in Grimsby in 1881 and initially stopped at the Park Street boundary. With the growth of New Cleethorpes it was extended into Cleethorpes as far as Poplar Road in 1887 and to Albert Road on the seafront in 1898.*

College had prepared for estate development. But once it started, house building spread rapidly, mostly in new streets on College land and laid out either side of Grimsby Road between Park Street and Manchester Street. A new suburb, which became known as New Cleethorpes, was formed. By 1895, New Cleethorpes contained a third of the resort's ratepayers. By 1913 over half the population and housing stock of Cleethorpes lay in this north-western area of the town.[1] The suburb was the result of a need to house Grimsby's rapidly expanding industrial workforce, coupled with the College's aspiration to increase the income from its Cleethorpes estate. New Cleethorpes was far from the resort area and, as a consequence, the town became divided into two separate communities (see map on page 89).

The attraction of both New Cleethorpes and 'Old' Cleethorpes as commuter suburbs was enhanced by the extension of the Grimsby tramway system into the town. A horse-drawn tramway had been introduced to Grimsby in 1881 by the Great Grimsby Street Tramways Company, a subsidiary of the Provincial Tramways Company based in Portsmouth. Initially the service stopped at the Cleethorpes boundary at Park Street, but in 1887 it was extended along Grimsby Road in New Cleethorpes and as far as Poplar Road, stopping short of the steep Isaac's Hill. In 1898 the gradient of the hill was eased and the line was extended to a seafront terminus at Albert Road. The system was subsequently electrified and a tram depot and electricity generating station were built on Pelham Road in Cleethorpes. The Cleethorpes section was extended to Brighton Street and electric trams began to run between Grimsby and the new seafront terminus in 1901. The trams were now competition for the other form of public transport in the town: the railway. The railway lost local traffic to the trams and in 1903 a fare war developed between the two companies.[2]

34 Electric trams superseded the horse-drawn trams in 1901; here is one at the Kingsway terminus near Rowston Street after the Kingsway was completed in 1906.

We have already seen that, in general, the houses on College land were built under leasehold tenure on 99-year building leases. This produced annual leasehold ground rents which, as more and more land was turned over to building, formed the major part of the College's income, and also enabled it to expand its buildings and teaching staff. The importance of this leasehold development to the College may be seen from the fact that, in 1890, its Cleethorpes estate produced £2,158, or 29 per cent of the College's income. Over the ensuing 10 years this amount increased rapidly: by 1900 the ground rents produced £5,589, or 50 per cent of its income.[3]

Leasehold tenure also enabled the College to control building by the use of covenants, or conditions, in its building leases. By controlling the nature of the layout and building on its land the College influenced the character of a large part of Cleethorpes. The College's local agent, solicitor W.H. Daubney, disapproved of the manner in which some of the Grant-Thorold land in nearby New Clee had been used for 'a paltry class of house'.[4] Daubney and the College wanted something better and planned the street layout accordingly. Most of the College's covenants were concerned with maintaining the fabric of the estate and ensuring that buildings were kept repaired and in good condition. In addition, however, the College wanted to maintain its estate as a pleasant and decent area in which to live. Accordingly, its leases included a detailed covenant regarding nuisances. This forbade the erection of a wide range of commercial buildings such as slaughterhouses, blacksmiths' shops and beer shops, and stipulated that the leaseholders and householders should not:

> harbour, lodge or permit to dwell therein any lewd or disorderly person or persons, nor keep thereon any hogs, boars, sows, pigs or other offensive beast or cattle, nor shall suffer anything to be done upon the premises … which shall or may grow to the annoyance, grievance, disturbance or damage of the Lessors or Lessees or tenants in the neighbourhood.[5]

This covenant was later amended to include prohibitions on selling any kind of intoxicating liquor and on fish curing houses, smoke houses and fried fish shops. However, despite its strictures against beer shops and the sale of intoxicating liquor, the College had a pragmatic attitude to the use of its land in this respect, where it was appropriate. New Cleethorpes lay astride the main route from Grimsby to the resort. It is not surprising, therefore, that the College permitted two public houses on its land there for the convenience of residents and those passing to and from 'Old' Cleethorpes.

One of the public houses became linked with the provision of a professional football ground, Blundell Park, which is still the home ground of the Grimsby Town Football Club. The club had played on a ground at Clee Park, which was a privately owned recreational area on land at the corner of Park Street and Grimsby Road, leased from the College. When the Clee Park lease expired in 1889, the College developed the land for housing and the *Clee Park Hotel*. Accordingly, the club moved to the Abbey Park ground in Grimsby owned by Edward (later Lord) Heneage. When this, too, was required for housing, the club moved to its present location on land purchased from the College by J.H. Alcock. He paid the College £7,500 for 7¼ acres for a hotel (the *Imperial Hotel*) and a football ground. The club moved to the ground in 1899.[6]

'A Sanitary and Pretty Place'

Although the College was the prime mover in developing its estate, it had to acknowledge the interest of the Local Board of Health. Here were two organisations obligated to serve the interests of the body they represented. For the former this was the College establishment in Cambridge with its buildings, staff and students; for the latter it was Cleethorpes and its residents. Neither organisation was entirely its own master and operated within legislation and regulation that limited its scope for action. An additional constraint on the actions of the Board was that it was beholden to a local electorate and local pressure groups. Circumstances dictated that the two bodies would be dependent on each other as the town grew. The College relied on the Board to provide the necessary structure of public administration and services within which it could develop its estate. In return, the Board relied upon the College to use its land responsibly in regard to local needs, whether this was for housing, public recreation, buildings or services, or road widening.

Whilst the College was building its new suburb, the Board endeavoured to control house building throughout the town; in 1885 it stressed that in future only building plans that showed nine-inch party walls would be approved because four and a half-inch walls gave no privacy to a family. Builders Henry and George Doughty were directed to conform to this decision with regard to houses they were currently building in the town. In 1887, the Board had to take action against George Doughty for breaching byelaws by

35 *Grimsby Road in New Cleethorpes, probably prior to the First World War. Two electric trams can be seen in the distance.*

36 *Blundell Street (later Avenue) in New Cleethorpes, probably in 1906. The street was named after Peter Blundell, whose legacy enabled Sidney Sussex College to purchase its local estate in 1616.*

erecting shops in Alexandra Road in front of Clark's Bazaar. In 1892 proceedings were taken against builders Wilkinson & Houghton for five houses in Phelps Street where the height of the rooms was less than that stipulated in the byelaws.[7]

The general sanitation of the town was another area to be tackled. Cleethorpes continued to be publicised as a 'health resort', and therefore became increasingly conscious of anything that would be to the detriment of this concept and deter potential visitors. In 1883, Dr Keetley reported on local health risks, such as the large number of pigs kept in an unclean state, and privies without boxes, in consequence of which 'the credit of the place as a health resort was lost'.[8] In 1886, a local government medical inspection of the town was carried out. Although the inspector made no damning comments he, too, was concerned about the pig-keeping, and recommended that byelaws prohibiting the keeping of pigs within 60 feet of dwellings should be revised to increase the distance. His other observations included the potential nuisance from the Clee nightsoil depot just beyond the town boundary, the disgraceful condition of some private roads, the need to carry out nuisance inspections more strictly, the need, in view of the increase in population, for a separate post of Inspector of Nuisances, and the desirability for the town to have a suitable place for the isolation of infectious diseases and cholera.[9]

The question of drainage and sewerage continued to be the subject of complaints. In the summer of 1885, MS&LR customers complained of 'awful' smells at Cleethorpes. These were brought to the attention of the Board by the railway company, which wrote that sanitary engineers had reported that 'the system of drainage in Cleethorpes is altogether improper and calculated to constitute great danger to health'. Its letter went on to say that 'The Company are of course greatly interested in the sanitary condition of this place, and I have been instructed to apply to you to at once provide your district with proper and sufficient sewers. I shall be glad to hear from you that this will be forthwith done.' The Board replied that the drainage system was as near perfect as could be.[10] One source of complaint was smelly water at the base of the promenade, samples of which were sent for analysis to the Local Government Board and to analysts at Manchester. Both

37 *Cloister Court, Sidney Sussex College, Cambridge. Its construction was largely financed with ground rents from the College's New Cleethorpes leases.*

reported that the smell was due to gases resulting from the reaction of sea water on the iron ore slag used by the railway company for filling the promenade. The MS&LR was still dissatisfied with the local drainage and the Board eventually borrowed £4,690 to improve the sewerage system and provide a northern outfall into the Humber.[11]

Yet another problem was outbreaks of infectious diseases, which could seriously undermine the resort's visiting trade. In April 1888, an outbreak of smallpox occurred in Grimsby and Clee-with-Weelsby, but was linked to Cleethorpes by rumours. This could affect the whole of the summer season. Railway excursions were cancelled at the request of mayors of a number of large towns, resulting in financial losses to both the railway company and tradespeople. A special meeting of the Board decided that bills should be posted in principal towns denying the rumours, and the railway company's Chief Medical Officer recommended running the trains past the stations at Grimsby, Grimsby Docks and New Clee without stopping. The Board's concern over reports of infectious diseases was also displayed in 1891, when a member contacted the *London Daily Telegraph* to correct its report of 200 cases of influenza at Cleethorpes; the real figure was twenty.[12] The resort had an outbreak of cholera in September 1893. There were several deaths in Grimsby, two visitors died in Cleethorpes and a party of 500 holidaymakers from Southwell cancelled their visit. A local newspaper remarked that 'the cholera scare has completely ruined the season at Cleethorpes'.[13] On the recommendation of health authorities, and despite objections from ratepayers, the Board appointed a Sanitary Inspector in October.[14]

An important consequence of the rapid expansion of housebuilding in New Cleethorpes was that the town had an increased rateable value, augmenting the Board's income from household rates. It was reported in 1892 that there had been an increase in the town's rateable value of not less than £6,000 during the past five years. In that time the number of ratepayers had grown from 750 to approximately 1,200.[15] This provided a firmer financial base for taking on commitments to improve the town. A local newspaper commented in 1893 that:

> The growth of Cleethorpes into a place of considerable more importance and popularity than it is at present is only a matter of a very few years away. The opening of the Sidney Sussex College estate at the Clee end of the parish is resulting in a great

increase of population and rateable value, and the Local Board are making arrangements for an extensive scheme of road improvements.[16]

One improvement the Board was able to finance resulted in controversy, and highlighted a dilemma caused by the building of New Cleethorpes: the division of the town into two distinct areas. New Cleethorpes and 'Old' Cleethorpes were separated by a large area of undeveloped land through which ran Grimsby Road, which linked the two communities. Controversy arose when the Board decided to 'flag' the town's footpaths, including a path alongside Grimsby Road. Public meetings were held by both the opponents and supporters of the policy. Opponents argued that the paving would benefit only the residents of New Cleethorpes and would be premature and a waste of money. Supporters argued that New Cleethorpes was providing a third of the town's rates and the paved path would make an excellent promenade to bring visitors into New Cleethorpes, instead of just the seafront.[17] In the event, the Board decided to go ahead with the scheme, and the paving of most of the town was completed in 1894. A local newspaper commented that the 'smart little town' had become entirely modernised and brought up to date. All the foopaths had been flagged and visitors could now walk around the town, after tiring of the promenade, without encountering mud and splashes.[18]

Also in 1894, the Board decided to provide a new drainage scheme, at an estimated cost of £4,500. Its main feature was a major new outfall at the south end of the resort which would deposit sewage in deep water. The chairman of the Board remarked that when the scheme was concluded Cleethorpes would be 'as sanitary and pretty a place' as any of the east coast resorts. The southern outfall was completed in 1895.[19]

38 *Part of New Cleethorpes development, which was essentially completed by the early 1900s but is seen here c.1994. Blundell Park Football Ground can be seen, with Grimsby Road running below it across the picture, Brereton Avenue running parallel to it and part of Sidney Park at the bottom of the picture. Barcroft Street is on the extreme left and Manchester Street on the extreme right.*

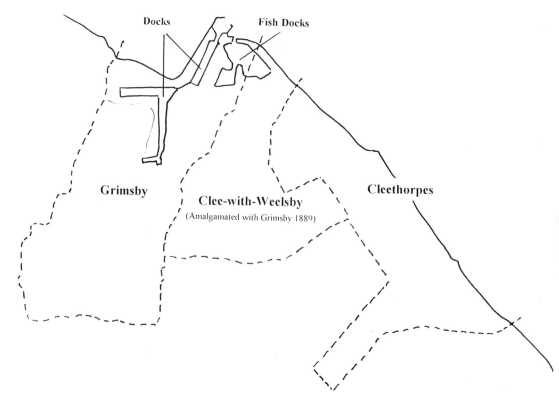

39 *Boundaries between Cleethorpes, Clee-with-Weelsby and Grimsby, 1873-89. In 1889, Clee-with-Weelsby was absorbed into Grimsby and from then on Grimsby's northernmost boundary with Cleethorpes ran along the middle of Park Street.*

A Stronger Voice for the People

This was the last major action taken by the Board because there soon followed a national scheme of local government reorganisation, under which the Local Boards of Health were replaced by Urban and Rural District Councils. Accordingly, the Board held its last meeting in December 1894 and was replaced by the Cleethorpes-with-Thrunscoe Urban District Council (UDC). The advent of the new local authority is significant because it would gradually acquire confidence and a stronger voice, leading to the eventual transfer of power in the resort from the railway company to the people, as represented by the UDC. In the meantime, in accordance with its new title and dignity, and its increasing income and duties, the UDC asked the College for a site for offices. The College offered 600 square yards at the top of Isaac's Hill, and the UDC's offer to purchase the land for two shillings a square yard was accepted.[20] In the event, the land was used instead for a Technical Institute which opened in March 1902 and later housed the town's public library.

Despite its new status, the local authority was not yet professionally mature, and in 1897 disparaging references were made to the casual manner in which it operated at its meetings: 'It appears to be the usual thing for the members to discuss a subject with one another across the table in the most offhand and familiar manner'. Improvement followed, however, and seven years later it was commented that 'We can remember the time when the meetings of the governing body used to be conducted on the most primitive lines … but now the place is governed on modern principles.'[21]

The UDC was still the public health authority, and was supported and encouraged in this work by the College. In 1899, the latter took the initiative and decided that leases for the building of new houses on its land would only be granted in future if the houses were provided with water closets, instead of the usual privy boxes. The privy box system was believed to be largely to blame for the prevalence of typhoid in Cleethorpes. Of the cases reported during August to October 1899, 24 had occurred where privy boxes were used and only four where there were water closets. At this time, the town had about 800 houses with water closets and 1,900 with wooden box privies. In the following year, the Council followed the College's lead and decided that all building plans in future must provide for water closets.[22] In the meantime, it started a programme of conversion of privies to water closets, and by 1902 nearly 500 had been converted, chiefly in the

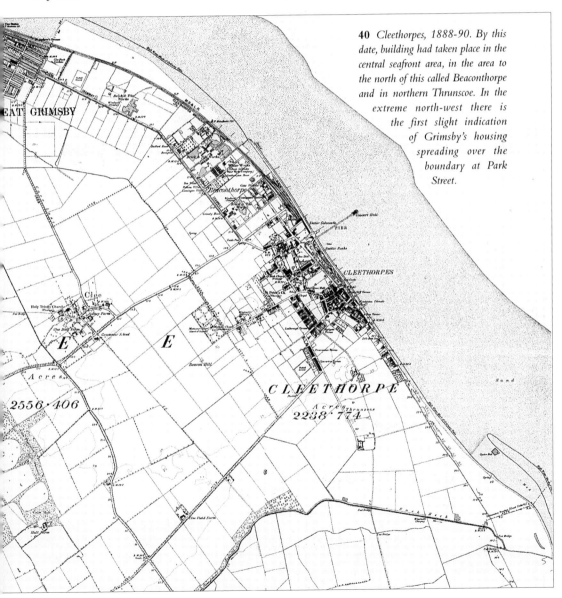

40 *Cleethorpes, 1888-90. By this date, building had taken place in the central seafront area, in the area to the north of this called Beaconthorpe and in northern Thrunscoe. In the extreme north-west there is the first slight indication of Grimsby's housing spreading over the boundary at Park Street.*

older part of the town. This work gained impetus under the UDC's Improvement Act of 1902, which included powers for it to convert privies at the expense of the property owner. Some 1,400 privies were converted under the Act.[23]

The UDC took the initiative in the provision of a public park. The rapid spread of housing in New Cleethorpes, and the need for leisure facilities for its rapidly increasing population, prompted the UDC to ask the College for land for a recreation ground. The College agreed to the request and donated 12 acres in 1898 for what became Sidney Park. The UDC engaged T.H. Mawson, the 'well-known gardener from Windermere', to design the park.[24] Mawson went on to become the leading landscape architect of his day. His clients included Queen Alexandra and Andrew Carnegie. He designed many public parks and was involved in major town-plannning schemes in Canada and Europe. The opening ceremony of the park in 1904 was performed by Charles Smith, the Master of the College, and the occasion was marked by mutually complimentary speeches by him and UDC members about the good relations between the two bodies. Certainly, apart from the benefits to the town, the development of the College estate had resulted in a vastly increased rental income for the College and a considerably increased rates income for the UDC.

Schools and Churches

The growth of the town also created educational needs. Two existing schools underwent major changes. The Humberston Foundation School (later Clee Grammar School) moved to new buildings in Clee in 1882, and the National School in St Peter's Avenue was enlarged in 1888 and 1891 to accommodate 900 pupils. A local School Board was created in 1894 in order to provide new schools; sites were purchased from Sidney Sussex College and work began on building schools in Barcroft Street in 1896, and Bursar Street in 1901. The School Board had a short life: it ceased to exist in 1903 when responsibility for schools in the town passed to the Lindsey County Council.

There was also development in church and chapel provision at this time including the construction of the new large Wesleyan Trinity Church on St Peter's Avenue, which opened in 1885. A Primitive Methodist Mission Room was provided in Beaconthorpe, and the present church there was built in 1914. The Park Street United Methodist Chapel opened in 1896, and the foundation stone of a Wesleyan Methodist Chapel was laid in Lovett Street in 1899.

VII

Changing Times
1900-1914

The 1880s and 1890s had seen significant changes in the resort. Sidney Sussex College had re-drawn the local map by building the suburb of New Cleethorpes, which had created a major increase in the population of Cleethorpes. The railway company had invested more than £100,000 in Cleethorpes, owned or controlled the main attractions, and was the dominant force in the resort. However, its authority was now being challenged by local groups and the inadequate Local Board of Health had been replaced by an Urban District Council with more powers and a sounder financial base.

Against this background, several events occurred early in the new century which appeared to symbolise the ending of one era in the resort's evolution and the beginning of another. An obvious national event was the death of Queen Victoria in January 1901 and the accession to the throne of Edward VII, ushering in the more relaxed Edwardian Age. Other events had more local relevance. The first, in 1901, was the death of Sir Edward Watkin, the main force in the MS&LR's investment in, and development of, Cleethorpes. Watkin had ceased to be chairman of the railway company in 1894, after 30 years in that position, but he remained a director. He had long promoted a direct line to London from Sheffield, and as its construction proceeded in the 1890s the MS&LR changed its name to become the Great Central Railway (GCR) in 1898. Although the company was still the strongest force in the resort as the new century began, Watkin's death presaged its eventual withdrawal from that role.

Another death, in 1903, was that of H.B. James, senior and supervising partner of Messrs. H.B. and A.F. James, the London contractors who had worked with the railway company in carrying out practically all the improvements at Cleethorpes. Sandwiched between these two deaths was the passing of the Cleethorpes Improvement Act in 1902 which was promoted by the UDC and gave it extensive authority over the further development and improvement of the town.

Extending the Resort into Thrunscoe

When the Local Board of Health was replaced by the UDC in 1896, the latter was soon faced with a major problem. Although erosion of the central cliff had been halted by the construction of the Central Promenade, the lower cliff to the south, in Thrunscoe, was suffering severe damage. The coastline here was surmounted by a muddy track called

41 *Sea Bank Road in the early 1900s, showing the eroded cliff before the Kingsway and Kings Parade were constructed. The first side street on the left is Haigh Street.*

the Sea Bank Road and the clerk to the UDC recalled that in the early 1870s this had been a broad roadway which had since been eroded by the 'ravages of the tide'. Houses had been built along the road and, in 1897, the UDC asked the railway company to continue its sea wall along the front of the Sea Bank Road in order to protect the road and adjoining property. The company declined to help. By this time it was heavily involved in its London extension.[1]

The owners of property along the road had already installed their own sea defence works in the form of rough wooden 'facings' to the cliff face, at an estimated cost of

42 *Sea Bank Road in the early 1900s, showing the wooden protection against cliff erosion, prior to work beginning on the Kingsway scheme. The first side street from the right is Rowston Street.*

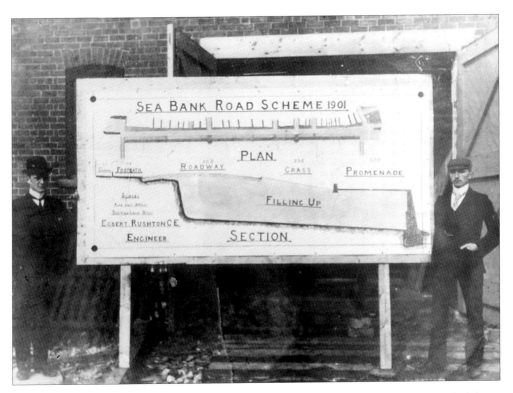

43 *Diagram of the Cleethorpes UDC's projected Sea Bank Road Scheme, 1901. The man on the left is believed to be Egbert Rushton, the UDC's Engineer in 1901.*

£1,200. In December 1897, these suffered storm damage and the following year saw increasing public discussion on the question of protecting the road.[2] The Council saw the possibility of linking the protection and improvement of the road with a scheme for the southerly development of the resort into Thrunscoe. Accordingly, it called a special meeting 'for the purpose of considering the dangerous state of Sea Bank Road and to form a scheme of improvement on the sea front'.[3]

A flurry of activity followed in 1898. Two private syndicates, based respectively in London and Hull, enquired into the possibility of obtaining land in Thrunscoe and providing a Winter Gardens or pleasure grounds, but nothing came of either approach.[4] Instead, the UDC itself began to look for land in Thrunscoe which might be used for visitor attractions. It asked Sidney Sussex College if it would sell an area of sand dunes and rough ground which was known as the 'Golf Links', although only a portion of the land actually formed part of the local golf course. The College refused to sell but offered to lease the land, an offer which the UDC declined.[5]

As the 1898 holiday season came to an end, the Council's Surveyor was instructed to prepare a plan for a new promenade along the length of Sea Bank Road. Also, the application to the College for the purchase of the 'Golf Links' land was renewed.[6] This land became an essential part of the Council's improvement plans because it lay on the coast at the end of the proposed new promenade and was seen as an ideal area to develop with visitor attractions. Therefore, 1899 began with a statement from the UDC that they were not prepared to proceed with the improvement scheme unless they could purchase

44 *Sea Bank Road in 1904, during the construction of the Kingsway and Kings Parade, showing the new sea wall being built on the right. The first side road on the left is Haigh Street.*

the 'Golf Links' from the College. The Council's justification for this stand was that the new work would bring financial benefit to the College by opening up the latter's other land in Thrunscoe for building. Consequently, there should also be some return to the ratepayers for the UDC expenditure. The Council's idea was to lay out the 'Golf Links' with gardens and other attractions from which it would derive an income.[7]

The first year of the new century saw further damage to Sea Bank Road and the portion near to the end of Rowston Street was undermined by the tide. Local press stressed the need for an improvement scheme to be undertaken and supported the UDC in its negotiations with the College. In 1901, the College's local land agent, F. Higgins, and solicitor, T. Mountain, recommended that the College should sell the land at the 'moderate price' of £1,000. They argued privately that if the College ever wanted to build on the land it would have to construct an expensive sea wall to prevent flooding. Therefore, the land would probably have remained undeveloped, in which case its sale would be to the College's benefit.[8]

Time was running out for Sea Bank Road in its battle with the elements and in March 1901 a 'tremendous storm' caused more damage. Soon afterwards the College wrote to the UDC that, subject to government approval, they would accept £1,000 for the 33 acres known as the 'Golf Links'. The Council offered £300 and negotiations produced a final price of £500 in 1901. A condition of the sale, imposed by the College, was that the land was sold as a public recreation ground and should remain so forever. Local press commented that: 'The development of the College estate would follow if the improvement was carried out. It would enrich the College and Council also. It was a mutual bargain.'[9]

Whilst engaged in its plans for Thrunscoe, the UDC had also been pursuing its aim of obtaining possession and control of the foreshore. In 1898 it was successful in being granted a lease by the Crown of the foreshore fronting Sea Bank Road, but the Great Central Railway refused its request to acquire the foreshore fronting the railway promenades.[10] Also to no avail was a petition to the company in 1901 from forty or fifty inhabitants and ratepayers maintaining that the UDC should have control of the foreshore and that only ratepayers of Cleethorpes should be allowed to trade thereon.[11]

Cleethorpes Improvement Act, 1902

Once the purchase of the 'Golf Links' was agreed with the College, much activity followed to advance the improvement scheme. An essential preliminary was a parliamentary bill to sanction the work and its finance. The likely financing of the scheme led to a very contentious dispute. Those who owned property along Sea Bank Road maintained that the ratepayers in general should pay for the improvement works. Those living in other parts of the town argued that the cost should fall only on the Sea Bank Road property owners because they would benefit financially when their property increased in value with the completion of the sea wall and road. In order to resolve the dispute it was decided to impose an improvement rate. This was a special municipal rate which would be paid in addition to the usual annual rate—but only by those owning property along the new road. It would be levied for 60 years at the rate of 2s. 6d. in the pound on property fronting the new road, 1s. on side streets and 6d. on certain property in the rear.[12] Some members of the Council continued to argue against promoting a parliamentary bill but Councillor George Moody replied that 'this was the chance of a lifetime and the opportunity for opening out and developing the southern end of Cleethorpes should not be missed … As Sea Bank Road now stood it was a disgrace to everybody'. The Council agreed to promote the bill and, in November 1901, approved plans and estimates prepared by W.T. Douglas, 'an engineering expert'.[13]

More debate followed in December, at a public meeting called to discuss whether or not to approve the bill. The meeting was well attended and lasted for three hours. It was chaired by Moody, who set out a detailed and persuasive case for proceeding with the bill and the improvement scheme. His speech was credited with breaking down opposition to the scheme and the meeting ended with an almost unanimous vote in favour of the bill. At the UDC's final debate on the matter in January 1902 the voting was eight in favour of the bill, one against and one neutral.[14]

Remaining opposition included the GCR, which argued that the UDC's proposed recreation grounds on the 'Golf Links' would compete unfairly with its own visitor attractions. This argument was disallowed by Parliament and the company withdrew all formal opposition in March 1902. The following month it agreed to relinquish its foreshore leases to the UDC. Agreements reached with the Crown agents and the Humber Conservancy regarding the acquisition of more of the foreshore by lease or purchase meant that, by 1903, the UDC had achieved its long-standing objective of ownership and control of all the resort's beaches.[15]

The UDC's bill became law on 31 July 1902 as the Cleethorpes Improvement Act. It marked a major advance for the UDC and confirmed its increasingly important and positive role in the administration and development of the town. In addition to authorising the Sea Bank Road improvements and granting sanction to regulate and control the all-important foreshore, the Act included powers regarding tramways, electricity, recreation grounds, sanitation, building and the control of infectious diseases. Authority to levy the improvement rate was also included.[16]

Kingsway and Kings Parade

The UDC now had the 'package' which enabled it to proceed confidently in its new role of resort developer. It had parliamentary sanction for the improvements, ownership and control of the foreshore and the 'Golf Links', and a rateable income large enough to finance the scheme. The improvements would consist of a road, called the Kingsway, which would be 35 feet wide, with pavements 10 feet wide. Running parallel would

45 *The official party and others at the opening of the Kingsway and Kings Parade on 12 July 1906. The opening ceremony was performed by Lady Henderson, the wife of the Chairman of the GCR. The buildings in the centre and to the left are on the corner of Brighton Street.*

be a width of 15 feet, separated from vehicular and pedestrian traffic, to be used for a double line of tramways. The project would be completed with a shrubbery five feet wide and a promenade 30 feet wide called the Kings Parade. In the meantime, Sea Bank Road suffered further damage. During the autumn of 1902 the condition of the road had become even more acute. It was now impossible for a horse and vehicle to proceed further along the road than Rowston Street, where the timber road had been undermined and a wooden footbridge provided in its stead. In January 1903, heavy downpours of rain following upon a keen frost dislodged large quantities of the bank, particularly near the *Lifeboat Hotel.* At the end of Segmere Street the only means of passage was via a timber footway.[17]

The UDC invited tenders for the scheme in November 1902 and the contract was awarded to Messrs J. & M. Patrick of Wandsworth, who started preparatory work on the construction site in March 1903; the contract price was £12,278.[18] The work was due to be finished by December 1903 but progressed slowly, probably because it needed a larger workforce. It was also bedevilled by recurring gales and storms, which damaged the work in progress, but by December 1904 the greater part of the sea wall was built. However, a severe north-easterly gale early in the new year brought the highest tide to the Lincolnshire coast for 20 years, and a length of about 100 yards of the new sea wall was demolished and sand scoured from behind it. This setback spurred the work on: the wall was rebuilt and by September 1905 was nearly complete. The finished wall was 2,000 feet long and 18 feet high plus a parapet wall. It was seven feet thick at the base, tapering to two feet at road level. A temporary railway was used to bring material, including 15,000 tons of concrete, to the site. About 100,000 cubic yards of sand from the shore were used for the back filling, which added four acres to the area of Cleethorpes. There were three stepways to the beach and four curved bastions along the wall, in two of which obsolete 64-pounder cannons were mounted.[19]

The UDC then completed the scheme: installing lighting, laying down lawns and paths, planting hedges and shrubs, providing public lavatories, shelters, a fountain and a bandstand and the fixing of a set of old-fashioned stocks presented to the Council by the Owersby (Market Rasen) Parish Council. A refreshment pavilion planned for the end of the promenade was not opened until May 1914. Named the Kingsway Pavilion it later became a popular dance hall and was renamed the Café Dansant.[20] One planned improvement which was not implemented at all was the tramway extension from Brighton Street to the far end of the Kingsway along the reservation which had been provided. The Council and the tram company were unable to agree upon the nature of the new track and a fare structure, so the UDC decided that the tramway strip should be laid out as parterre gardens. The tramway was extended for a short length only, to a new terminus at the commencement of the Kingsway.[21] As the work neared completion a public meeting was held to discuss the question of financing the opening celebrations, as they could not be paid for out of the municipal rates. A collection at the meeting raised £116 12s. 6d. and a committee was formed to start collecting subscriptions. Contributions included 20 guineas from Sidney Sussex College.[22]

The Chairman of the UDC, Councillor E.J. Brockway, appealed to employers to make the opening day a general holiday as far as possible. He was the manager of the Cleethorpes gas works and set an example by granting his employees a full day's holiday. The formal opening of the improvements was performed on Thursday, 12 July 1906 by Lady Henderson, the wife of the Chairman of the GCR; on the same day, she also turned the first sod to initiate work on the Immingham Dock. With regard to the Kingsway opening it was said: 'Crowds of people lined the route and almost every window was occupied. Cleethorpes was bathed in sunshine during the early morning and again in the evening, but at mid-day the rain fell in torrents.' Lady Henderson's entourage was greeted at Park Street and proceeded along Grimsby Road which was decorated with arches and flags. At Isaac's Hill she was met by the Church Lads Brigade and the Boys

46 *The Kingsway and the Kings Parade promenade, which were completed in 1906. The central linear gardens were originally planned to be a tramway which never went ahead.*

47 *The Kings Parade, with the Kingsway to the left. Completed in 1906 and seen here c.1910. The three-storey building with double windows is on the corner of Segmere Street. The pier can be seen faintly in the distance.*

Brigade, who formed a guard of honour and marched in front of the carriages to the Kingsway. Lady Henderson cut the ribbon and a choir of 2,000 schoolchildren sang the National Anthem. Lady Henderson and her party walked a short distance along the Kings Parade and were then taken to the Pier Pavilion for a reception and speeches: 'The only regret was that as the guests were proceeding to the Pavilion a sharp shower of rain fell.' Celebrations continued to Sunday and included a procession of decorated floats, pierrots, a battle of flowers, a 'confetti fête', thousands of fairy lights illuminating the Pier Gardens, fireworks, entertainment in the Pier Pavilion and a military tournament on the beach.[23]

The new promenade was credited with bringing record crowds to the resort and 1906 was described as a 'boom' year by a local newspaper:

> 1906 has provided one of the greatest advances, one of the largest strides in progress within living memory ... the town has begun to reap the invaluable reward of municipal enterprise. 1906 is the crowning point of many years' work ... and we seek perennial good in the beautified appearance, the enhanced value of the south end, the laying out of new estates, the impetus in building and the vastly increased influx of spectators, bringing with them prosperity to residents, tradesmen and others.[24]

The success of the improvements rubbed off on the UDC. Local press commented that the Council had become more progresssive and cited Councillors Moody, Grant and Brockway as being primarily responsible for carrying through the negotiations for the completion of the Sea Bank Road improvements. Reference was also made to the:

enhanced importance of the duties of the Council. Cleethorpes has been fortunate during recent years in securing the services of some of her best citizens to represent her municipal interest ... the lax manner of discussing matters in a desultory way, which savoured of the smoking room and the dismal surroundings of the old regime, have all disappeared.[25]

It was also hoped that the new road would lead to better quality accommodation being built to attract longer-term visitors to the resort. The newspaper wished that by following the Council's lead:

private enterprise will now come to the front in Cleethorpes. Some of the property joining the Kings Parade is scarcely worthy of its position. It was built when but a lane existed there. Here is the finest situation in Cleethorpes; will the builders put up some pretentious boarding houses ... and so provide accommodation for a class of people who might be inclined to visit Cleethorpes were they able to secure satisfactory board and residence.[26]

Visitor Attractions

The Kingsway and Kings Parade gave good road and promenade access to the 'Golf Links', which the UDC could now consider converting into a recreational attraction. We have seen that only some of the land was used for golf, and this portion was leased to the golf club accordingly. When the club's lease expired in 1908, the Council took full possession of the land and the club had its course rearranged on other land nearby. This cleared the way for the Council to develop the 'Golf Links' and, in 1910, it approved plans for its development into the 'South Pleasure Grounds', which would include a sea wall, promenades, a marine lake, a sunken bandstand and walks. The plan was subsequently amended and revised, but no action had been taken by the time that the outbreak of the First World War intervened.

In the meantime, the resort continued to be very busy. It was reckoned that during June, July and August the number of visitors increased the population by up to 6,000, and that on Bank Holidays there were between 30,000 and 50,000 trippers in the town.[27] Amusements included the Fairy River, Helter Skelters and Aerial Flights. In 1903 the Empire Theatre was advertised as a variety theatre and, in the afternoons, a 'café chantant'. A sign of the changing times was a cinematographic entertainment given in 1902 by T.R. Watkinson in the Primitive Methodist schoolroom. Other early film shows were given in the Kursaal on the North Promenade. Another innovation was pleasure drives in the new-fangled motor cars. Some entertainments did not have total support and local residents complained in 1908 of pierrots singing in the Pier Gardens from 10 in the morning till 11 at night.[28]

Other attractions included a new switchback railway, a 'Water Shute' and the Hotchkiss Patent Bicycle Railway. For the latter, the riders propelled themselves around a track raised about five feet above the ground. The outstanding new attraction in 1908 was the 'Figure 8 American Toboggan Railway', which stood on nearly an acre of land at the northern end of the promenade. Its cars held four passengers and were hoisted up an inclined track to a height of 50 feet and then released automatically. At the Whitsuntide Bank Holiday it was reported that the attraction 'has taken Cleethorpes and the visitors by storm and must have carried somewhere near 30,000 passengers on Monday alone'.[29]

Such attractions involved large-scale capital outlays and brought more outside investment and influence into the resort. For instance, when the Cleethorpes Switchback Company was incorporated in 1910, its three initial directors were all businessmen from Bolton in Lancashire. By 1916, there were 19 shareholders, of whom 10 were from Bolton, three from Cleethorpes, and one each from Leeds, Nottingham, London, Blackpool, Rotherham and Edinburgh.[30] A major instance of incoming investment was the Warwick Revolving Observation Tower, which graced the North Promenade for a short while. The first tower was constructed at Atlantic City, New Jersey, in about 1895. Thomas Warwick, a London engineer, held a licence to build towers in this country and his Warwick Revolving Towers Company was incorporated in December 1897 with 50,000 £1 shares. Shares were held nationwide, and by March 1899 100 shareholders held 32,690 shares. Towers were built at Great Yarmouth, Morecambe, Scarborough, Douglas in the Isle of Man, Margate and Southend. In July 1898, Warwick acquired a lease from the GCR to construct a tower on company land adjacent to the North Promenade. A local newspaper saw the tower as a great step forward for the resort: 'with the construction of this tower next October—and its completion by the following Easter—Cleethorpes will be in the way of coming into line with flourishing resorts which have so far outrivalled it'.[31]

In the event, construction was delayed and the tower did not open until June 1902. It was about 150 feet tall and was encircled by a gallery. This was in effect a lift that rotated around the tower as it was raised to the top, where passengers could disembark and take in the view. On the opening day 'those making the first ascent ... were nearly all of the gentler sex'. On one ascent nearly 70 passengers were carried at one time. At the base of the tower was a pavilion which accommodated stalls, slot machines and the like. Despite initial interest, the venture was not successful, and did not operate as a revolving tower after the summer season of 1905. In 1906, the entire framework was removed to Healing to become a water tower, which was itself demolished in 1959. The other towers had similarly short lifespans and only one, at Great Yarmouth, lasted any length of time, running until 1938, despite operational difficulties.[32]

The Cleethorpes inshore fishermen, their boats and their catches were an 'attraction' which was of both visual and gastronomic interest to visitors. The Cleethorpes inshore

48 *Concert party performing in the Kingsway Enclosure and Bandstand, which was superseded by the Kingsway Pavilion (Café Dansant) which opened in 1914.*

industry peaked during 1895-1915, when there were upwards of a hundred fishermen working from Cleethorpes. They had to be versatile and, according to the season, fished for crabs, lobsters, dogfish, eels, mussels, shrimps, cod, whelks, sprats, cockles and oysters. They fished the Humber and along the Lincolnshire and Yorkshire coasts. The Cleethorpes oyster beds provided income for local fishermen and traders. In the 1890s there were about fifty beds opposite Brighton Street slipway containing an estimated ten million oysters. All this came to an end following complaints from public health authorities in Sheffield and Gainsborough in 1902 and 1903 that the Cleethorpes oysters had been the cause of outbreaks of typhoid. The beds were found to be polluted and were closed for good in April 1904.[33]

Regardless of such setbacks, the time was one of optimism. In tune with a rising spirit of 'boosting' the resort, the Cleethorpes Advertising Committee was established in 1905, composed of councillors and others. The UDC had no authority to spend its rates income on advertising and the new committee relied on donations from businesses and the public. During its first year, it had 10,000 guide books printed, plus 10,000 booklets entitled 'Children's Paradise' and 'setting forth the attractions of Cleethorpes as a health and pleasure resort for children'. Several articles appeared in daily papers and journals, and 10,000 posters were ordered. A successful sandcastle competition was held in August, with prizes provided by the *Daily Mirror*. The committee reported that the opening of the Kingsway and the festivities connected therewith had attracted large numbers of visitors, and the establishment of a three-day carnival to be held early in the season would probably prove of equal value.[34]

Certainly, the innovations and enterprise of this period attracted increasing numbers of visitors to the resort, as described in the following extracts from a lengthy press account of the August Bank Holiday weekend at Cleethorpes in 1908. Initially, the reporter describes the influx of visitors over the weekend and where the trippers came from:

> Bank Holiday ... has come and passed again, and ... never before have the crowds been larger or the weather more brilliant. Before the morning dawned the place was full of visitors, and on Saturday night the inhabitants had the glorious pleasure of seeing people walking street after street endeavouring to find a house where there was still one bed left unoccupied. Fourteen trips swelled the total on Sunday, and yesterday [Monday], all through the morning, the crowds came in a deluge. Train after train arrived, long strings of carriages full from end to end. Without counting duplicates there were five from Leicester district, five from Nottingham district, four from the Sheffield district, and others from Deepcar, Attercliffe, Heanor, Manchester, the Lancashire district, Leeds and the Yorkshire district, Burton, Chesterfield, etc., many specials from Hull and Lincoln, and others on the GNR from Louth, Boston and Spalding. By midday the front was a seething mass of happy humanity ...

He then describes the beginning of the weekend on Saturday, and the following two days:

> The holiday really commenced on Saturday, when the great army of holiday makers began to pour into Cleethorpes. Fortunately large numbers were going outward, and from many streets in Cleethorpes loads of luggage were being despatched to the station, or how in the world Cleethorpes would have accommodated Saturday's arrivals one dares not venture to suggest ... But the day wore on, Cleethorpes became crowded, the shops found their stacks of provisions rapidly declining, and by night many visitors were walking about the street in an effort to find houses where there were still apartments to be let. On Sunday morning there were more arrivals, and more

luggage, with a correspondingly increased difficulty of securing beds, and there was a rush of trippers, but the great siege occurred on the Bank Holiday. The recent hot weather had driven the thousands out of the heat-laden towns, away from whirring wheels and throbbing machinery to the seaside, just to catch a glimpse of the sunlit dancing waves, to loll outstretched on the sand, to paddle in the cooling waters, or ride out along country roads in the shadow of the quiet trees. But there was such a crowd that all could not paddle or loll on the sands together, and from the Figure 8 to the golf-links the front yesterday was one surging mass of humanity.

Mention is made of the heavy patronage of the amusements and rides:

> All are familiar with the amusements at Cleethorpes, though very few could give a list of them, they are grown so numerous. Not one of them but reaped a rich harvest yesterday, for the crowds were squeezed into every nook and cranny. The Figure 8 and the switchback were literally 'howling' places of fun and gaiety, the aerial flights and helter skelter were as busy as the proverbial bee on a summer afternoon, and in every direction the people perspired, laughed, shouted and were merry.

The report concludes with reference to the value of the new Kingsway development in providing an alternative and more relaxed recreational area:

> There was a slight difference on the Kingsway and on the Golf Links. Those who came for the picturesque, for flowers and plashing fountains, and who delight in taking their pleasures quietly and aesthetically, had made for this end of Cleethorpes, but whether gay or grave, boisterous or smilingly happy, there were visitors everywhere. Cleethorpes has never known a busier day, nor a brighter.[35]

The Pier Fire

Under the railway company's management, the pier was still a major attraction, but it suffered a setback on 29 June 1903, when the Pier Pavilion Concert Hall was destroyed by fire:

> Yesterday, the Cleethorpes Pier and Pavilion provided a spectacle for the visitors which was of quite an unexpected character. A fire broke out shortly after noon underneath the Pavilion which spread so rapidly that within an hour it completely wrecked the far end of the Pier, removed all traces of the concert hall and refreshment bar, and left but a charred and blackened end; jagged with half-burnt timbers and twisted girders ... [fortunately the morning band performance had finished and the pavilion was practically empty] ... The heat was intense and had the wind been blowing in from the sea, instead of out towards sea, it was questionable whether any portion of the Pier would have been left standing.

Visitors and residents flocked to view this thrilling and unexpected, if short-lived, event and the watching crowds included 70 children who absented themselves from Bursar Street School:

> Exactly an hour after the fire had been noticed the Pavilion collapsed with a loud crash, sending up a shower of flames and sparks which provided an exhilarating spectacle to the many onlookers who were provided with such an admirable position on the promenade and sands for watching the progress of the conflagration ... The [tram]cars from Grimsby arrived crowded with people who were anxious to see what a few minutes before, had been an attractive sight. Within a short time after the alarm sounding the news had spread far and wide that Cleethorpes Pier was on fire, and practically hundreds at once made for the scene. [Grimsby] Pontoon

49 *Pier fire, 6 July 1903.*

workers even suspended operations for a while in order to get a better view of what they had already seen from Grimsby docks; while numbers of the braiders and other employees on the docks lost an hour's work to witness the fire ... By half past two the flames were practically subdued, and it took very little time after this to completely extinguish the fire.[36]

In fighting the fire, the Cleethorpes Fire Brigade had to be assisted by the Grimsby Borough Brigade and the Grimsby Docks Brigade. This emphasised the inadequacy of the equipment and facilities available to the Cleethorpes Brigade (which had been formed in 1901 with eight men), and improvements followed: a new fire station opened in Poplar road in 1904, complete with a new fire engine. More immediate action was required from the pier management in the aftermath of the fire. Artistes had been booked to perform on the pier, including 'Miss Ada Phillips, contralto, Mr Percy Honri, song and concertina artiste, Mr A. Ulph-Smith, humourous musical performer and Mr Nelson Hardy, ventriloquist'. A marquee was quickly made available, the pier orchestra played to accompany dancing in the evening and a stage was soon erected so that the week's entertainment could proceed.[37]

With regard to the longer term, the railway company directors decided to exercise the option to buy out the pier company. The purchase, for £11,250, was completed in 1904, and they agreed to build a temporary pavilion at an estimated cost of £450 for the coming season. They also engaged R. St George Moore of Westminster to design a permanent replacement 'on the most economical lines possible'. He estimated this would cost £6,000.[38] Moore was a well-known engineer whose achievements by this time included the pier at St Leonards and the most famous of piers, the Brighton Palace pier. The contract for constructing the Pavilion was placed with Alfred Thorne of Westminster for £5,224 2s. 10d. Thorne was an experienced contractor and had already constructed piers at Dover, Bangor, Cromer and Cowes. The Pavilion was rebuilt nearer the shore and the opening took place with a 'grand concert' on Whitsun Saturday, 11 June 1905. The pierhead had not yet been restored after the fire and in 1906 the GCR decided

50 *The pier, showing the new Pavilion, which was completed in 1905 to replace the one at the end of the pier that had been destroyed by the fire of 1903. The building in the distance is the tearoom which was built later at the end of the pier.*

to carry out the necessary restoration and provide a tearoom, at an estimated cost of £2,156.[39]

Its actions and expenditure after the fire, affirmed the railway company's interest in the resort. Even so, a few years later, the UDC, flushed with the success of its Kingsway scheme, approached the company with a view to leasing or buying the pier and the pier gardens. In 1908, the GCR declined to sell on the grounds that 'they formed part of an estate which, with the sea wall, cost a very large sum of money'.[40] The matter would come to the fore again in the 1920s.

Respectability and Regulation

At their simplest, the new Kingsway and Kings Parade provided protection against the ravages of the sea and a pleasant new walk for visitors. However, the UDC and some residents saw the development as the first step in the creation of a more 'respectable' part of the resort. The 'Golf Links' was a popular informal recreational area but produced complaints of gaming and bad language. In a 1904 court case six local men pleaded guilty to gaming at pitch and toss there on Sundays. A local newspaper commented that 'the Golf Links were a favourite public resort but the presence of men like the defendants had made the place intolerable'.[41] The Council's aspirations for the area were summed up by Councillor Grant, who remarked that 'they got all the rough element at the north end, therefore they ought to make the other end so that a better class of people could visit Cleethorpes'.[42] Some residents yearned for a return to the 'respectability' of the days when Cleethorpes had been a 'select' resort, and they saw the Kingsway and the Kings Parade, and the creation of a regulated recreational attraction on the 'Golf Links', as a means of turning Thrunscoe into an area which would attract a better class of visitor.

Others, however, ridiculed the idea of Cleethorpes attracting visitors from higher social groups. A resident wrote to the local newspaper that: 'We want the masses who spend their money in the place, not the [upper] classes. It is useless spending money on

Cleethorpes. It will always be an ordinary looking place ... there is no natural beauty anywhere.'[43] Despite such pessimism, the press commented: 'We trust that the new Kingsway will be the means of spreading Cleethorpes' fame, and that it will attract a better class of summer resident and raise the status of the township in every possible way.'[44] The Council also hoped that the Kingsway would help attract a better class of visitor and refused to have slot machines and the like on the Kings Parade.

In addition to its aspirations for the new Thrunscoe development, the UDC also saw the need to control and improve the 'image' of the resort generally. Under its new powers, it adopted byelaws regulating various aspects of town life, including the sands and seashore, tents, vans, sheds and similar structures; and whirligigs, swings and shooting galleries.[45] They covered the provision of booths, shows and games, selling and hawking, riding, bathing and boating and the preservation of good order and conduct in general. Some of the implications of the Council's newly acquired control of the foreshore were set out in the local press:

> Considerable speculation was rife as to the means that would be adopted for the regulation of the sands during the Easter season, and people who have been in the habit year by year of monopolising 'pitches' there have been anxiously inquiring about the subject. It was only as recently as Wednesday night that the Council decided to let these people have their last 'fling' during Eastertide. By another Bank Holiday season, however, matters will assume a different aspect, and sites on the sand will be allocated according to the discretion of the Council and to whom they think best, preference in the matter of applicants being of course given to local people.[46]

The Council took its new powers seriously, as this press report from 1910 shows:

> On Monday next the Sea-shore Committee will meet at the Council House for the purpose of letting space on the sands for stalls, etc., for the coming season and applicants are asked to attend and make their application on that day, for no spaces will be let afterwards. The rules laid down are fairly stringent, but they all make for decorum and a good beach. For instance no spaces will be let for tea booths—this, we believe, at the request of the restaurant keepers—nor for fried fish, fried potatoes nor hot peas. No coke or coal fire will be allowed on the sands. As many as 25 ice-cream stalls will be allowed but that is the maximum number.[47]

Something which had been a topic of discussion and concern for many years was the question of bathing. The byelaws adopted by the Local Board in 1875 stipulated that bathing machines containing males should not to be placed in the water nearer than 25 yards to machines containing women (and vice versa). No person was to bathe except from a bathing machine or be naked on any part of the sand between the Life-Boat House and the Volunteer Gun Battery (in modern terms approximately between the Leisure Centre and Wonderland). Bathing machines were to be provided with 'a sufficient number of woollen or cotton drawers, or such other dresses as may be effectual to prevent indecent exposure'. Offenders in this department would incur a penalty of £2. Despite this, there was a complaint in 1878 of nude male bathing near the pier.[48] In general the two sexes bathed on different parts of the beach, but mixed bathing was gaining ground at resorts. There was also criticism of bathing machines in 1905:

> It is deplorable that the antique discomfort of the bathing machine still reigns paramount. It is dear, dirty and stuffy; yet those ladies not possessed of a private tent ... have to perform their toilet under wretched conditions ... the bathing machine has not moved an inch with the bustling times.[49]

Sunday Observance

The UDC also decided in 1906 that the proposed Refreshment Pavilion in the Kingsway Gardens would not be opened on Sundays. This highlights another aspect of the quest for respectability, the question of Sunday observance, which was a long-standing local issue. We have seen that the Cleethorpes grocer, E. Turner, who provided transport between Grimsby and Cleethorpes in 1831, did not offer the service on Sundays. The issue came to the fore when the arrival of the railways produced increasing numbers of visitors and excursionists. In 1859 and 1865, requests from local residents for the MS&LR to stop running excursions on Sunday were rejected by the company. In 1858, fisherman and trader Levi Stephenson was charged with Sunday trading in his booth on the sands. He was discharged with a caution not to sell during the hours of divine service.[50] Part of the dispute which Richard Thorold and others had with booth-holders on the beach in the 1860s was that some of them traded on Sundays.

In later years, residents continued to protest at Sunday rail excursions and about boatmen giving pleasure trips on Sundays. In 1896, a public meeting 'to which hundreds were unable to obtain admission' passed a unanimous resolution viewing increasing Sunday rail traffic with alarm and urging the MS&LR to discontinue Sunday trips: 'the same being detrimental to the religious, the moral, the social and the pecuniary interests of the place'.[51] Later in the same year, the UDC held a special meeting at which the 'desecration of the Sabbath' was the chief item of business. Members agreed to ban boating, touting and hackney carriages on Sundays, but the Council's decision was criticised in the national press: a sign of changing public attitudes.[52] The pier's entertainment on Sundays was limited to afternoon and evening 'Sacred Concerts'.

The completion of the Kings Parade raised comparisons with the railway promenades regarding Sunday trading:

> I and many others are glad our Kingsway is quiet and respectable but the 'Sodom' end of the old Promenade is abominable every Sabbath Day. Rock sellers, photograph shops, Fairy River, Helter Skelter and roundabouts are all in full swing.[53]

Many visitors, especially Sunday excursionists, expected to experience the full range of entertainment and facilities which were available during the rest of the week, whereas religious groups and others wished to preserve the sanctity of the Sabbath:

> To take a walk along the Promenade at Cleethorpes on a Sunday afternoon or evening it is difficult to realise that it is not an ordinary holiday day. It becomes one mass of blazing colour, a living stream of gaily dressed people.[54]

In 1908, a local newspaper argued the need to curb the opening of attractions without being 'Puritanical' about it: 'When Sunday excursionists find the roundabouts, the waterway, and the "slipping the slip" are closed they will philosophically turn their attention to other and perhaps quieter and better things'. Even the provider of a visitor attraction agreed with the proponents of 'respectability' and said that: 'In my exhibits on Sundays at the Kursaal I seek to elevate the race.'[55]

The UDC also restricted Sunday trading by requesting the police to initiate action under the Lord's Day Observance legislation. In response to this policy, traders argued in 1910 that 'the restriction has had an effect of considerably retarding Cleethorpes' progress as a seaside resort, because Sunday excursionists cannot secure all that they require, even to the extent of the necessaries of life'. A deputation met the UDC, which maintained that the matter was now in the hands of the police authority, the Lindsey County

51 *The Empire Theatre, which was opened in 1896 as the Alexandra Hall and designed for a wide range of public functions. Four years later it was altered and re-named the Empire Theatre. It currently accommodates an amusement centre.*

52 *The Warwick Revolving Observation Tower on the North Promenade opened in 1902. The venture was unsuccessful and it was dismantled in 1906, the framework being used in the construction of a water tower at Healing.*

Council. The UDC asserted that every religious denomination had asked it to continue prohibiting Sunday trading and that it had received many letters expressing approval of its action. It was also reported that 'Councillor Moody objected to Cleethorpes being turned into a Continental Sunday holiday resort'.[56]

Building and Services

The new century saw little slackening in the rapid growth of the town. During the decade 1901-11 the population increased from 12,578 to 21,417, and the number of houses

53 *'Dipping the Dip' and other amusements on the North Promenade before the large Wonderland building was constructed.*

from 2,926 to 5,145. Most of the new houses were smaller working-class accommodation, which was in line with local demand. However, the town's drainage and sewerage facilities were still inadequate. This was a particular problem in New Cleethorpes, which was on low-lying land. Accordingly, in 1902, the UDC asked Sidney Sussex College to curtail its house building there. Fortunately for the College, its estate included high ground either side of Isaac's Hill. Development of this area for housing had started in 1897 but now gained momentum: during 1903–5 applications were made to build 222 houses there, in roads such as Bursar Street and College Street. Isaac's Hill was the main route into the town, and the College imposed a condition that the sum spent on building each house on the hill should be not less than £300, and not less than £275 on the side roads.[57] This building development compensated the College to some extent for the restriction on building in New Cleethorpes.

The other new large area for house building was in Thrunscoe. It was evident that the completion of the Kingsway in 1906 would open up land there for building. The major landowner in Thrunscoe was Sidney Sussex College which held 242 acres at the very end of the Kingsway. One of its conditions for selling the 'Golf Links' to the UDC had been that it would be permitted to build a road to the urban district boundary in continuation of the new Kingsway. This road (now called Kings Road) would run along the boundary of the College estate and make it easier to open up for building.[58] Consequently, even before the Kingsway was completed, the College submitted plans to the UDC for two new roads, one in continuation of the Kingsway and one at right angles to it (the future Cromwell Road).

However, the development of College land was once again to be frustrated by poor drainage.[59] The only building permitted was the detached house that is currently a masonic lodge on the corner of Kings Road and Cromwell Road. Plans were approved for the house in 1906 and it was built for trawler owner (later Sir) Thomas Robinson.

In contrast to the poorly drained College land, another area in Thrunscoe was suitable for building. This land lay directly behind the Kingsway and had comprised White's Farm. It was now owned by the Boulevard Estate Company. Development started in 1906 and continued throughout the pre-war period. Extensions were made to older streets that predated the building of the Kingsway, such as Haigh Street, Segmere Street and Bradford Street (later Avenue). New streets were laid out during 1907–9, including White's Road, Nicholson Street, Queens Parade and Oxford Street. In 1912–13, the

54 *Amusements and stalls on the North Promenade beach.*

UDC approved company plans for further streets, such as Seacroft Road, Lindum Road and Signhills Avenue.[60]

Building on the College's Thrunscoe estate was still held up, but it indicated to the UDC its intentions for the land. For many years the College had envisaged this area as a residential quarter with better quality houses. The Boulevard Estate Company's land abutted that of the College, and the latter did not want the development of its potential residential estate blighted by the erection on adjacent land of small working-class houses—known locally as 'cottages'. The College wished that:

> the Boulevard Estate Owners shall not erect cottage property abutting upon and along the Northern boundary of the College Estate. The last mentioned is essential because it is the present intention of the college to make this part of their Thrunscoe Estate a residential one and not to have cottages built thereon.[61]

Despite its intentions, the College could not move until drainage was improved. In the meantime, the growth in population led to the need for all manner of services. Since becoming an Urban District Council, and with the New Cleethorpes development providing it with increased income from rates, the local authority had acquired both the confidence and ability to take its part in improving the town. However, it still had no meeting place of its own, meetings being held in such places as the Oddfellows Hall at the junction of Yarra Road and Cambridge Street. Accordingly, the UDC purchased from County Councillor H. Kelly 2,382 square yards of land for new council offices at the junction of Cambridge Street and Knoll Street. The price was 7s. 6d. a square yard, considerably more than the 2s. per square yard the Council paid Sidney Sussex College for its land on Isaac's Hill, where it had originally decided to build a Council House.

55 *The Cleethorpes UDC's Council House (Town Hall), which was completed by 1905.*

In 1903, a tender of £5,968 was accepted for the erection of a Council House on the new site and the UDC held its first meeting in the building in 1905.[62]

Other developments in the growing town were the introduction in 1900 of 'telephonic communication', to which 'several residents' were subscribers, and a water tower provided in Pelham Road in 1908 by the Great Grimsby Waterworks Company. Constructed of 'ferro-concrete', the latter was over 160 feet high, held 250,000 gallons and was intended to be used for auxiliary supplies during repairs and stoppages to the water supply. Because of the increase in population, the Barcroft Street School became seriously overcrowded: built for 900 pupils, it had more than 1,200 in 1901. Temporary schools were set up and in 1902 the Bursar Street School, which would accommodate 950 pupils, was opened. Elliston Street School was opened in 1907, and enlarged in 1910, and the Reynolds Street School was opened in 1914.

Advances were also made in the provision of churches and chapels. To serve New Cleethorpes, St Aidan's Church Institute was erected in 1899 and St Aidan's Church was consecrated in 1906. Christ Church Mission Hall opened as a branch of the Clee parish church in 1911 to serve the Beaconthorpe area. Local Baptists worshipped at various places, including the Oddfellows Hall, and held 'Pleasant Sunday Afternoons' in the Empire Theatre. In 1910 they built a church in Alexandra Road; after it was bombed in 1916, the members used other premises and then a hut on the church site until a new church was built in 1927. The Bethel Mission opened in Tiverton Street in 1903 to minister to the fishing community and the Salvation Army commenced their local ministry in Cambridge Street in 1896.

Drainage

The constraints on building on College land in Thrunscoe and New Cleethorpes because of poor drainage were symptomatic of a problem facing the entire town: despite various schemes carried out in the past, the town needed a major new drainage system. With the exception of the central area of the resort, most of the town was low-lying. A condition imposed by the College on the sale of the 'Golf Links' was that the UDC would provide sufficient outfall drainage to the College's Thrunscoe estate when the College was ready to develop it for building.[63] Accordingly, when the Kingsway was completed in 1906, the College asked the UDC to provide the agreed drainage. As an inducement, it offered to pay £1,500 towards the cost. It was also anxious to re-start building in New Cleethorpes and offered six acres to extend Sidney Park and eight acres for another recreation ground, subject to the Council carrying out a drainage scheme for the whole town.[64]

In 1907, the UDC committed itself to carrying out a scheme under which a new main sewer would commence in north Cleethorpes, and make its way through the town and across Thrunscoe to a pumping station and tidal outfall near to the resort's southern boundary. The cost was estimated at £37,200, but the Local Government Board deemed the scheme inadequate, and delays followed whilst a revised scheme was being prepared. At a public inquiry in 1910 the College's solicitor remarked that the College owned all the land on the west side of Grimsby Road but building had been stopped there because of the want of sewers. He stressed that whilst the scheme was of vital importance to the College it was also important to the further development of the town and should not be delayed. Current building was largely restricted to the Boulevard Estate Company's land in Thrunscoe.[65]

The scheme was eventually approved and in his annual report for 1914, the Medical Officer of Health reported that the new sewerage system should be in operation soon, the building trade should revert to its normal state and the scheme should also reduce flooding. He also commented that the foreshore, which was crowded with trippers during the summer, would be free from sewage pollution, at any rate from Cleethorpes.[66] In the event, the scheme was not in operation until October 1916, at an estimated cost of £90,000.

Expansionist Grimsby

The growth of the town on College land in New Cleethorpes was of financial benefit to both the College and the UDC, but this happy state of mutual benefit was threatened when Grimsby expressed a wish to extend its boundaries into Cleethorpes. A commentator of 1890 described the contemporary situation:

> Grimsby ... and Cleethorpes, are about as unlike as any two places can well be. You always hear them spoken of in connection with each other, and, indeed, it is not easy to dissever them in the mind, as there is only the distance of a threepenny tram-ride between them—a matter of a couple of miles or so—and it cannot be very long before the two places join hands, so rapidly are they both increasing and extending. Practically they will become one town, having Grimsby for its strictly business ... portion, and Cleethorpes for its ornamental pleasure-taking, and holiday part. Grimsby is business. Cleethorpes is all pleasure.[67]

As early as 1893 the Grimsby Corporation had proposed extending its boundaries to the foot of Isaac's Hill, but it withdrew in view of uncompromising opposition from the Local Board and Cleethorpes residents. However, the danger of annexation was not over. In 1895, the point was made that the growth of New Cleethorpes was creating a divided town with two main centres of population which had differing social backgrounds. It was remarked that: 'There were two different races of people in Cleethorpes. Those in the south portion wished to go to bed at ten, whilst those in the north wanted to

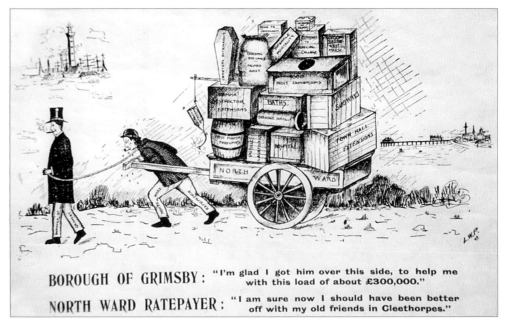

BOROUGH OF GRIMSBY : "I'm glad I got him over this side, to help me with this load of about £300,000."

NORTH WARD RATEPAYER : "I am sure now I should have been better off with my old friends in Cleethorpes."

56 *Cartoon, c.1906/7, arguing against Grimsby's bid to absorb the North Ward (New Cleethorpes). The self-satisfied figure represents the Grimsby Corporation leading the perspiring North Ward ratepayer, who would have to take on Grimsby's financial commitments. These are illustrated on the barrow and include Town Hall Extensions, Cemetery Extensions, Privy Conversions, Municipal College Extension and so on.*

stay up till eleven.' It was feared that there was a danger of the residents of northern Cleethorpes asking to be annexed by Grimsby if they had grievances, which would be unfair to other ratepayers of Cleethorpes.[68]

Such thoughts were in the minds of Cleethorpes councillors when, as part of Queen Victoria's Diamond Jubilee celebrations in 1897, an opportunity came for urban districts to petition the Privy Council for municipal borough status. Boroughs were of a higher status than urban districts and if Cleethorpes was successful in its petition it would be in a stronger position to fight off any future expansion proposals from Grimsby. Accordingly, the UDC petitioned for borough status. The Grimsby Corporation opposed the petition and remarked that: 'The residents in New Cleethorpes come to Grimsby to work, and were really Grimsby people, and it was thought unfair that those people should benefit from Grimsby while the rates went to Cleethorpes.'[69] The mention of the rates emphasised that New Cleethorpes represented a sizeable, and annually increasing, rateable value and would be a welcome addition to the Grimsby municipal treasury. Privy Council officials recorded that the Grimsby Corporation opposed the granting of a charter 'on the ground that Cleethorpes should properly be joined to Grimsby'. They also noted that 'the place appears not to be of sufficient size and importance', and the petition was refused.[70]

Despite Cleethorpes' opposition to annexation, the College had a positive view of the importance of Grimsby industries to the development of its estate. This was shown when it agreed to join with large landowners in Grimsby in helping to finance a bonus of £5,000 per annum to the GCR for seven years. This would help pay for the construction of a new dock which the railway company proposed building at Grimsby. The College agreed to give £250 annually towards the bonus 'on the ground that this [dock] extension will hasten the development of the College estate'.[71] In the event, the bonus was not paid because the railway company built the dock at Immingham. Further evidence of the link between New Cleethorpes and Grimsby came in 1901 with a report that: 'The lock-out at the Docks affects the North end of Cleethorpes much more seriously than the South end, as the number of fishermen and engineers resident in New Cleethorpes is very large.'[72] Even the opening of the Sidney Park in 1904 attracted the remark that 'the new park is placed in such a position that Grimsby folk can easily use it … The

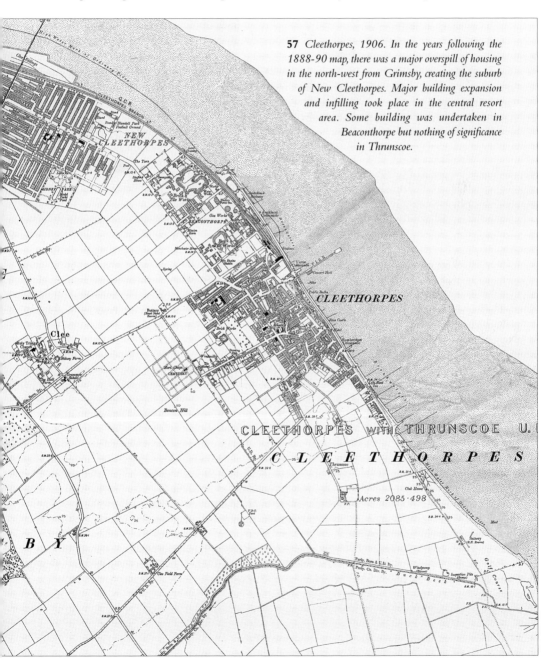

57 *Cleethorpes, 1906. In the years following the 1888-90 map, there was a major overspill of housing in the north-west from Grimsby, creating the suburb of New Cleethorpes. Major building expansion and infilling took place in the central resort area. Some building was undertaken in Beaconthorpe but nothing of significance in Thrunscoe.*

two places will really have to be amalgamated ... and it is hard to see ... how the two communities are to remain apart'.[73]

With such obvious economic and social connections between New Cleethorpes and Grimsby, it is not surprising that matters came to a head in August 1907, when the Grimsby Corporation once more considered extending its boundaries. A local newspaper carried a leader on 'Pot-Bound Grimsby' and its need to extend in all directions, including taking in Cleethorpes up to the bottom of Isaac's Hill. The paper also commented: 'There is a sort of panic at Cleethorpes over the agitation now going on [in New Cleethorpes] ... for incorporation with Grimsby. On all hands people who live in and around the Park Street district say they ought to be governed by Grimsby.'[74] Letters from residents of New Cleethorpes complained that they were under-represented on the Cleethorpes Council, that their revenue was being milked by 'Old' Cleethorpes, and that there was 'an overwhelming majority of residents in favour of incorporation'. The Grimsby Corporation eventually proposed to incorporate Cleethorpes up to the bottom of Isaac's Hill, plus taking in the new dock under construction at Immingham and parts of adjacent Little Coates, Great Coates and Weelsby.[75]

The UDC resolved to 'resist to the utmost' the proposed incorporation. It was supported by the College, which also opposed the proposal. Other opponents included the Lindsey County Council and the Grimsby Rural District Council, both of which would lose land and rateable value under the proposals.[76] In view of the opposition, the Grimsby Corporation cut back its submission. The boundary extension in Cleethorpes was to be only as far as Suggitts Lane. Parts of Little Coates and Weelsby were to be taken in but, significantly, the proposal to take in the Immingham Dock was dropped entirely. The cutting back of Grimsby's proposed extension into Cleethorpes was something of a cosmetic exercise, because whilst Grimsby would lose about a third of the land which it had originally proposed taking it would keep the most valuable built-up area of New Cleethorpes. Despite this reduction in Grimsby's proposals, there was still determined opposition. Opponents argued that Cleethorpes had a better record on public health, sanitation and death rates and a meeting of Cleethorpes ratepayers voted overwhelmingly against incorporation.[77]

A Local Government Board public inquiry into Grimsby's proposals was held in February 1908. Despite the College's interest in the well-being of the Grimsby economy, and its disappointment at the inadequacies of the Cleethorpes drainage system, it still supported the Cleethorpes Council. The Master of the College, Charles Smith, gave evidence and said that he was 'thoroughly well satisfied' at the way the Council administered the district. Smith agreed that all the College wanted was an effective system of drainage but said that Cleethorpes could do it better than Grimsby. He acknowledged the College's self-interest when he stated that if New Cleethorpes was taken into Grimsby, it would be impossible for the Cleethorpes Council to carry out a major drainage scheme because of the loss of rateable value, with the result that the College's Thrunscoe land would have to be left undeveloped.[78]

During the course of the public inquiry, the UDC committed itself to carrying out the comprehensive sewerage scheme which has already been referred to, and the question of public health became one of the inquiry's major issues. Cleethorpes had a far better record and could also point to the better quality housing in New Cleethorpes than in Grimsby. The Local Government Board subsequently rejected Grimsby's proposals, and the College's support of the UDC at the inquiry helped cement good relations between the two bodies.[79]

VIII

War and Expansion

1914-1929

The first decade of the new century had been eventful for the expanding town. Outside investment had brought in new attractions and the Council defeated an attempt by Grimsby to absorb New Cleethorpes. Most notable, however, had been the enterprise of the local authority in obtaining its Improvement Act in 1902 and extending the resort to the south with the Kingsway development. Such action marked the beginning of a crucial change in the control of the resort as the UDC began to exert its authority and make inroads into the supremacy of the railway company.

First World War

Not surprisingly, the outbreak of the First World War had serious effects on the locality. Local employment was completely disrupted and house building was put on hold. The Grimsby fishing industry, in which many Cleethorpes men were employed, was put in disarray, and about three-quarters of the steam fishing vessels were taken for minesweeping and other Admiralty purposes. Some of the displaced workers went into the armed forces; others were employed in government work such as munitions or constructing local defence works. The proposed development of the 'Golf Links' was not begun and other resort service industries were affected owing to the disruption of the holiday trade. The poor relief figures for Cleethorpes in 1915 show 901 persons receiving outdoor relief (compared with 410 in 1914) and 87 workhouse inmates (compared with 46 in 1914).[1]

The resort was effectively taken over by the military and put on a war footing. On 8 August 1914, a contingent of 1,437 members of the 3rd Battalion of the Manchester Regiment came to the resort by train:

> On arrival at Cleethorpes the battalion found rumours of all sorts, and a good deal of excitement and 'wind up' generally. The whole battalion was made to line the promenade all night from the pier up to Humberstone Foreshore, ready to repel a German invasion. It makes one smile now at the thought of it, but it was real enough then, and the promenade made an agreeable resting place for some who had bade fond farewell to friends and relations in a true Lancashire fashion the evening before.[2]

By 12 August the the battalion was installed along the coast between Cleethorpes and Tetney and had settled down to its responsibility of guarding the coastline. Battalion headquarters occupied 4 Highcliff and, as the weather became colder, billets were acquired in Cleethorpes. In general, private houses were not commandeered for billets. Buildings

58 *Members of the 3rd Battalion, Manchester Regiment at Humberston in 1918. The battalion was stationed in Cleethorpes and guarded the local coast. It was a training battalion and trained approximately 32,000 recruits locally during the war.*

used included Sunday schools, the gasworks offices, a cinema, restaurants and empty boarding houses. Further effects of war on the populace were felt when the military authorities asked the UDC to extinguish some of the street lamps, which 'owing to their great brilliance … would be of great advantage to the enemy'.[3]

The battalion was essentially a training unit whose primary functions were training new recruits and getting wounded men fit again for battle. Drafts of untrained recruits kept arriving to replace the men who had been sent to the battle front. It was reckoned that 32,000 recruits passed through the town over the course of the war. The health and cleanliness of the men was of concern to the authorities. The UDC supplied large quantities of disinfectants and arranged baths for soldiers suffering from infectious diseases, as well as disinfecting their clothes.[4] In 1915, as part of the battalion's cleanliness regime:

> An attempt was made to have a bathing parade in the Humber once a week, but it was soon discontinued, as when, after a lengthy march across the sands, one did reach the sea, the water was so full of foreign and decaying matter from Grimsby and Hull that the cleanliness of the men was not increased by the performance.[5]

In order to protect the coast, seven 24-hour pickets were established along the coastline, their strengths ranging from seven to 14 men. In 1916 a Machine Gun School was established at the resort, where it remained for the duration of the war with its headquarters in a girls' school on the Kingsway.

The resort suffered bomb damage from Zeppelin raids. In the early morning of 1 April 1916 a bomb hit the town's Baptist chapel, which was being used overnight as a temporary billet for 70 recruits who had arrived on the previous day; 31 were killed and many others injured. Members of the local Voluntary Aid Detachment (VAD) attended to the dead and wounded. A military funeral was held on 4 April, when most of the dead were buried in the Cleethorpes cemetery. Others were taken to their home towns for burial. A memorial cross was ceremoniously unveiled in the cemetery in March 1918.[6] In his history of the battalion, C.M. Thorneycroft commented that:

> After this unlucky raid the inhabitants of Cleethorpes got very jumpy, and the moment a raid warning was received must needs come out and parade the streets instead of going to bed and hoping for the best. All troops too had now to be marched from their billets and scattered along the sea-shore or various hedges and lanes in the country ... The light restrictions were very much enforced and if a glimmer was seen round the edge of the blinds or curtains, raucous voices would be raised from the street or the local policeman would hammer on your front door. Even striking a match in the street was looked upon as a risky proceeding. However, every one after a time calmed down and it was agreed that the disastrous result of this bomb was due more to good luck on the part of the enemy than to good management on their part.[7]

The lighter side of air raids was also commented upon:

> The shelter opposite the *Cliff Hotel* close to the Battalion Headquarters was always occupied by a small crowd of local inhabitants on air raid nights. On the night in question the 'All Clear' having just come through on the 'phone, the Adjutant thought he would slip round in his car to the various Companies so as to enable the men to get back to billets as soon as possible. The car which was in the *Cliff Hotel* yard was started up and a nervous member of the crowd in the shelter, not knowing the 'All Clear' had come through, shouted out 'Here are the Zepps, I can hear their engines and they are flying low'. At once the whole crowd of about 30 to 40 men headed by the local policeman took to their heels and stampeded in every direction.[8]

59 *Memorial in Cleethorpes cemetery to soldiers of the Manchester Regiment who were killed by a bomb dropped on Cleethorpes from a Zeppelin in 1916.*

School attendance was affected by the Zeppelin raids and an entry in the National School log book on 7 April 1916 reads: 'the average attendance this week has only been 169 out of 261, many people having left the town for a time on account of the frequent Zeppelin raids'. The Bursar Street

60 *The local V.A.D. on parade at Well Vale in Lincolnshire. Their Commandant, Mrs T.W. Ellis of Grimsby Road, Cleethorpes, stands in front. During the First World War they staffed the hospital that operated in the St Aidan's Church Mission Hall.*

School was occupied by the military during 1916 and 1917, and pupils were dispersed among other schools.[9]

By October 1916 the battalion was over 4,000 strong. Yarra House on Alexandra Road was taken over as an officers' mess and the Arcadia Restaurant was used for meals for the military. A sergeants' mess had been opened at 21 Market Street in 1915. Many of the men were Roman Catholics and a Mass Centre, served by a priest from Grimsby, was opened in the Pier Pavilion. The battalion's relaxation activities included football, hockey, gymnastics and cross-country running, and a military band gave Sacred Concerts on the pier every Sunday evening. The Council's newly-built Kingsway Pavilion was taken over as an armed forces social centre and, owing to its structure, was nicknamed 'The Glass House'. It was run and staffed by the local Women's Emergency Corps, who were reported to be 'in constant attendance upon Tommy and Jack':

> The moment they [soldiers and sailors] turned into 'The Glass House' the hearty welcome, the cheery atmosphere and the generous hospitality soon made each one forget his grouse and once more feel normal and cheerful. During the time the Battalion was at Cleethorpes over two and a quarter million meals were served at 'The Glass House', over 500 free concerts were given, at many of which the attendance was close on a thousand sailors and soldiers, to all of whom free refreshments and smokes were served. Over 300 free whist drives were held besides innumerable billiards handicaps, and skittle and dart competitions, all of which were free and the winning competitors were all given prizes … Besides 'The Glass House' there were several other places that were always open to the soldier and ready to help him.[10]

Appreciation was also shown for the Red Cross Auxiliary Hospital, which was housed in St Aidan's Church Mission Hall from November 1914 to March 1919, and which was run and staffed by members of the VAD under their Commandant, Mrs T.W. Ellis. A total of 966 patients were treated in the hospital, of which more than 150 were army personnel.[11]

An incident in July 1917 tarnished the battalion's reputation. It concerned Private J. Brightmore, a conscientious objector, who refused to obey a military order and was confined for 11 days in a deep pit dug in the foreshore. The case created a public outcry and was raised in the House of Commons. As a result, several officers were moved from

61 *Humber Forts, January 2000. Haile Sand Fort, with the Bull Sand Fort visible in the distance.*

their posts and a new commanding officer was appointed to the battalion in August 1917.[12]

Huge visible reminders of the war that can still be seen from the Cleethorpes promenade are two military structures in the Humber: the Bull Sand Fort, which lies off the northern, Yorkshire, bank of the river, and the smaller Haile Sand Fort off the southern, Lincolnshire, bank. Their construction was started in 1915 and they had a variety of armaments including six-inch and two-pounder guns as well as small arms. An anti-submarine net of steel mesh (known as the boom defence) was stretched between the forts. Neither fort, however, took any active part in the war; they were not officially completed until March 1918 (Haile Sand Fort) and December 1919 (Bull Sand Fort).[13]

In the war's final year a large proportion of the town's men were away on war service. The 1918 register of electors shows about 2,700 absent on war service, a figure which omits those in the services who were not eligible to vote. Of those listed, a random sample suggests that over half were in the army and more than a quarter in the navy. The remainder were divided fairly equally among the RAF/RFC, minesweeping, the merchant marine, fishing, and other duties.[14] It is not apparent how many women were away in the services or on other wartime duties.

As the war neared its end the resort acquired its well-known decorative statue 'The Boy with the Leaking Boot'. It was donated to the resort by Swedish shipbroker, businessman and Swedish Vice-Consul, John Carlbom, who came to England in the 1890s and founded a successful company in Grimsby in 1897. He lived on the Kingsway until 1910 and presented the statue in appreciation of the time he and his family had lived in the place where his two sons had been born. On 5 March 1918 the UDC minutes recorded that:

> A gentleman, who formerly resided in Cleethorpes was desirous of presenting to the Council an ornamental Fountain for erection on the Kingsway. The Fountain in question was a reproduction of an ornamental Fountain erected in Stockholm by a celebrated sculptor. The design is that of a lad who is wearing one boot only; the other boot is being held in his hand and through this boot the water percolates.[15]

The offer was gratefully accepted and by 8 May the statue was in position on the Kingsway. However, it quickly attracted some unwelcome attention. Soon after its installation, two Special Constables caught two boys throwing stones at it. The boys were brought before the magistrates on 1 June, reprimanded and bound over to keep the peace. The UDC's Pleasure Grounds Committee recommended that 10s. be paid to each of the Special Constables for catching the boys.[16]

A whimsical reporter suggested the reason for the incident as follows:

> Youthful Cleethorpers are warned that the statue of the boy holding a boot at arms length has been placed in the Kingsway Gardens as an ornament and not as a target. The insularity of the Cleethorpes boy may be responsible for him showing resentment at an imported specimen of a foreign boy being given a place of honour in the Kingsway Gardens.[17]

The statue continued to be vulnerable to those bent on mischief and was eventually moved and displayed in the safer surroundings of the resort's Council House. Proposals are afoot to return it to the Kingsway Gardens in 2005. The statue has continued to be popular with residents and visitors, reflected in its extensive use as an advertising logo for the resort.

Although the resort's visitor industry suffered during the war, attractions were still ready for business and the brilliant weather of Whitsun 1918 brought record wartime crowds to the resort:

> Cleethorpes was invaded by a huge crowd of visitors from the usual centres of industry, which included Manchester, Sheffield, Nottingham and Hull. They poured into the township in their thousands—the rush commencing on Saturday … Many of the visitors arrived on Friday, and in a number of instances they will prolong their stay over a week, but in the majority of cases the stay was not protracted beyond Monday, on account of the brief nature of the holiday.

Reports showed the difference in attitudes and activities on Sunday, a day for quiet relaxation, and Monday, which saw more extravagant enjoyment:

> The promenade on Sunday afternoon and evening was ablaze with colour, the light summer attire most beloved of ladies making a pleasing contrast with the more sober hues of dress affected by the men. Naval and military uniforms were also much in evidence. The sacred concert on the pier proved another source of attraction and was thoroughly enjoyed … On Monday … the proprietors of the numerous side shows, 'dip the dip' and the switchback reaped a rich harvest. There seemed to be no stinting of money in any direction, everybody being bent on securing the maximum of pleasure in the time available. Another source of attraction was the Pier Pavilion where many tripped the 'light fantastic' to the strains of Mr McCall's orchestra.

Even the military entered into the spirit of the weekend:

> A group of pierrots connected with the Manchester Regiment provided another source of entertainment on behalf of the Prisoners of War Fund and the extent to which their offerings were appreciated was shown by the liberality of the contributors. Except for this little incident and the khaki uniforms there was no sign of the great upheaval which is taking place in another part of the hemisphere.[18]

Peace

Soon after news of the Armistice had reached the town in November 1918, Cleethorpes was decked out with bunting. The band of the Manchester Regiment marched the streets playing Rule Britannia and the national anthem. Members of the Women's Army

62 *'The Boy with the Leaking Boot' statue in the Kingsway Gardens. Donated to the resort in 1918 by John Carlbom, local businessman and Swedish Vice-Consul.*

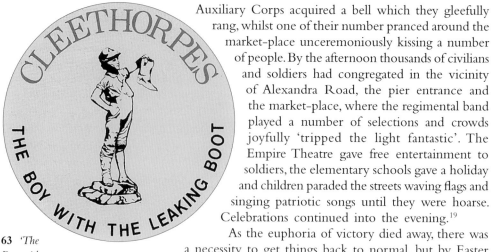

63 *'The Boy with the Leaking Boot' advertising roundel.*

Auxiliary Corps acquired a bell which they gleefully rang, whilst one of their number pranced around the market-place unceremoniously kissing a number of people. By the afternoon thousands of civilians and soldiers had congregated in the vicinity of Alexandra Road, the pier entrance and the market-place, where the regimental band played a number of selections and crowds joyfully 'tripped the light fantastic'. The Empire Theatre gave free entertainment to soldiers, the elementary schools gave a holiday and children paraded the streets waving flags and singing patriotic songs until they were hoarse. Celebrations continued into the evening.[19]

As the euphoria of victory died away, there was a necessity to get things back to normal, but by Easter 1919, the first peace-time holiday, the resort still bore signs of military occupation and wartime shortages. It still, however, saw a multitude of visitors:

> Dip-the-Dips [the Big Dipper rollercoaster] and the Figure of Eight were firm favourites with the youths and maidens. The public houses did a big trade and the supply of beer and whisky available fell short of the demand, and in consequence there were muttered imprecations.[20]

By the early 1920s holiday traffic was back to pre-war levels. Monday 2 July 1923 saw excursion trains from Sheffield, Leicester, Nottingham, Derby, Mansfield and Chesterfield. Two special trains from Conisborough brought 800 adults and 950 children. Over 30 charabancs brought nearly 1,000 people. A few weeks later, on Saturday 11 August, 23 special trains brought about 12,000 visitors. A different aspect of the times was a day's treat organised at the resort by the Cleethorpes Labour Party for 1,600 poor children from Grimsby and Cleethorpes.[21]

The period also saw the construction of what became Cleethorpes' distinctive visitor attraction, the Wonderland amusement centre. It had opened as an open-air facility in 1911 and continued to operate during the First World War. In 1921 it was bought by entrepreneur George Wilkie, who rearranged the site and created an indoor complex. Elsewhere, films were shown in the largely wooden Royal Kinema, which was used as a billet for the Manchester Regiment during the war. It reopened after the war but, after burning down in August 1919, it was rebuilt as the Theatre Royal, which operated as a cinema but also staged variety shows and musical productions by local amateur groups. The Empire Theatre operated as a cinema until 1939.

An exciting new attraction, amphibious 'Sea Cars', provided rides over both beach and sea. Possibly even more thrilling were the aeroplane pleasure flights which could be taken from the beach.

Thrunscoe Recreation Ground

Although the resort eventually returned to normality, and visitors continued to enjoy its attractions, the UDC was intent on adding to these its proposed Thrunscoe Recreation Ground on the 'Golf Links'. But first the land had to be cleared of its wartime legacy. The

64 *Cartoon from 1919, reproduced in 1949, emphasising the housing shortage after both World Wars. The estate agent is laughing in derision at the man who has asked if he has a house to let.*

1919 (could just as easily be 1949!): *The man who asked a house-agent if he had a house to let.*

military had constructed barbed wire entanglements, trenches, redoubts and strongpoints along the coast and, although it set out to remove them, the job was left unfinished when the batallion departed from the resort on 28 February 1919.[22] The 'Golf Links' was in particular need of attention and the UDC received £1,526 in government compensation. Most of this was spent in 1921, when 30 unemployed men completed the restoration, which included forming a shallow lake measuring approximately 400 feet by 150 feet—this was later referred to as a paddling pool.[23]

In 1919 the Council formulated a revised scheme for the 'Golf Links', which included reclaiming 43 acres of foreshore and constructing a sea wall, promenade, bathing pool, marine boating lake, bandstand, tea rooms, model boat pond and large turfed area. The work was intended to be carried out in three stages, the first of which was to create the Bathing Pool. In 1922, the Unemployment Grants Committee awarded a grant towards the cost of the pool. This was on condition that the scheme commenced by 30 April 1922 and that preference was given to the employment of ex-servicemen.[24]

Work commenced but no provision was made at this stage for changing accommodation for bathers. The Council suggested the building of changing rooms as a scheme of unemployment relief. The scheme was rejected by the Unemployment Grants Committee because of the national shortage of skilled building workers, who were needed to build houses.[25] In the meantime, the UDC prepared for the pool's completion. It hired two marquees as temporary changing accommodation (one each for men and women), appointed four attendants, ordered 250 bathing costumes and 100 bathing caps to hire out at 2d. and 1d. respectively and fixed the admission prices at 6d. for adults and 4d. for children.[26]

The pool opened to swimmers on Monday 6 August 1923 but there was no official opening at this time. However, it was proudly noted that, with measurements of 400 feet by 200 feet, it was larger than the comparable pool at Blackpool. During its first two days, approximately 6,000 bathers used it. The following Saturday was reckoned to be the busiest day in the history of the resort and 12,000 visitors came by train. Twenty-three special trains brought visitors, and a further 13 were needed to carry away the visitors who had been staying during the week.[27]

65 *A Whit Monday outing from Ashby (Scunthorpe) to Cleethorpes in 1919.*

The pool closed at the end of the season on 22 September. It was subsequently open annually from May to September and proved to be a popular facility. The attendance on 12 July 1924 was 1,170 bathers and 159 spectators. The initial stock of bathing costumes proved to be insufficient and was increased, intially by 450 costumes and then by a further 288.[28] Such success encouraged the Council to construct the changing rooms and other buildings which would complete the scheme: the official opening of the completed project finally took place on 1 July 1925. During that year's season, the pool had 34,829 bathers and 25,578 spectators. It hired out 6,858 costumes, 11,660 towels and 1,026 bathing caps.[29]

This spurred on the UDC to enlarge the paddling pool and convert it into a Boating Lake. The work was intended to provide labour for the unemployed during the coming winter, but the Unemployment Grants Committee turned down repeated requests for financial help arguing that it was 'still unable to regard the extent of unemployment in the District as sufficiently exceptional'.[30] Despite this setback the Council decided to go ahead with the Boating Lake which would measure 850 by 160 feet. Four islands would be created from excavated material and there would be a boathouse with a landing stage, trees, shrubs and seats. A loan of £4,000 was sanctioned and the contract was awarded to local builders Taylor & Coulbeck. Tenders were accepted for the supply of 40 boats, and two attendants were appointed. The lake was opened on 25 May 1928 and proved to be another triumph. In the first six days 3,126 boating tickets were issued and it was decided to purchase another 10 boats and a motor launch that would carry 12 passengers. Later in the year a tender was accepted for installing electric illuminations on the lake.[31]

The lake closed at the end of the season on 15 October 1928. In December the Council, emboldened by its success, decided to have it extended to the north, nearly doubling its length. New features were to include two bridges, a band enclosure, a children's paddling pool, and more trees, shrubs and turfing. The estimated total cost was £9,500, for which the Unemployment Grants Committee agreed to give a grant provided that most of the workmen were either ex-servicemen or from depressed areas of the country. A new motor launch to carry 30 passengers was ordered, and a new engine was fitted to the old one.[32] The enlarged lake was available for boating on Sunday 30 June 1929. The receipts for the season showed a healthy increase on the previous year, up from £2,089 in 1928 to £2,456 in 1929.[33] In addition to its normal use, the lake was also the venue for occasional special events. For seven years, the 'Biggest Ever' committee had been organising an annual gala in Grimsby in aid of the Grimsby and District Hospital. The committee now organised a Carnival and Gala to take place on Saturday 24 August 1929 in aid of hospital funds. Events included a regatta on the Boating Lake and a fancy dress parade.

The Boating Lake also became embroiled in the persistent dispute over Sunday observance. The UDC was heavily involved in the issue during the 1920s and 1930s but held an indecisive and uneasy position on the matter and, in 1925, agreed with the police to take a relaxed stance on instances of Sunday trading. There were complaints against this policy from officials of three Methodist Sunday schools that had a total of 1,320 scholars. They argued that Sunday trading was harmful to the best interests of young people and made it more difficult to train them to be loyal and worthy citizens.[34] The Boating Lake became involved when the UDC decided to permit Sunday boating. Objections came from the Grimsby Second Circuit of the Primitive Methodist Church and the Correspondent of the Cleethorpes Council Schools. The latter stated that the school managers were of the unanimous opinion that Sunday boating would have a detrimental effect on young people saying 'the Council's recent tendency to encourage the approximation of Sundays to the ordinary days of the week was against the best interests of children and was much to be deplored'. The Council refused to alter its decision.[35]

Boundary Extensions, 1922 and 1927

The post-war period saw the Council striving to extend the boundaries of the resort. In 1920 the Marquess of Lincolnshire auctioned his estate in the adjoining parish of Humberston and the UDC purchased 217 acres of land which lay just outside, and adjacent to, the urban district's boundary. The UDC then applied to the Lindsey County Council for permission to extend its boundaries to take in this and other undeveloped land in Humberston totalling 583 acres, plus 392 acres in neighbouring Weelsby. The County Council held a public inquiry in September 1921. The UDC's main argument was that because of rapid growth in population and housebuilding the town needed more land for its natural development but it contained a much smaller area than comparable urban districts such as Scunthorpe. Other arguments were that the Weelsby land included the Cleethorpes town cemetery, that 217 acres of the Humberston land were already owned by the UDC and that the land contained an insanitary bungalow camp near to the resort's boundary, for which the necessary sanitation could be best supplied by Cleethorpes.

Supporters of the UDC included Sidney Sussex College; opponents included the Grimsby Corporation, which argued that Grimsby, too, was growing rapidly and the land in Weelsby would be better served by being taken into Grimsby. In November 1921 the County Council agreed to the UDC taking all the Humberston land it had requested and about half of the Weelsby land.[36] A few years later, in 1926, the UDC petitioned to take in the remaining 185 acres of the Weelsby land. Once again, the Grimsby Corporation objected and bad feeling was expressed between the two local authorities. The UDC's clerk, A.S. Barter, remarked that if Grimsby Corporation members wished to have a better understanding with the Cleethorpes Council, they should leave Cleethorpes alone and 'mind their own business'. A member of the Grimsby Corporation, Frank Barrett, stated that most of the Cleethorpes population depended upon Grimsby for their daily bread and they only went to Cleethorpes to sleep.[37] Later in the year, Cleethorpes Council's George Moody remarked that:

> During the last ten years half-a-dozen mayors [of Grimsby] have professed that they wished to live in harmonious relationship with Cleethorpes and when that expression had been used he had always noticed that an attack had been launched immediately.[38]

The UDC petition succeeded and the boundary was extended in 1927 to take in the extra 185 acres. Thus, owing to the efforts of the UDC, Cleethorpes' acreage had nearly doubled, from 1,185 in 1921 to 2,117 in 1927. Grimsby Corporation was also seeking boundary extensions to the south and west of the borough and, also in 1927, Grimsby's acreage was increased from 3,260 to almost 6,000 acres.

Marine Embankment

The Humberston land now within the Cleethorpes boundary lay to the south of the new Thrunscoe Recreation Ground. The golf course took up 113 acres of the 'new' land and the remaining 104 acres consisted of rough saltmarsh, which was often flooded by the tide, making it waterlogged and unsuitable for any practical public purpose.[39] When the Council purchased the land it had the idea of eventually using it as a further recreation area and, in 1928, it was decided to go ahead with a scheme for the relief of unemployment that would entail constructing an embankment to protect the land from flooding. This would enable it to be drained and would also provide a seafront walk to the resort's boundary with Humberston. Plans were prepared by the Council's Surveyor and in January 1929 the Unemployment Grants Committee gave a loan for the scheme plus a grant. A condition of the grant was that half of the labour should be from the distressed areas, the remainder to be unemployed men, particularly ex-servicemen.[40]

Work commenced on 11 February 1929 and a maximum of 161 men were employed at any one time. Soon after it had begun, Primitive Methodist minister the Rev. F.H. Edwards arranged a club room and evening entertainment for the men who had been brought in from the distressed areas. The work was completed on 11 June 1930, having cost about £27,000.[41] The total length of the embankment was 5,475 feet—just over a mile. In 1933 the embankment was embellished with a brass tread that marked the line of the Greenwich Meridian and refreshment could be obtained at the far end of the embankment from Mrs L. Egarr's wooden hut. The Thrunscoe Recreation Ground's embankment was extended by about four hundred yards to link up with the new Marine Embankment and the resort could then boast of a seafront walk of nearly three miles.[42]

Railway Promenades and Pier

A significant event in 1923 affected the ownership of railway property in the resort. The 'grouping' of the national railway system saw the existing railway companies being absorbed into four new companies, each covering a large geographical area. Locally, the GCR was merged into the newly-created London and North Eastern Railway (LNER), which became the owner of the railway property in Cleethorpes. It was crucial to the resort's development that this took place at a time when the UDC was interested in extending its control of the seafront, whilst the new company, with its much larger geographical remit, did not have the GCR's proprietorial interest in the resort. This is shown in an LNER internal memorandum of June 1926:

> It is felt that the business of the administration of the pier and pleasure gardens is scarcely one for a railway company to undertake, and that a great deal more could be made of the premises by the Council who would be keenly alive to doing everything possible to develop the estate to attract visitors to Cleethorpes and so benefit the ratepayers as well as the Company.[43]

In the same year, the Council asked the LNER for a lease of the Pier Gardens; the company responded that it was willing to sell the UDC the bulk of its Cleethorpes estate. This comprised the pier, with the pavilion and cafe, the Pier Gardens with tennis courts and bowling green, the promenades and sea wall, the swimming and slipper baths, five lock-shops in the Central Colonnade, a further eight in the Humberston Colonnade and the Grotto refreshment rooms. The cost of the property had been £106,000 and the net receipts for the year 1925 were £1,787, a return of only 1.69 per cent on the capital outlay. Preliminary discussions took place between the two parties.[44]

The UDC would need parliamentary authority to proceed with the purchase. It was also interested in acquiring extra powers to provide a wider range of services in order to forward local development. Accordingly, in December 1927, the UDC decided unanimously to promote a bill in parliament which, according to a local newspaper, was:

> calculated to give the township a better standing and to render it more attractive as a place for holidaymakers … The object is to promote the better government of the township and an improvement in its physical attractions in order to draw a bigger influx of visitors … Other seaside towns are sparing no expense in catering for the

66 *Grimsby-Cleethorpes Provincial Tramways bus.*

visiting public. Cleethorpes would be wise to follow suit if it desires to maintain its custom against the competition of its enterprising rivals ... It must go forward or be outstripped in the race. Its Councillors are showing themselves to be men of wisdom and are entitled to the fullest support.[45]

At a public meeting on 16 January 1928, a resolution approving the promotion of the bill was carried by a large majority, only four people voting against it.[46] The bill received the royal assent on 3 August 1928 as the Cleethorpes Urban District Council Act. It authorised the Council to purchase and manage the pier, Pier Gardens, and promenades. The UDC was given sanction to purchase and operate the tramway system, to operate trolley buses and regulate traffic, powers regarding electricity supply, streets, building, drainage and infectious diseases, and authority over the seashore, parks, promenades, baths and public buildings. The UDC was now set to make extensive use of the many powers authorised by the Act, but agreement with the LNER over the purchase of the railway property lay several years in the future.[47]

Public Transport

The powers regarding public transport that the Council had obtained in the 1928 Act emphasise the changes taking place in transport during the post-war period. Before the war, the railway and tramway systems had been the main providers of public transport, but the arrival of motor buses offered greater flexibility and new financial opportunities. Prior to 1914, the tramway company had provided bus services to local villages such as Waltham and Caistor and after the war it expanded these services. In 1919 it introduced 'toast-rack' buses along the seafront, which were very popular with visitors, and, in 1926, it started a bus service from Cleethorpes to Humberston that carried 14,301 passengers in the first two months of operation. There was also a steadily expanding stream of private bus operators and by the mid-1920s most villages of any size in the locality had some sort of bus service. Charabancs had become commonplace in Cleethorpes, leading to complaints that touts offering trips were annoying holidaymakers.

However, the urban tram service was becoming inadequate and overcrowded. This was despite an increase in the number of trams in service from 22 in 1911 to 31 in 1921. The system was becoming inadequate and its lifespan was uncertain. Changes were already taking place in Grimsby: the Grimsby Corporation had purchased the Grimsby section of the tram system in 1925 and started replacing trams with trolley buses. It also started to

67 *Provincial Tramways charabanc, c.1920, advertising a seven-mile circular tour through the countryside with fine scenery, fare 6d.*

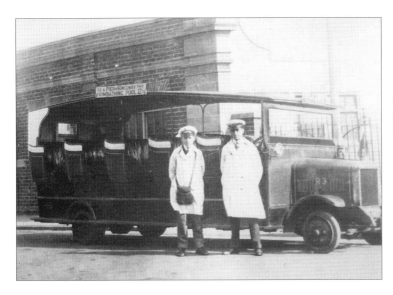

68 *'Toast-rack' bus which ran along the seafront between the Pier and the Bathing Pool, c.1930.*

operate motor buses and had 17 by 1929. The tramway company continued to run the tram service in Cleethorpes but this could only be looked upon as a temporary measure. The UDC's new powers authorised it to purchase the tramway system and then, if need be, discontinue the service and replace it with trolley buses. It was also empowered to run motor buses and started its first experimental service in 1929. By 1935 the UDC had 12 buses, which carried 1,713,111 passengers in the year ending 31 March 1935.[48]

Roads and Building

The new motor buses were being joined on the roads by increasing numbers of cars and motorcycles which called for wide smooth roads. Good roads into the resort were needed, not only to ease travel for visitors but also to give a good impression as they entered the town. Consequently, the two main roads into the resort, Grimsby Road and Clee Road, were both widened during the 1920s. Because of existing built-up frontages, Grimsby Road could only be widened between Bramhall Street and Isaac's Hill. Clee Road's entire length, from Isaac's Hill to Love Lane Corner, was widened. Existing trees along Clee Road were retained as far as possible and, in 1925, additional trees were planted.

Another entry road, Taylors Lane, was renamed Taylors Avenue in 1925, but plans to increase the width of the section within the town boundary from 32 feet to 60 feet wide were prevented by Sidney Sussex College refusing to give land for widening. Another landowner, W.T. Hewitt, had already given land for the widening of Clee Road and gave further land so that a 'circus' could be constructed at the end of Taylors Avenue in 1930. Accordingly, the crossroads was named Hewitt's Circus.

The differing policies of the UDC and Sidney Sussex College in 1921 delayed the extension of the Kingsway to form the Kings Road. The College owned the land needed for the extension but would not agree to any work taking place unless it was permitted to develop its adjacent Thrunscoe land with more expensive higher-quality houses at the same time. The completion of the major drainage scheme in 1916 had made this feasible but stalemate ensued because the UDC insisted that the remaining College land in New Cleethorpes, which was destined for working-class housing, should be developed first because of the shortage of smaller houses.[49]

69 *Bathing Pool, c.1923, with changing marquees on the left. Partly because of government building restrictions, the entrance building and changing rooms were not completed until 1925.*

There was certainly a desperate need for more housing. While the population of the town had continued to rise, from 21,417 to 28,155 between 1911 and 1921, house building had been halted by the war and so the number of houses increased by only a few hundred, from 5,145 in 1911 to 5,711 in 1921.[50] These factors combined to produce a major housing shortage in the post-war period. As well as sharing houses, people also took up residence in caravans, garages, outhouses and sheds. The UDC tried to prevent residence in the more unsuitable, insanitary premises, but its largest single problem was the holiday bungalow site that had come within its orbit when it purchased the Humberston land in 1920 and which became part of its public health responsibilities when the town boundary was extended in 1922. The site probably started out as a military encampment during the war, and it was known as 'First Camp' although its official name was the Black

70 *A later view of the Bathing Pool. It was advertised as the largest open-air pool on the east coast. Many bathers reckoned it was also the coldest.*

71 *The Boating Lake, initially opened by the UDC in 1928 as part of its Thrunscoe Recreation Ground development. Because of its success the lake was extended and the much larger lake was completed for the 1929 season.*

72 *A paddling pool provided by the Cleethorpes UDC as part of the Thrunscoe Recreation Ground facilities.*

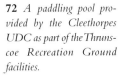

73 *The busy sandpit near the Boating Lake, seen here in the 1930s. It was provided by the UDC as part of its Thrunscoe Recreation Ground development.*

74 *A crowded North Promenade and beach in the 1920s.*

Bear Camp. The camp was located on the coast in the region of the present Cleethorpes Showground and a press report in 1920 referred to it as the 'Bungalow Town':

> The residents here may be divided into two classes—people who are there for health reasons, and others of the great army of homeless, who are only waiting for the opportunity to get into a house of more adequate proportions elsewhere … The people … who cannot get a house in town simply make the best of their lot—and wait. The ex-soldiers living here will find the conditions not far-removed from army life.[51]

It was reported in 1921 that: 'These bungalows are the only homes of some of the people there. They were taken when the house shortage became very acute, and what was at one time purely a summer camp has become a residential quarter.' Of the 30 bungalows on the camp at the time, 25 were used as permanent accommodation. In September 1921, an abnormally high tide flooded the camp: about half the bungalows were either damaged or moved from their positions by the force of the sea. Despite this onslaught, the camp remained in use. Because of the housing shortage, the UDC reluctantly allowed the bungalows to continue to be used for residential accommodation. However, the respite was only temporary and the 'Bungalow Town' ceased to exist in 1930, after the UDC insisted that all the huts or bungalows be removed from the site.[52]

Central government encouraged local authorities to help meet the demand for accommodation by building government-subsidised council houses. The Cleethorpes Council only got involved with great reluctance. It paid Sidney Sussex College £3,250 for land adjoining Clee Road and had 136 council houses built. By April 1922 over 930 applications had been received for the 136 houses and more were being received. There was a severe shortage of working-class houses, but the Council saw private subsidised building as the answer to the demand and decided there was no need to build any more council houses.[53] Consequently, the remainder of the 1,187 houses completed in the town during 1920-29 were built by private enterprise. More than half of them (587) were aided by central government subsidies to builders. The College was now building again in New Cleethorpes and building also took place in Thrunscoe, on the Boulevard Estate and on roads in the area of Sherburn Street.

The increase in the number of houses in the 1920s was not matched by population growth. The town had experienced 30 years of rapid growth, but the 1920s showed a sudden check, and the population increased by only a few hundred from 28,155 in 1921 to 28,621 in 1931. To some extent this is explained by the growth of nearby commuter villages. For example, during the decade the population of Humberston increased from 609 to 1,096 and that of Waltham from 978 to 1,896. Yet because of this standstill in population, the increase in the number of houses during the decade helped to alleviate the housing shortage.

As building restarted in New Cleethorpes, the question of a recreation ground came to the fore. We have seen that Sidney Sussex College offered the UDC land for a recreation ground if it proceeded with a comprehensive drainage scheme for the town. Accordingly, in 1919 the College offered 14 acres in Brereton Avenue, which became the Sussex Recreation Ground. The land was offered provided that it would be maintained as an open space for the free use of the public and as a playground for children, and for cricket, football and other games.[54] Work on the ground was carried out in stages during the 1920s and 1930s, with government financial support on condition that unemployed men undertook the work. By June 1923, 40 previously unemployed men were at work and the resort guide reported in 1927 that 'Fifteen tennis courts have been constructed … also an excellent bowling green—all of which are open to the public at very reasonable charges'.[55] Work followed on setting out a children's play area and constructing two pavilions.

There was still a need for more and better provision of education. The National School was showing its age. In 1922, it had 703 pupils in inadequate buildings with

75 *Kings Parade and sea wall. The foreshore here was built up with sand by the Borough Council in the early 1950s to form a new beach, which is currently above tide level.*

76 *Kingsway and Bathing Pool c. 1930, showing the housing development which took place in Thrunscoe after land was opened up by the building of the Kingsway in 1906. In the top right-hand quadrant can be seen Hardy's Farm buildings. The site is now occupied by the Signhills Schools.*

77 *Matron and staff of the Croft-Baker Maternity Home in Mill Road. It was formerly the residence of Alderman W. Grant and was purchased by Alderman Mrs. Croft-Baker, who presented it to the town for use as a Maternity Home. The Home was opened in 1929, closed in 1984 and then converted into apartments.*

poor facilities. In 1928, the Girls' and Infants' Schools were modernised and the Boys' School was to cease being used when alternative accommodation became available. In 1926, the Lindsey County Council had provided a new Secondary School for Girls on Clee Road, with eventual capacity for 400 pupils. The same year saw the opening of the Public Library in the Technical Institute on Isaac's Hill.

Coming of Age
1930–1939

The 1920s had certainly been a decade of great change for Cleethorpes including the doubling of its acreage, the southerly extension of the sea wall with the Marine Embankment, and the completion of two popular new attractions in the shape of the Bathing Pool and Boating Lake. All this had been due to its energetic and enterprising UDC, which, as the decade came to an end, had also acquired new parliamentary authority to improve, control and extend public services. There was, therefore, the strong probability of further significant changes as the resort entered a new decade.

Railway and Trams

The 1930s opened with the UDC still involved in discussions on the purchase of the railway company's seafront estate. A price of £27,500 was eventually agreed and the purchase was finalised in February 1936. This was much less than the railway company's earlier expectations and provoked the LNER internal comment that the price was 'much below what the Company have in mind [but] the fact remains that during the last five years, the loss on the working of the Pier and Gardens has averaged £670 per annum and … there is no prospect of the property becoming a paying proposition under existing conditions'.[1]

Discussions were also taking place over the purchase of the tramway system. Across the country generally, trams were being replaced by motor buses and trolley buses. In 1930, the UDC offered to buy out the tramway company for £20,000 but the offer was turned down, as was an increased offer of £30,000 in 1933. A course of action would have been to go to arbitration but the Council was chary of doing so in case too high a value was arrived at by the arbitrator. Councillor Moody, who was leading the UDC negotiations, advised against going to arbitration 'over what may be called an obsolete service of trams'. He did not want to commit ratepayers to paying for what might be turned into scrap metal in the next year or two. However, the Grimsby Corporation was working on replacing its trams with trolley buses and, in 1935, the tramway company signalled its intention to introduce a bill in parliament authorising it to replace the trams in Cleethorpes with trolley buses. This caused the UDC to come to a decision to buy out the company and then replace the trams with trolley buses. Accordingly, it bit the bullet and went for arbitration.[2]

Twelve Reasons why you should Live at Cleethorpes

To those seeking desirable seclusion and retirement, Cleethorpes offers advantages which will on comparison compare most favourably with claims of any other town or resort. Amongst the advantages not already named, may be claimed as follows :—

1. Low Mortality Rate.
2. Exceptionally high sunshine record.
3. Equable climate.
4. Superior range of villas and residences moderately priced.
5. Exceptionally moderate cost of living. Public services, cheap electricity, gas, rates, water, buses, etc.
6. Its abundant and varied supply of high-class entertainments, social life and functions.
7. Its hospitable inhabitants and friendly social spirit.
8. Its fine geographical position, attractions of beauty and interest of surrounding country.
9. Its excellent shopping and recreation centres.
10. The nearest resort to industrial England.
11. Good train and travel services.
12. 1st Division Football.

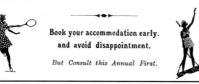

**Book your accommodation early.
and avoid disappointment.**

But Consult this Annual First.

78 *'Twelve Reasons Why You Should Live at Cleethorpes', from the resort's guide for 1936.*

In 1936, the arbitrator settled on a price of £50,000, which was much higher than the UDC's offers and justified the fears of some of its members. However, Moody said that the matter had dragged on for years and it was the best bargain that could be made:

> They had the buses, and when they got the trams, which they intended changing over to trolley buses, they would be able to give the public a very good service. Grimsby was to have trolley buses, and they hoped to run jointly with Grimsby, as the trams had been run. That, he believed, was in the best interests of the public.[3]

The UDC took over the service in July 1936, only five months after acquiring the LNER's seafront estate. It quickly replaced the trams with trolley buses, which started to run on 18 July 1937. Thereupon, the Grimsby Corporation and the Cleethorpes UDC were able to co-operate in running trolley bus services between the two towns. When the tram service ceased it was ironically commented that 'No more will the public get the thrills of a sea trip to Cleethorpes—they will glide along in comfortable ease, and about twice as fast'. By the end of the 1930s both Grimsby and Cleethorpes were served by modern public transport systems.[4]

Civic Pride

While the UDC was flexing its muscles in relation to purchasing the railway company's seafront property and the tramway system, it was also thinking about other municipal advancement. In 1933 the Council was once more considering whether to petition the Privy Council for a charter of incorporation as a municipal borough. The 1897 petition had been unsuccessful but Cleethorpes had grown considerably since then, both as a resort and as a residential town. It had also considerably improved as a local authority and appeared to be a suitable candidate for achieving the enhanced status of municipal borough.

At a meeting of the UDC on 4 July 1933, members heard that achieving municipal borough status would not mean that Cleethorpes would have the same powers of self-government as Grimsby, which had the much higher status of county borough and ran all its own services. The services which a municipal borough could provide differed little from those provided by a UDC. The Lindsey County Council would continue to provide major services such as elementary education and police. One obvious effect of municipal borough status would be the added dignity of having a mayor, aldermen and civic regalia. Other benefits, though important, would be less obvious. For example,

79 *On the Central Promenade in 1937. In the background, the pier entrance crosses above the promenade. In 1939, the Borough Council replaced it with an entrance direct from the promenade.*

it was understood that government departments gave more consideration to boroughs than to urban districts and that parliament was loath to interfere with the independence of boroughs. The implication of this latter benefit was that, as a municipal borough, Cleethorpes would be in a stronger position to counter the long-standing arguments of Grimsby that the two towns should be amalgamated. In view of the conflicts with Grimsby in the past, it is not surprising that the ensuing local discussion about getting a borough charter became more about its use as a bulwark against Grimsby's hopes of expansion than any concrete benefits which it might bring to Cleethorpes. The Council voted by 12 to one, with one abstention, in favour of petitioning for borough status.[5]

Several groups and individuals expressed opposition to the petition on the basis that it would hinder amalgamation with Grimsby, which they thought would be in the best interests of both towns and which, they argued, was bound to happen at some time in the future. These included the Cleethorpes Labour Party, the Cleethorpes Ratepayers' Association and Lord Yarborough. Even the *Hull Daily Mail* joined in and supported amalgamation. Sidney Sussex College sat firmly on the fence and argued that whilst it agreed that the best long-term outcome would be amalgamation it took no sides regarding the petition.[6] The Cleethorpes Advancement Association voted in favour of borough status and at a meeting of the Cleethorpes Chamber of Trade, the chairman of

80 *Central Promenade in the 1930s.*

the UDC, Councillor A.W. Cox, commented on Grimsby's 'interference' in Cleethorpes' domestic matters. He said that Cleethorpes had a great future as a seaside resort and residential area whilst Grimsby had a great future as a fishing port: 'we are two distinct entities and have each our own destiny'.[7]

A public inquiry into the petition was held by a Ministry of Health inspector in November 1934. The UDC argued that the town had progressed well in the previous 60 years and that its development was what would be expected of a seaside and health resort. This line of argument was undoubtedly in order to draw a distinction between the seaside Cleethorpes and the industrial Grimsby. The point was also made that in terms of population Cleethorpes was the fourth largest urban district in Lincolnshire, after Grimsby, Lincoln and Scunthorpe, and successfully provided a wide range of services. Grimsby opposed the petition and argued that the resort was heavily dependent on Grimsby's industry, stating that five out of seven males and nine out of 24 females in Cleethorpes worked in Grimsby. Comment was made that the inquiry was being asked to countenance two boroughs, 'one of which contained people who had retired, well-to-do, and the other contained those less aesthetic places where the money was made'.[8]

The inquiry decided in favour of Cleethorpes and a royal charter of incorporation as a borough was granted on 8 July 1936. So in the same year that the purchases of the railway company seafront estate and the tramway system were completed, the increasing capabilities and confidence of the local authority were marked by the achievement of borough status. The new borough was proud to record in its celebratory souvenir booklet that:

> It is generally recognised that a Royal Charter of Incorporation is conferred only in those cases where satisfactory proof has been given of the efficiency of the Local Government Administration in the district and the capacity for further development.[9]

It took further pride in the new civic regalia, which emphasised its new-found achievement and dignity. Many organisations and individuals subscribed to provide the accoutrements of borough dignity. Heading the list was Sidney Sussex College, which provided a heavily ornamented silver gilt mace over five feet long. An element from the College's coat of arms was included in the new coat of arms which the borough adopted as a further mark of its new status.

The importance the local authority attached to the granting of borough status can be gauged from the fact that the programme of celebrations to mark its municipal coming of age covered five days. On Wednesday 23 September 1936, a procession of dignitaries culminated with the official presentation of the royal charter in a ceremony at Sidney Park. This was followed by the singing of 'Jerusalem' by a choir of schoolchildren, a short religious service, music by the Cleethorpes Silver Band and a display of country dancing by schoolchildren. A Charter Ball was held in the evening in the Pier Pavilion and a fireworks display took place near the Bathing Pool. The next few days of celebrations included souvenirs and free use of attractions for children, dances, a free meal for old people, free film shows for the unemployed and the poor, band concerts, more dancing displays by children and more fireworks. The celebrations concluded on Sunday with a civic church service and an evening concert in the Pier Pavilion. Coming down to earth with a bump, elections for the new Borough Council were held on 2 November and the Charter became fully effective when the new Council held its first meeting on 9 November 1936.

Regardless of the persuasive arguments that more long-term benefit would have accrued to both towns if Cleethorpes had accepted amalgamation with Grimsby as an alternative to borough status, the Charter can be seen as a deserved symbol of the energetic expansion of municipal enterprise in the resort during the previous decades. The new borough was proud to list the services and work in which it was now engaged. These included: public health and drainage, the collection and disposal of house refuse, food inspection, the provision of parks and open spaces, recreation and entertainment, highways, the fire brigade, an ambulances service, the promenades, the pier and pier gardens, the tramways, the electricity undertaking and housing. It also listed the services provided in the town by, or in conjunction with, the Lindsey County Council, such as the public library, education, public assistance, maternity and child welfare, and the police.[10]

Redeveloping the Seafront

The newly installed Borough Council now set about the job of improving the seafront. Its initial idea of deciding on a suitable scheme by competition did not comply with the requirements of the Town Planning Institute. Accordingly, it invited a well-known landscape architect, E.P. Mawson, to prepare a scheme. It was Mawson's father Thomas, the eminent landscape architect and town planner, who had prepared a layout for the resort's Sidney Park earlier in the century.[11] Mawson was asked to submit drawings and estimates for a crescent extension on the promenade opposite Sea Road, the widening of Sea Road by the provision of a dual carriageway, a new pier entrance direct from the promenade, the development of the Pier Gardens frontage to Sea Road to include shelters, licensed premises, shops, gardens and so on, and, finally, the improvement of the High Cliff Steps.[12]

The estimated cost of the scheme was £54,000 and application was made to the Ministry of Health for sanction to borrow £12,090 to implement the first stage of the project. The Council stressed its desire to start the work as soon as possible in order to

81 *Central Promenade, probably early 1950s, and the new pier entrance of 1939 direct from the promenade. The truncated pier was shortened during 1948-9 after being breached in the war.*

82 *High Cliff Steps leading down to the Central Promenade and built by the MS&LR in 1885. The Cliff Hotel is in the background.*

83 *High Cliff Steps, May 2000. They were constructed in 1938 by the Borough Council to replace the MS&LR's steps. In the background is the old* Cliff *Hotel building transformed into 'JD's Nightscene'. It is currently being replaced by luxury apartments.*

provide work for the unemployed. The work on this first stage was grouped under three headings. Firstly, the provision of improved access from High Cliff to the promenade in place of the existing steps; secondly, the construction of a bow wall bastion near the Sea Road slipway and the provision of an entrance to the pier from the promenade; thirdly, the widening of Sea Road.[13] Sanction to take out the loan was granted and work began in 1938. The stylish art deco steps at High Cliff were completed on 31 October and proudly bore the new borough's coat of arms. During the ensuing year, improvement continued at a quick pace. The new pier entrance and kiosks were completed, which meant demolishing that part of the pier which had run over the promenade. Sea Road was widened, and the Sea Road slipway, kiosks and bastion bow wall were completed. Alexandra Road, too, was widened.

One improvement led to a local storm in a teacup—or in a tankard. New licensed premises had been planned to replace the refreshment pavilion on Sea Road. Plans prepared by Mawson were accepted by the Council for what became the *Submarine* public house (currently called the *Bucket and Spade*). However, there was still a temperance presence in the resort, and the Cleethorpes Branch of the National British Women's Total Abstinence Union, the St Peter's Church Mothers' Union and the Cleethorpes Trinity Methodist Church protested, albeit unsuccessfully, against the council decision to have licensed premises on its land.[14] On completion, the premises were leased by Samuel Smith's brewery, which entered into occupation on 6 June 1939. The old refreshment pavilion (by then isolated in the middle of the widened Sea Road) was demolished.[15]

Vandalism sometimes bedevilled the Council's improvements. Shortly after acquiring the Pier Gardens, the Council opened them free of charge for a trial period of four Sundays. A total of 7,240 people passed through the gates, 80 per cent of whom were young people, but it was agreed that free admission should not be extended for the time being. A later decision, in 1939, to open the gardens free of charge ran into trouble because of vandalism and the Council decided that the gardens might have to be closed to the public if it continued. The new High Cliff Steps were soon defaced by young people. Accordingly, an ex-policeman was engaged at £3 per week to check unruly behaviour and to prevent damage to Council property.[16]

In 1939, the Council intended to continue improvement work at the end of the summer season, and Mawson was asked to prepare drawings and estimates. The new work would entail improvements to the Pier Gardens, which would include a café to replace the existing Grotto Café, shelters with public conveniences and kiosks, and new garden layouts with the provision of a car park immediately joining the promenade. New swimming baths were also planned to take the place of those built by the railway company. Unfortunately, all development was put on hold with the outbreak of war in September.[17]

Entertainment and Attractions

The acquisition of the seafront estate and the pier involved the Council in a new range of activities. Early in 1936, the coming season's programme had to be organised for the pier. Tenders were invited for the provision of a dance band and that of Robert (Bob) Walker was accepted. He would supply a band of 10 performers plus conductor and provide music for all dances and orchestral concerts in the Pier Pavilion on weekdays and Sundays for £52 10s. per week. The Council agreed to the BBC broadcasting dance music from the pier for two five-minute slots on 26 June and for 15 minutes on 24 July 1936.

However, even the provision of a dance band involved the Council in controversy. During 1937, around thirty complaints were received from trade unions regarding the appointment of Bob Walker's band at the Pier. The complaints referred to the level of wages and the fact that the band was 'employing men who already have regular employment instead of musicians who have lost their employment since the advent of the Talkies'. All the allegations were refuted but the granting of a tender for the 1939 season produced

84 *The Kingsway, Olympia and Café Dansant (previously the Kingsway Pavilion) in the 1930s.*

85 *Winter Gardens, previously Olympia, September 2003.*

more controversy. Some Council members wanted Bob Walker's tender accepted but it was finally decided to accept that from J.D. (Don) Twidale of £865 15s. for the season.[18] Other dances were put on by national magazines, such as the Carnival Dances sponsored by *Answers* magazine in 1937. Admission was 1s., and each patron would also receive a copy of *Answers*. Prizes would be provided by the magazine publishers to the value of £8 or £9 each evening. The publishers of *Picture Post* magazine asked permission to hold *Picture Post* nights at the pavilion each Friday during the season, and to sell the magazine at the pier entrance, paying the Council ½d. for each copy sold. The sponsors would also supply spot prizes to dancers holding a copy of the magazine. In 1937 potential visitors were deprived of a thrilling act, when the appropriately named Mr B. Dolphin was refused permission to give diving exhibitions from the pier. The Oberon Cruising Company operated river cruises from the pierhead landing stage with its vessel *White Lady II* during 1936-8.

In the final season before the outbreak of war, visitors were enjoined to 'Come to the Pier for Health and Entertainment!' The admittance charge was still 2d. and attractions included dancing to Don Twidale and his Band afternoon and evening. Special prominence was given to 'Celebrity Concerts each Sunday with Britain's Premier Vocalists'. These ran from May to October and included well-known tenors of the day such as Webster Booth and Frank Titterton. Other concerts featured local groups, including the Grimsby Madrigal Society, the Cleethorpes Festival Choir and the Thrunscoe Boys' Choir. Refreshments, in the form of morning coffee, luncheons, grills, teas, fruit drinks, ices, chocolates and cigarettes, could be obtained at the Pier Café.[19] Other events included a 'Red Haired Beauty Contest', organised by the Cleethorpes Advertising Committee.

Meanwhile, the Empire Theatre and the Theatre Royal were still showing films. The latter was advertising itself as 'The Premier Cinema and Variety Theatre in the District' and proclaimed in 1931 that 'You have not heard the "talkies" at their best until you've heard them at the Royal'. A rival appeared in 1937 with the building of the up-to-date

86 *Cleethorpes High Street, c.1930, looking in the direction of Isaac's Hill.*

Ritz Cinema on Grimsby Road.[20] Another new attraction was Olympia, an amusement hall built on ground opposite the Bathing Pool. It contained a rifle range, hoop-la and various other stalls and later became a roller skating rink. After the war it was transformed into the present-day Winter Gardens.

The concept of an annual Carnival, as tried out in 1929, was revived and extended in 1932 and the Cleethorpes Carnival took place on Friday and Saturday, 12-13 August. Friday's events included a Carnival Procession starting from Sidney Park at 6.30 p.m. and ending at the Boating Lake. The many prizes included one for the Best Decorated Donkey, and the Best Comic Costume. An evening regatta at the Boating Lake included rowing races, Bladder Fights in Boats, Pillow Fights on Poles and a Tug of War in Boats. The evening also saw Carnival Dances on the Putting Green, at the Royal Café and at the Kingsway Pavilion. The Carnival continued on Saturday with the election of the Cleethorpes Beauty Queen and a Bathing Pool Gala, which included Water Polo, a Blindfold Swimming Race, a Needle and Thread Race and Comic Diving. Both evenings concluded with dances and there was a firework display on the Saturday evening. The following year's Carnival was extended to a full week of activities.[21]

Sunday Trading

Sunday trading was still a contentious matter and the Council was divided on the issue. This produced a confused situation. The early 1930s saw repeated requests from stallholders for permission to open on Sundays turned down, but petitions in 1933 resulted in stalls on the north foreshore being permitted to open. However, letters from several clergymen and ministers early in 1934 conveyed their 'deep concern for the due observance of Sunday during the forthcoming season' and expressing the hope that the Council would 'stand firm for a dignified and respectful observance of Sunday'. Consequently agreements for the 1934 season prohibited Sunday opening[22] and the Council turned down petitions from foreshore traders requesting Sunday trading. Yet it was then decided by eight votes to seven to take no action against reported instances of Sunday trading.[23] In January 1935 it decided that stalls other than entertainment sites would be allowed to open on Sundays for the season.[24] Clarification was then sought on what constituted 'entertainment sites'; the Lincolnshire Aero Club was permitted to make Sunday flights from the foreshore, despite having been refused permission to do so

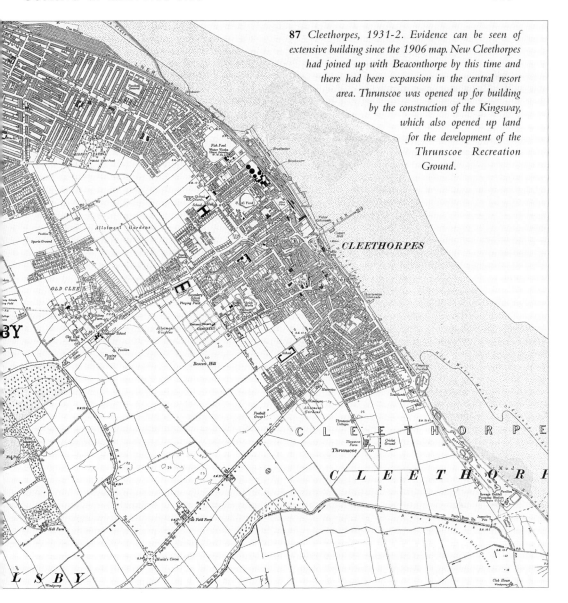

87 *Cleethorpes, 1931-2. Evidence can be seen of extensive building since the 1906 map. New Cleethorpes had joined up with Beaconthorpe by this time and there had been expansion in the central resort area. Thrunscoe was opened up for building by the construction of the Kingsway, which also opened up land for the development of the Thrunscoe Recreation Ground.*

in 1933.[25] The prohibition on 'entertainment sites' operating on Sundays continued into the 1939 season. Restrictions on Sunday opening were even applied to the Council's Sussex Recreation Ground when the UDC decided in 1935 that only the eastern portion of the ground would be open to the public on Sundays and the use of the children's games equipment would be prohibited on that day.[26]

The situation with regard to Sunday trading by shops was rationalised throughout the country by the passing of the Shops (Sunday Trading Restriction) Act of 1936. The basic premise of the Act was that shops would be closed on Sundays, except for certain specified categories. In addition, local authorities of holiday resorts could make an order permitting Sunday opening on up to 18 Sundays in the year subject to two-thirds of the shops voting in favour. The UDC issued such an order and although the vote throughout the town did not reach the requisite two-thirds majority, it did so in the resort area. The order was confirmed accordingly, and shops in the resort area were permitted to open on Easter Sunday, Whit Sunday and Sundays from 4 June to 17 September 1939.[27]

Building and Services

Although there was much activity in the resort, and visitors continued to flock in by road or rail, the standstill in population growth which had been apparent in the 1920s continued into the 1930s. Because of the outbreak of war in 1939 there was no national census in 1941, but the National Registration figure for Cleethorpes in 1939 gives a total of 27,142 people. Although no accurate comparison can be made with the 1931 census figure of 28,621, the 1939 figure does indicate a continued lack of population growth. House building continued and the years 1930-9 saw the building of 1,251 houses.[28] The College continued its leasehold development, concentrating on building in the Queen Mary Avenue and Brereton Avenue areas of the town. It also belatedly began development of its Thrunscoe land with building in Cromwell Road. Building continued on the Boulevard Company estate in Thrunscoe. Six houses were built by the Council for the closely-packed Wardall Street area residents dispossessed as a result of the demolition of houses under the Council's slum-clearance scheme. The survey into slum housing was carried out under national legislation and it is an indirect compliment to the quality of housing in the town that the survey considered only nine houses to be slum property which should be demolished.[29]

A sign of the changing times was the 1937 opening of the art deco electricity showrooms at the bottom of Isaac's Hill. Electricity supply had been extended in the town during the 1920s in response to demand. The number of consumers increased from 32 in 1913 to 973 in 1929 and the units of electricity sold increased from 9,019 in 1913 to 387,265 in 1929. Under the 1928 UDC Act, the Council gained extra powers to lay mains cables, erect sub-stations and charge for electrical fittings. Accordingly, there were further large increases in the 1930s, the number of consumers to 6,007 in 1937 and the number of units sold in the same year to an estimated 3.8 million.[30] There was also competition from the gas company and a large gasholder was constructed near the railway line in 1931 (and subsequently demolished in 1967).

The 1930s also saw improvements in education. The Thrunscoe Senior School on Highgate was opened on 17 June 1933 enabling major changes to take place at the National School. The Boys' School was closed, the Girls' and Infants' Schools became a Church of England Junior Mixed School and the older boys and girls were transferred to the Thrunscoe Senior School. The old Boys' School was replaced by the present Church Hall in 1935. In 1937 major extensions to the Humberston Foundation School (Clee Grammar School) on Clee Road were opened.

Another significant event was the building of the first Roman Catholic church in the town, Corpus Christi Church, which was completed in 1930 on Grimsby Road. Hitherto, Roman Catholics had worshipped in several venues. In earlier years they had attended St Mary's Church in Grimsby. During the First World War, because of the needs of Catholic members of the Manchester Regiment stationed in the resort, a Mass Centre was held in the Pier Pavilion. Church members later met in a hut in Reynolds Street and then in a room in the Reynolds Street School.

X

War and Recovery

1939-1974

The 1930s had been a decade when the several strands of the resort's advancement came together. The railway company's seafront estate and the tramway system had been taken into public ownership and the town had acquired the enhanced status of a municipal borough. Then followed the modernisation of the town's public transport system and the beginning of a major scheme of seafront improvements. Cleethorpes had probably reached its highest point as a popular seaside resort when yet another outbreak of war halted its progress.

In the forefront of change had been Alderman Sir George Moody. He died in October 1939 and, like that of Sir Edward Watkin, his death symbolised the end of an era. As one of the major improving forces on the Council, Moody epitomised aspects of the history of Cleethorpes. His parents were incomers to the town and his father made his mark in the Grimsby fishing industry. Moody carried on this family tradition of 'having a foot in both camps' and was extolled as 'An outstanding personality in the Grimsby trawling industry and the most prominent figure in the development of Cleethorpes'. Despite his prominence in the Grimsby industry he was in the forefront of the opposition to any moves by Grimsby to extend its boundaries to take in Cleethorpes. He became one of the 'progressives' on the Council and supported moves to improve the town and its services, especially the construction of the Kingsway improvements, the creation of the Thrunscoe Recreation Ground and the purchase of the pier, Pier Gardens, promenades and tram service. He became a member of the local authority in 1882, was elected chairman on eight occasions and was knighted in 1926 for his political and public services. He worked tenaciously at getting borough status for the resort and local appreciation of him was expressed when he was made the Charter Mayor in 1936 and the new borough's first honorary freeman in 1938.[1]

Second World War

Well before the outbreak of war, preparations were being made for the conflict. In May 1939, about 8,200 gas respirators were issued to the public. In June, a branch of the Women's Voluntary Service (WVS, later WRVS) was established in the resort; in July, a voluntary evacuation scheme was prepared for children, expectant mothers, the blind and the disabled covering an area either side of Grimsby Road between the borough boundary and Manchester and Bramhall Streets, although consideration was to be given to extending the area of the scheme. War was declared on 3 September and two days later the evacuation of children was started. On the same day sanction was received for the construction of 14 public air raid shelters to accommodate a total of 2,500 persons.[2]

With the coming of war the Council's projected seafront improvements were suspended. The foreshore was closed to civilians by the military authorities on 30 June 1940 and barbed wire entanglements were placed on it. Anti-tank precautions and pillboxes were constructed. The two Humber forts had been manned on a care and maintenance basis between the wars and were soon fully manned; the combined garrison of the forts totalled 10 officers and 245 men of other ranks during the war. The boom defence was once more put into effect, anti-aircraft guns were installed and the forts saw action against enemy aircraft and E-boats.[3]

Naval authorities considered that the Humber and the Humber ports were adequately protected from enemy landings by fixed defences and by the inherent navigational difficulties of the river. However, the beach between Grimsby and Cleethorpes was regarded as 'vulnerable'. It was considered that some obstruction would be presented by the sea wall at Cleethorpes but that the slipways could be used by tanks: it was urged that they should be rendered useless as a matter of urgency. The main danger from invasion was seen to be on the beaches between Donna Nook and Gibraltar Point but one authority considered that the prospect of landing in sufficient force to constitute an effective invasion would be outweighed by the risks to an invasion force whilst at sea. However, it was reckoned that tanks could be easily landed and the wide beaches would provide excellent landing grounds for aircraft. Once ashore on the Lincolnshire coast, it was suggested, enemy forces could press inland to the heart of England.[4] It was in this context that the Cleethorpes pier was breached in 1940 by the military as an anti-invasion measure. This left a large gap in the pier structure. Other piers around the country were also breached in order to prevent them being used for the landing of enemy troops, light vehicles and military supplies. Although the action has since been criticised and derided, it was taken at a time when the north-east coast was identified as one of the prime areas for an early invasion.[5]

Petrol rationing came into effect on 16 September 1939 and there were cut-backs in both petrol and trolley bus timetables. Local attractions such as Wonderland and Hawkey's Capitol Café were closed and requisitioned by the War Department for the duration of the conflict. Wonderland was initially used for the maintenance of military transport and later for the assembly of American military vehicles that arrived in crates at the Grimsby and Immingham docks. The Winter Gardens were used as an officers' mess and canteen. The Marine Embankment remained available for civilian use and the Bathing Pool and Boating Lake retained their popularity. Theatres and cinemas stayed open and dances were held at the Café Dansant and other venues. Travel was discouraged during the war

88 *Crowds near Wonderland on the North Promenade, post-1945.*

and special 'holidays at home' events in parks and elsewhere were organised for the local populace. Local organisations provided social facilities for members of the armed forces: a weekly social evening called 'Monday Night at Seven' was organised by the Trinity Methodist church, with entertainment by local artistes, and the WVS provided a canteen; the Empire Theatre was transformed into a forces' canteen and social centre, providing a piano, dartboards, dominoes, a radio set, and informal concerts.[6]

The resort suffered from air raids but not to the same extent as Grimsby. During 1940 small-calibre bombs landed in local fields and the Humber but the resort's first air raids occurred in May 1941. In the course of two raids, houses were damaged in Bursar Street, Wollaston Road, Clee Road, Bentley Street and Mill Road. Several people

89 *Crowds on the North Promenade and beach, 1957.*

were injured but there were no fatalities. No one was injured in an incendiary raid in December but houses suffered fire damage in Queen Mary Avenue, Daubney Street, Phelps Street, Clerke Street and Park Street.

The worst raids occurred in 1943. On 14 June, the Whit Monday Bank Holiday, a raid took place on both Grimsby and Cleethorpes. Incendiary bombs, high explosive bombs and 3,000 anti-personnel ('butterfly') bombs were dropped. Altogether, the two towns suffered 66 deaths, and 1,000 people were made homeless. The overwhelming majority of the deaths and damage occurred in Grimsby, with many people killed or injured by the anti-personnel bombs. These lethal weapons were dropped along a corridor from Isaac's Hill through to Grimsby. They caused two deaths in Manchester Street. Many fell in the area of Sidney Park, resulting in one death; the park was closed for months afterwards. Trains between Grimsby and Cleethorpes were stopped because of anti-personnel bombs along the line. Other bombs caused damage to houses in Hart Street, Brereton Avenue and Mill Road. Cleethorpes suffered eight deaths in the raid and many injuries. Another heavy raid on the two towns occurred a month later. Structural damage was sustained in Grimsby Road, Brereton Avenue, Sidney Street, Frankland Place and Daubney Street.

JUGS OF TEA

This was the final air raid of the war. In addition to the deaths and injuries, a total of 64 houses were effectively destroyed in the town during the war and many more were damaged.[7]

The memorial plaques in the town's Memorial Hall list 368 war dead. These consist of 112 crew members of minesweepers and fishing vessels, 83 soldiers, 60 sailors, 53 airmen, 35 civilians and 25 merchant seamen.[8] A town meeting in 1946 decided unanimously that a war memorial should take the form of a community Memorial Hall. The land was donated by Sidney Sussex College but an expected government grant towards construction was not forthcoming. This caused some changes in the building plans, and delays in carrying out the project, and the hall was eventually opened in 1960.[9]

Peace

As an allied victory became a certainty, the foreshore was released for civilian use on 1 April 1945.[10] With the declaration of peace in Europe on 8 May 1945 (VE Day) a United Service was held at the Trinity Wesleyan Church. Bonfires were lit on the same evening and the following day. Street parties were held, effigies of Hitler were burnt and shops soon ran out of fireworks. The succeeding Whitsun holiday was the first post-war holiday weekend and the resort was very busy. Signs of war, such as the anti-tank measures, pillboxes, barbed wire and static water tanks, began to be removed. The army continued a presence on the Humber Forts until 1956, after which the forts were maintained by civilian workers.[11]

Normal seaside activities were gradually resumed. The Capitol Café was released for civilian use in August 1945 but Wonderland was not released until Easter 1946, and had only six weeks to prepare for Whitsun. There was dancing at the Pier Pavilion and the first Cleethorpes East Coast Dance Festival was held. The Empire Theatre re-opened as a theatre with a resident seaside show. Thanks were expressed to the military when crowds lined the seafront to see the troops of the Lincolnshire Regiment march past after being presented with the Freedom of the Borough. Wonderland was in full swing by 1947 with dodgems, big dipper, roller skating rink, ghost train, cartoon cinema and so on. Other attractions were also back in business. The winter of 1947 was one of the coldest on record: the Boating Lake was frozen and used for skating and impromptu ice hockey; Olympia was transformed into the Winter Gardens and re-opened as such in December of that year. The highlight of 1949 was the reappearance of the seafront illuminations, which had not been lit since 1939.[12]

By the end of the 1940s, the resort was almost back to pre-war normality, with one major exception—the pier. Although government compensation was available to repair breached piers, and other piers were indeed repaired, the Borough Council judged the compensation to be insufficient for the task. The estimated cost of putting the pier into good repair was £26,000 and in 1948 the Council decided instead to demolish the isolated seaward end and spend the compensation on improving the Pier Pavilion.[13] Demolition contractors began preparatory work in 1948 and the demolition of the isolated section of the pier was completed in April 1949. Most of the 200 tons of salvaged timber decking was used in the rebuilding of Leicester City Football Club's war-damaged grandstand.

90 *East Coast Floods, 1953. Damage to Arcadia (Hancocks Palace of Pleasure) on the North Promenade beach.*

91 *East Coast Floods, 1953. Marine Embankment was demolished by the sea at the Buck Beck Outfall.*

Some steel girders and timber were used in Wonderland and nearly 300 tons of girders and scrap iron went for re-smelting. The result of the work was that the pier's original length of 1,200 feet was reduced to its present length of 335 feet.[14]

Although the nation had seen an end to war, the advent of peace saw a further skirmish in the persistent conflict between Cleethorpes and Grimsby over the question of amalgamation. In 1946, the Grimsby Borough Council proposed amalgamation with Cleethorpes. The Mayor of Cleethorpes, Alderman Cox, summed up local feeling when he commented:

How much better it would be for the boroughs of Grimsby and Cleethorpes to concentrate the whole of their energies and resources on solving the immediate problems than in wasting time, energy and money upon this foolish talk of amalgamating Grimsby and Cleethorpes.[15]

The proposal came to nothing but it recurred in 1963 with a suggestion from the Boundaries Commission that the two towns should be joined in one administrative unit. The Cleethorpes Council voted by 14 votes to five to oppose the proposal.[16]

Highs and Lows

The ensuing two decades saw a high point in the popularity of the resort and then the beginning of a decline. The 1950s began on an optimistic note: Whitsuntide 1950 experienced temperatures of 80 degrees Fahrenheit or more; petrol rationing had just ended and the resort was crowded. Cleethorpes celebrated the Festival of Britain in 1951 with beacons on Beacon Hill and at points along the town boundary. Amongst the delights available in 1953 were films at the Theatre Royal and the Ritz (ABC) cinema, plays at the Empire Theatre, dancing at the Café Dansant and 'Family Nights' at the Winter Gardens with 'Prizes Every Dance'. However, a major disaster was imminent. A storm surge in the North Sea on the evening of 31 January 1953 caused flooding and destruction along the east coast of England from the Humber to the Straits of Dover, and saw the loss of 300 lives. In Lincolnshire, the greatest destruction took place in the area of Mablethorpe, Sutton-on-Sea and Ingoldmells, where 41 deaths were suffered.

Cleethorpes escaped lightly by comparison with no fatalities. Even so, there was extensive damage to the resort. The sea broke though the sea wall in north Cleethorpes between Suggitt's Lane and Fuller Street, destroyed the railway line, and flooded and damaged houses in that area. The greatest havoc on the seafront was along the North Promenade. The promenade sea wall was damaged in many places, the road surface was destroyed and iron seafront railings were snapped by the sea. There was flooding and damage to amusement arcades, shops, cafés and stalls, creating a major blow to the town's holiday industry. The pier escaped comparatively lightly with some damage to its decking. Wonderland and the Bathing Pool were flooded and damaged. The Marine Embankment was broken through and the land behind was flooded. The sea broke through dunes and banks further south and flooded farmland and the holiday bungalow camp in nearby Humberston. However, the storm solved one problem for the Council. It had decided in 1951 that an amusement building on the sands, Arcadia, should be removed, but the owners had been given a stay of execution. In the event, the building was wrecked by the storm and the remnants were subsequently removed.

The Cleethorpes Publicity Manager, H.A. Ingham, described the storm disaster as 'the worst Cleethorpes has ever known'. He added that the town would have to put in several months of tremendously hard work to be ready for the 1953 holiday season. The cost of the damage at Cleethorpes was estimated at £100,000 with the damage to the sea defences being the heaviest item.[17] Work started quickly on plugging the gaps in the sea banks and clearing away debris. But the elements were by no means finished with Cleethorpes and, in March the following year, high tides and strong winds caused more damage to the railway line and embankment near Suggitt's Lane. In the meantime, 1953 saw a happier occasion with the coronation of Elizabeth II. Celebrations included football and cricket matches, a swimming gala, a firework display and a coronation ball. After a week of festivities the celebrations closed with a Grand Coronation Display and Searchlight Tattoo at the Blundell Park Football Ground.

92 *Captain Jim Crampton in the mid-1950s and his Auster aircraft, in which he gave flights from the beach.*

In August 1953, the Council approved a scheme of improvements to the Pier Pavilion, at an estimated cost of £10,000, but some councillors argued that the pier was a 'white elephant' and said it should be put out to private enterprise.[18] A major improvement of the year was the completion of a three-year operation to move sand and create a sandy beach in front of the Kings Parade. Hitherto a dismal stretch of mud and pools, it was now an attractive area for family enjoyment.[19]

1955 proved to be a good year for the resort and was described as 'a year that must surely go down in Cleethorpe's history as one of the best on record'. Easter saw car parks full to overflowing. Nineteen special trains ran on Easter Monday and such was the influx of trippers that cafés ran out of bread. The weather was good in July and August with high temperatures. Twenty special trains ran on the August Bank Holiday, all accommodation was booked up and more than 7,000 people were admitted to the Bathing Pool in a day. A new, if short-lived, attraction was the Cleethorpes Showboat. This former Goodwin Sands lightship, made to look like a Mississippi River showboat, was beached at the north end of the promenade and described by some councillors as 'a great monstrosity'. It spent the following winter moored in the Grimsby docks, after which its contents were auctioned off.

Despite the influx of holidaymakers during the early 1950s, changes were afoot which would radically affect the resort. Holidaymaking in static caravans and chalets was becoming very popular. The number of caravans along the coast between Cleethorpes and Skegness rose from 4,200 in 1950 to 21,000 in 1974, in addition to self-catering holiday chalets.[20] The Cleethorpes Council provided a trailer caravan site with a limit of 30 caravans but had strong competition from the Grimsby Rural District Council,

93 *Trolley buses at the Park Street and Grimsby Road junction, mid-1950s. The boundary between Cleethorpes and Grimsby runs along the middle of Park Street and the left-hand bus is in Grimsby, whilst the right-hand bus is in Cleethorpes.*

94 *A busy North Promenade on a rainy day. On the right is the railway station and trains, showing the immediate accessibility of the promenades and beach for rail travellers.*

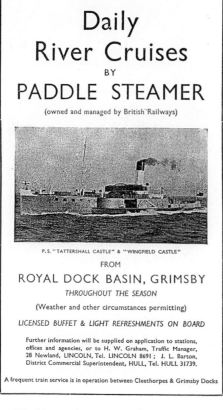

Daily River Cruises

BY

PADDLE STEAMER

(owned and managed by British Railways)

P.S. "TATTERSHALL CASTLE" & "WINGFIELD CASTLE"

FROM

ROYAL DOCK BASIN, GRIMSBY

THROUGHOUT THE SEASON

(Weather and other circumstances permitting)

LICENSED BUFFET & LIGHT REFRESHMENTS ON BOARD

Further information will be supplied on application to stations, offices and agencies, or to H. W. Graham, Traffic Manager, 28 Newland, LINCOLN, Tel. LINCOLN 8691 ; J. L. Barton, District Commercial Superintendent, HULL, Tel. HULL 31739.

A frequent train service is in operation between Cleethorpes & Grimsby Docks

95 *River cruises on British Rail paddle steamer, 1959.*

which owned a coastal holiday chalet site in Humberston. It lay just beyond the resort's southern boundary and was known as the Humberston Fitties. In the early 1950s the Rural District Council began to offer caravan facilities on the site and in 1957 started a major scheme to provide a large site for static caravans on adjacent farmland. The new site was quickly filled up and extended, so that by 1971 it contained 1,383 caravans.[21]

The lure of cheap package holidays abroad was also beginning to be noticed. Replying to complaints of a slow start to the 1956 season, the Cleethorpes Publicity Manager commented, 'One reason for the slow start may be that every year now more and more industrial workers can afford to go abroad for their holidays'.[22] But even though holiday tastes were changing, Cleethorpes still offered a good range of customary attractions to keep loyal visitors from its traditional catchment area. Towards the end of the 1950s the official local estimate was of over one million visitors a year. They were attracted by the resort's easy accessibility by rail and coach and the close location of the railway station and coach drop-off points to the promenade and beach. After arrival, visitors could spend the day on the beach, stroll along the promenade, hire a day chalet, paddle, bathe in the sea or open-air bathing pool (advertised as 'The Largest Bathing Pool in the Country'), sample the fun in amusement arcades and visit Wonderland ('one of the largest indoor amusement areas in the country providing all the fun of the fair'). They could play bowls or tennis, go boating on the sea or the boating lake, visit the cinemas, or take in a variety show at the Empire Theatre (repertory in the winter). They could even venture a paddle steamer cruise across the Humber to Spurn Point or take an aeroplane flight from the foreshore. Entertainment was provided through the day at the Pier Pavilion, and the seafront illuminations lit up the evening.[23]

If the 1950s ended in a reasonably confident manner, the 1960s began with more signs of changing tastes. The Empire Theatre closed in 1960 and was transformed into an amusement arcade and bingo hall. In 1963, the Theatre Royal also closed; it was later demolished and replaced by a ten-pin bowling centre. Local public transport was experiencing difficulties. As far back as the 1930s, concern had been expressed at the high price of £50,000 which the Borough Council had paid for the antiquated tram system. A further £14,000 had to be borrowed in 1937 to convert the system to trolley buses. The Grimsby Corporation had also incurred high capital charges in acquiring and improving its own system. Consequently, during 1938 and 1939 talks were held about the benefits of setting up a joint transport undertaking. The outbreak of war interrupted discussions and the delays and strictures of the war did not improve the situation. Finally, in 1957, the two systems came together under the Grimsby and Cleethorpes Joint Transport Committee, controlled by councillors from each authority.[24] Both towns' trolley bus services were showing signs of wear and were replaced by the more flexible petrol buses on 4 June 1960.

Growing car ownership and coach travel was reflected in the fact that three-quarters of the resort's estimated one million annual visitors in the mid-1960s travelled by road. Not surprisingly, the decade saw a further decline in railway involvement in the resort. On the nationalisation of the railways in 1948, the LNER had been absorbed into the Eastern Region of British Railways. Money was spent in 1961 on modernising the resort's station, but the resort lost its link to London via the East Lincolnshire Line in 1970 under the Beeching cuts and lost its final direct rail service to the capital in 1993.[25] Meanwhile, on 17 September 1964, the British Railways Board put its leasehold and rented property on the North Promenade up for auction. This consisted of all the property along the promenade

WONDERLAND
AMUSEMENT PARK

The Finest Covered Amusement Park in the Country

Main Hall accommodates 20,000 people

OPEN SEVEN DAYS A WEEK

with the Holiday Spirit every day!

★ Attractions include: Big Dipper, Dodgem, Ghost Train, Flying Jets, Cartoon Cinema, Boating, Miniature Railway and scores of others . . . . .

SPECIAL CONCESSION TICKETS FOR PARTIES

Write: Wonderland, Promenade, Cleethorpes.

Printed by The Swindon Press Ltd., 100 Victoria Road, Swindon.

96 *Wonderland Amusement Park, 1959.*

between Sea Road and Wonderland and included bazaars, cafés, shops, kiosks, amusement arcades, a public house and Wonderland itself.[26]

The appeal of package holidays was spreading and local travel agents were advertising cheap 'all-in' holidays in hotels by the sun-bathed Mediterranean. Also, car-owning families and their vehicles could embark on Tor Line ferries at nearby Immingham for cheap trips to the European mainland. It is not surprising, therefore, that a local journalist commented in 1965 on the resort's need to lure back 'fickle' holidaymakers. She reported that the resort was smartening itself up and creating a new image and that the resort's 'ace card' was the new Marineland and Zoo which was due to open in June. The Publicity Manager said it would act as a boost for attracting visitors.[27]

In the early 1970s, the resort was essentially as it had been in the 1950s, but some changes had been effected or were in hand. The popular but ageing dance hall and rendezvous the Café Dansant closed in 1966 and was demolished, but its expected replacement did not materialise. The Ritz (ABC) Cinema closed in 1972 for major alterations in order to create a bingo centre and smaller cinema. On a more positive note, the Marineland and Zoo was operating and the extended and modernised Pier Pavilion featured summer variety shows. The old Grotto and indoor bathing pool on the promenade had been demolished and replaced with a waterfall, fountain, and flower beds. Publicity drew attention to such attractions as the miniature railway, ten-pin bowling, sea angling, folk festival and South Beach trailer caravan site.

97 *Thrunscoe in 1962, with the Bathing Pool in the top right-hand corner. Cromwell Road runs diagonally across from the Bathing Pool to meet with Hardy's Road, which was being developed for housing. The housing to the north of Cromwell Road was largely built in the 1920s and 1930s. The housing to the south dates predominantly from the 1950s. In the bottom right-hand quadrant at the end of Hardy's Road are the buildings of Hardy's Farm, now the site of the Signhills Schools.*

98 *St Peter's Avenue after the Second World War. Its original houses have been transformed into shops and business premises.*

99 *Holiday chalet and caravan development, c.1970, on the Humberston Fitties to the south of Cleethorpes, which illustrates changing tastes in holidays. The chalet camp on the right dates from the 1920s and the caravan development started in the late 1950s. The road in the top left-hand corner is South Sea Lane.*

100 *Beaconthorpe area of the resort, c.1961. The large central open area is the Sussex Recreation Ground straddling Brereton Avenue. Off the avenue is the Sidney Sussex College leasehold development, largely of the 1930s. In the bottom right-hand quadrant is the rectangular estate of council housing built by the local authority in the early 1920s and bounded by Clee Road, Wollaston Road, Bentley Street and Beacon Avenue.*

101 *Miniature railway with the Boating Lake in the background.*

102 *The Big Dipper and Wonderland on the North Promenade and the railway lines leading to the seafront railway station. Chapman's Pond, an old clay pit, is in the bottom right-hand corner. The large gas holder to right of centre was built in 1931 and demolished in 1967. The smaller water tower in front of it was built in 1908.*

Growing Again

The population of the town had remained fairly static for several decades, rising from 28,155 in 1921 to 29,557 in 1951, an increase of only 936 people over 30 years. This stagnation was balanced by a significant increase in population in nearby commuter villages, such as Humberston and Waltham. However, the ensuing 20 years saw notable population growth in Cleethorpes, from 29,557 to 35,837, an increase of 6,280 people. The new population needed houses and in the decades following the war central government

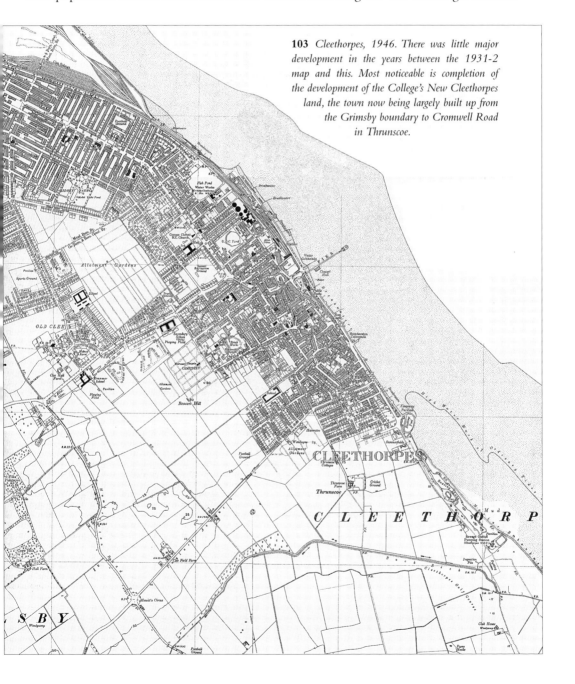

103 *Cleethorpes, 1946. There was little major development in the years between the 1931-2 map and this. Most noticeable is completion of the development of the College's New Cleethorpes land, the town now being largely built up from the Grimsby boundary to Cromwell Road in Thrunscoe.*

policy emphasised the necessity of providing municipal housing. Dr O.A. Hartley, in his study of local housing policy, has described how the Cleethorpes Council was reluctant to provide council houses, but was obliged to do so. In 1946, it purchased 17½ acres of land for council houses from Sidney Sussex College, at a price of £8,000. The Council 'celebrated' its reluctant foray into municipal housing in 1955 with the completion of 1,000 council houses. The Council's dominant policy in so far as housing was concerned has been described by Dr Hartley as 'to encourage private enterprise and owner-occupation, and to avoid involvement in building for letting'.[28]

In all, during 1946-60, the Council provided 1,260 council houses, which were matched by 1,182 privately built houses.[29] Some of the latter were provided on the initiative of Sidney Sussex College. During 1954-62, it developed its land in the Beacon Hill area with leasehold housing, but this was the College's last major piece of leasehold development in Cleethorpes. Its leasehold ground rents had declined in value in the inflationary economy. Consequently, in the 1950s, the College began selling building land in Thrunscoe and in 1965 it sold 90 acres there for the building of 900 houses. Overall, the College's entire landed estate (in Cleethorpes and elsewhere) was producing an annual return of only one per cent, whereas its equities were producing over four per cent. Accordingly, between 1963 and 1968 the College sold all its Cleethorpes leasehold property and building land and invested the proceeds in the stock market. This ended the College's long and close association with the town, which had begun in 1612. The relationship had been mutually beneficial: whilst the College had obtained good financial returns from its Cleethorpes land, the town gained from having a sympathetic landowner which faced the challenges of urban estate development with a high degree of integrity and social conscience.[30]

Other developments in the town included the provision of new schools such as the Signhills Infant and Junior Schools, which were built to serve the new housing in Thrunscoe and opened in 1970 by the then Secretary of State for Education, one Margaret Thatcher. At long last, in 1960, St Peter's Church gained the status of parish church of Cleethorpes and in 1961, because of the expansion of housing, dedicated its daughter church of St Francis on Sandringham Road.

Recent Times

The late 1940s and the 1950s saw the resort getting into its stride and working to achieve its pre-war level of activity and popularity. This had been achieved by the mid-1950s, which were certainly a high point for the resort. However, the rise of cheap overseas package holidays and other changing tastes then led to a decline. This provided an inauspicious beginning to the final quarter of the 20th century, during which we shall see the resort experiencing a roller-coaster ride of hopes and disappointments. In the event, the period got off to a bad start with a resurgence of the town's old adversaries—storms and flooding. In 1976 and 1978, the sea caused extensive damage to houses, the railway track and the Bathing Pool. During 1977-8, the Anglian Water company constructed a new concrete sea defence wall between Wonderland and the Grimsby fish docks to put a stop to this recurring event.[1]

An event of a different nature which had long-term local repercussions was the 1974 reorganisation of local government. Under this, the northern part of Lincolnshire, including Cleethorpes and Grimsby, was incorporated into the new county of Humberside, which also included East Yorkshire. Within Humberside, several new local government districts were created. One of these was the Cleethorpes District, which consisted of the Borough of Cleethorpes and the adjacent Grimsby Rural District. Thus the new Cleethorpes District included Cleethorpes itself, the major port of Immingham, villages, an extensive area of agricultural land and major petro-chemical works on the bank of the Humber. For over a century, Cleethorpes had a local authority charged with one limited task: namely, the well-being of the town as a seaside resort and residential area within its tight boundaries, an area of 2,268 acres in 1951. Under the new system, the local authority had members from all parts of a district covering 40,582 acres. Similarly, the resort's 1971 population of 35,837 became part of the new district's population of 66,767, rising to 68,724 in 1981. The new local authority had many varied responsibilities, of which the well-being of Cleethorpes was only one. The new district was granted the status of a borough and its central offices and meeting place were at the Cleethorpes Council House.

The new local government structure was two-tier, with functions divided between the Humberside County Council and the districts. Cleethorpes had worked within this system with the previous Lindsey County Council. However, Grimsby had been a unitary

104 *The seafront, c. 1993, including the pier, Sea Road, the railway station and part of the North and Central Promenades and Pier Gardens. The* Dolphin Hotel *can be seen left of centre and the Market Place and the area of the ancient hamlet of Oole is above it in the upper left quadrant.*

authority and, therefore, responsible for all its own services. Accordingly, although Grimsby remained a separate district and borough under the new system, it lost many powers to the Humberside County Council. The latter became the target of much animosity. The unitary authorities of Grimsby and Hull resented the loss of control of local services. In addition, pressure groups on both banks of the Humber campaigned for a reversion to their historical counties of Lincolnshire and Yorkshire.

In the year that this reorganisation took place, a survey of English seaside towns by the English Tourist Board classed Cleethorpes as 'lively' and catering largely for working-class visitors and families with children. The report also stated that resorts in general were not responding to a changing market.[2] Certainly, the early 1970s showed few signs of change at Cleethorpes. The pier still provided a wide range of entertainment including concerts, wrestling, children's shows and a 'Big Star Variety Show'. Other attractions included a narrow-gauge railway, ten-pin bowling, sea angling, an annual folk festival, a Carnival Week and Crazy Week, and the Carnival Parade, which was resurrected in 1976. Notice had been taken of the popularity of caravan holidays with the creation of the Council's South Beach caravan site.

But several major attractions began to have serious problems. Councillors were unhappy at the losses being sustained in running the pier and the pier shows, and in 1981 it was sold for about £55,000 to Funworld Ltd, an amusement company from Skegness. The company had ambitious plans but its summer show flopped and by 1983 the pier was closed. The Council declined an offer to buy it back because of the estimated renovation costs of £200,000. Rescue came in 1985 in the form of businessman and club owner Mark Mayer who bought the pier. He spent £300,000 converting the Pier Pavilion into a nightclub. Changes in ownership followed but it is still currently a popular nightspot under the name 'Pier 39'. Other casualties were Wonderland and the Big Dipper. Wonderland closed as an amusement centre but re-emerged as a large-scale and popular year-round Sunday Market. The Ritz (ABC) Cinema showed its last films in 1982 and the site is now occupied by a fast-food restaurant.

The Bathing Pool was never repaired after damage sustained from a storm in 1978. In 1983 a modern Leisure Centre opened on the site, containing a swimming pool and other sports, fitness and leisure facilities. The Marineland and Zoo was in trouble and spawned a series of unhappy ventures. In 1973 it became the Cleethorpes Adventureland and Zoo, with a smaller zoo and a children's adventure playground. Two years later it became a 'safari park' with glass-fibre animals but was closed after a few years. In 1981, despite fierce local objections, a stadium was built on the site for stock car and greyhound racing. Part of the site was taken up by a lacklustre leisure park. Unfortunately, the stadium was in close proximity to a large residential area and numerous complaints followed about the noise from the stock car racing. The 1980s were marked by much controversy regarding the development of the land.

In addition to the increasing popularity of cheap holidays abroad, there was a growing trend towards taking short breaks and self-catering holidays. There was also heavy competition from other resorts and attractions such as theme parks. The effect of these changes was exacerbated by the countrywide recession in heavy industries which had a serious effect on the resort's main market, the industrial areas of South Yorkshire and the East Midlands. Cleethorpes and Grimsby also suffered directly from the collapse of the deep-sea fishing industry and the attendant decline of associated industries. In the mid-1980s, local unemployment rose to 15 per cent and more than 18 per cent amongst men.

105 *The Leisure Centre, built to replace the storm-damaged Bathing Pool, opened in 1983.*

By 1985, the resort was in a state of decline and it was considered that Cleethorpes' future lay in enticing day visitors with the aid of a major new attraction. Accordingly, the Borough Planning Officer produced a feasibility study on creating a new 85-acre seafront Leisure Park in Thrunscoe and beyond, which would be aimed in particular at the day-visitor market. It was an ambitious plan to reinvigorate the deteriorating area (which included the Boating Lake and the controversial stadium) and would stretch from the Leisure Centre to the borough boundary. It would incorporate existing facilities that were suitable for improvement, but others would be replaced by new attractions. The park would aim to have attractions to suit all ages and a wide range of tastes—whether for quiet strolling, indulging in relaxed activities such as bowls and tennis or enjoying the fun of a lively fairground—but no stock car racing. However, there were immediate objections to some aspects of the scheme from nearby residents. A major objection was about the likely noise from the proposed funfair. There was also apprehension that the Boating Lake area would be fenced off and have an admission charge imposed. In the event, the Council adopted the scheme, but decided not to have either 'noisy rides' or fencing around the Boating Lake.[3]

Parts of the scheme were introduced over subsequent years but there was a need for large-scale private investment to create a major central attraction for the park. Privately financed schemes were put forward in 1987 and 1988 for creating a multi-million pound shopping and leisure complex on the land but both fell through. Salvation appeared to come in 1989 when the Pleasureworld company proposed a multi-million pound American-style theme park. The proposal was supported enthusiastically by the Council and construction work began, only to come to a halt a year later when Pleasureworld pulled out. However, the owners of the successful Flamingo Land Family Fun Park and Zoo in North Yorkshire stepped in and spent about £12 million in constructing the Pleasure Island Theme Park, which opened on 27 May 1993. At a time when the area had an unemployment rate of about 12 per cent, the park was said to provide more than 200 jobs, mostly seasonal. The 1980s had been a difficult decade for the resort but

106 *The Central Promenade and Pier Gardens, c.1993. The Council House (Town Hall) is visible left of centre. Sea View Street and the area of the ancient hamlet of Itterby is in the lower left quadrant.*

107 *A sign of the resort's southerly expansion, the Pleasure Island Theme Park, opened in 1993.*

the 1990s and the construction of Pleasure Island ushered in a more hopeful period. The Council's business plan of 1992 emphasised the importance of creating an 'operating climate' which would encourage private sector investment. It also highlighted the value of tourism in the overall economy of the borough.[4]

More multi-million pound investment followed from another major leisure company, Bourne Leisure, in creating a large up-to-date caravan park, called Thorpe Park. Under the local government reorganisation of 1974, the Council inherited the Humberston Fitties holiday bungalow and caravan sites from the old Grimsby Rural District Council. During 1986-96 there was a recurring and contentious debate on the future of the sites, which were deteriorating and in need of major capital outlay to bring them up to what were considered to be acceptable modern standards. A strong body of opinion in the Council argued that they should be sold to private developers who would finance improvements. Eventually, in 1992, Bourne Leisure was granted a 99-year lease of the Humberston Fitties

108 *A major element in the Meridian Point development, the new nine-screen Parkway Cinema opened in 2004.*

and South Beach caravan sites, but not the bungalow site. Several years of multi-million pound investment by the company followed and Thorpe Park was provided with many attractions including a swimming pool, tennis courts, bowling green, entertainment centre, children's activities, fishing lakes and a nine-hole golf course. More controversy followed as the company tried to acquire the holiday bungalow site. Determined opposition by the site residents and others led to the Council declaring the site a Conservation Area in view of its historical significance. It is now termed the Humberston Fitties Chalet Park and remains in full local authority ownership and control.

Other private investment included the opening of the Fantasy World children's attraction, transformation of the narrow gauge railway into the vastly improved Cleethorpes Coast Light Railway, the building of a Deep Sea Experience (later converted into an amusement arcade and cafe), new and refurbished public houses and restaurants, a new ten-pin bowling centre on Kings Road, a seafront 'Tonka' road train, and the construction of high-quality seafront apartments. Public investment resulted in the redevelopment of the old Café Dansant site with toilets, sales kiosks, flower beds and public seating, improvements to the Paddling Pool and Boating Lake, construction of a new Kings Road, improvements to the Central and North Promenades, including their complete re-paving, the creation of the seafront Cleethorpes Showground, and the opening of a new public library on Alexandra Road in 1984. The RNLI also restored its service in the resort with the establishment of an inshore lifeboat station on the Central Promenade in 1987. An independent Vigilantes Inshore Lifeboat Service had been operating in the resort since 1969 so henceforth the resort operated two sea rescue services.

A major, privately-financed improvement to the town came in the form of a £47 million investment by the regional water company, Anglian Water. The town's sewerage system was largely out of date and was unable to cope with the increasing demands of the area. Major problems were frequent flooding during heavy rainfall and untreated sewage contaminating the sea and beach. The large-scale improvement work took place during 1992-5 and doubled the capacity of the system. Improvement soon followed in the quality of the resort's bathing water, which was in line with increasing public interest in environmental issues.

Examples of how the resort responded to changing attitudes and tastes may be found in the establishment of a popular Nature House illustrating local natural history, which was eventually upgraded and replaced with a purpose-built Discovery Centre with a similar purpose, the creation of a Country Park, the private development of a Tropical Butterfly House (later called the Jungle) illustrating more exotic wildlife, and an annual Kite Festival. The resort's annual guide began to emphasise such changes, its content drawing more attention to the natural attractions of the area, such as the beauty of the local countryside, the attractiveness of local villages and market towns, the merit of the resort's beaches and dunes as natural resources, and the value of the foreshore for bird-watching—all in addition to the fun of traditional seaside facilities.

But the resort had to undergo a further upheaval in local administration. There was widespread national dissatisfaction with the 1974 reorganisation of local government. Locally this was expressed in antagonism towards the county of Humberside and its County Council. A Local Government Commission was set up in 1992 to examine the provision of local government throughout the country. Grimsby remembered the days when it had been a County Borough with control over all its local services and, not surprisingly, the Borough Council quickly came out solidly in support of a single unitary or all-purpose authority combining Grimsby and Cleethorpes. This would be

109 *The Kingsway and Kings Parade with Cromwell Road running inland from the Leisure Centre, c.1993. To the right of the road is the area developed after the opening of the Kingsway in 1906. Cromwell Road itself began to be developed in the 1930s and to its left is part of the extensive area developed from the 1950s.*

large enough not to be subject to any County Council control, and would revert to being in the county of Lincolnshire.[5]

The Cleethorpes Borough Council was still chary of being 'taken over' by Grimsby and argued that the post-1974 Cleethorpes District should become a unitary authority in its own right. However, a sample survey of Cleethorpes residents carried out in September 1992 did not show whole-hearted support for their Council's preference. Of those surveyed, 40 per cent agreed with the Council, 33 per cent preferred merging with Grimsby and 14 per cent preferred the option of becoming part of a two-tier structure in an enlarged county of Lincolnshire. The remainder were 'don't knows'.[6] In the event, the Local Government Commission recommended that the county of Humberside should be abolished and that Grimsby and Cleethorpes should combine to form a unitary authority and county called North East Lincolnshire. This was quickly followed by a decision of the Cleethorpes Borough Council on 20 July 1993 to merge with Grimsby. The local newspaper remarked on this momentous decision:

> Cleethorpes last night cast aside the rivalry of decades—and agreed to walk hand in hand with Grimsby into the 21st century. Grimsby proposed and Cleethorpes eventually said Yes in an historic vote in the resort … It took just 15 minutes at a Cleethorpes council meeting to bring to an end years of bitter wrangling between the two councils, who now see their future as better together.[7]

Although only three Cleethorpes councillors voted against the merger, others expressed their reluctance, with remarks such as 'Sadly there was no viable alternative'. The agreement received government ratification and the first elections for the new 'shadow' authority took place on 5 May 1995. However, there was still suspicion of Grimsby and a Conservative party leaflet for the election stated 'Don't let Grimsby dominate. Keep the Cleethorpes voice heard'.

The new unitary authority of North East Lincolnshire came into being on 1 April 1996 and the resort became part of an even larger local government unit whose councillors were responsible for a total population of 157,979 in 2001, of whom only 34,907 lived in Cleethorpes. But even before the new Council took office concern was expressed about its inadequate initial funding. Cuts of over £10 million were anticipated in its provisional budget for the coming year, with consequential cuts in services. The new Council expressed its priorities as education and social services, so budget cuts would affect other services more drastically. A public consultation exercise revealed that the public thought the Council's priorities should be to reduce crime, provide good social services and create jobs. The provision of 'Leisure' services was relegated by the public to the bottom of a long list of services.[8]

These Council and public priorities raised questions over the future well-being of resort development, which was founded on the provision of leisure facilities for visitors. However, the manufacturing sector was still in difficulties nationally and there was increasing awareness of the importance of service industries, including leisure and tourism, in creating jobs and bringing money into the area. In addition, Cleethorpes and its leisure attractions were seen as an important part of the 'portfolio' which would be used in trying to attract new industries and businesses to the district. Consequently, local authority publicity paid even more attention to emphasising the wide-ranging seaside, urban and rural attractions of the area, including facilities in Grimsby such as the National Fishing Heritage Centre and the Freshney Place Shopping Centre. At the same time, effort was put into developing vacant Council land along Kings Road in Thrunscoe. This development was given the designation Meridian Point Leisure and Retail Park, and the existing ten-pin bowling centre was joined by a fast-food restaurant, a children's play centre, a fitness and health club and a nine-screen cinema. Sites were also designated for a hotel, a public house, restaurants, leisure facilities and retail outlets. Development is still in progress at the time of writing.

Summary and Conclusion

At the beginning of the book the question was asked: how did the resort of Cleethorpes come into being and why has it developed in the way that it did? Certainly, during the course of this account of the making of the resort, we have seen a variety of influences at work. Some were intrinsic to the place itself, such as its location, geology, natural features and local residents. It was certainly the residents who provided the initial 'drive' in the resort's early days and who continued to be essential to its development. Relevant to this was their enterprise, their adaptation to change and their involvement as traders, service providers and public servants. One particular group of residents has been highlighted by Dr Frank Baker in his history of Methodism in Cleethorpes, in which he argues strongly in favour of the important and enterprising part played by local Methodists in the early days of the resort.[9] In addition to their involvement in business and trade, a large number of Methodists served on the local authority and were thus in a position to make significant decisions affecting the resort. They also had an important role in the local temperance and Sunday observance movements. Methodist influence declined in the 20th century but it still figured in the background of a good number of the local entrepreneurs and 'progressives' who performed notable roles in the later development of the resort. Of course, other members of the community also played their parts, whether or not they had any particular religious affiliations.

Local residents were also an important influence in their role as landowners. The many residents who owned small plots quickly turned their land over to building and, in the absence of any general plan of development, determined the character of a good part of the central resort area. In some resorts this function was carried out by a large landowner but not in Cleethorpes. Sidney Sussex College was in a position to shape the character of an important stretch of the seafront, but relinquished any potential role of resort developer when it disposed of its prime seafront land. However, the College came to the fore later when it created New Cleethorpes, which gave the local government authority a large income from rates, enabling the latter to adopt the role of resort developer. The College was also instrumental in the southern spread of the resort into Thrunscoe when it provided land for recreational purposes. The College had a good relationship with the local authority and the two worked together in providing good housing and a healthy environment.

Outside influences included the countrywide popularity of seaside holidays in the 19th century, followed by the shifts in holiday habits in the 20th century. However, the major single outside influence was the coming of the railway. This created a resort which came to be dominated by the railway company, whose shareholders regarded it as 'their' resort. Because of the massive investment in promenades and attractions made by the company, Cleethorpes became a significant Victorian resort. The railway interest also led to more investment from other outside entrepreneurs. Thus Cleethorpes ceased to be a purely local enterprise and became part of the national mainstream of resort development.

At the time, the most obvious effect of the railway was its radical influence on the character of the resort and its clientele. Cleethorpes was transformed from a quiet,

110 *More southerly expansion. This photograph shows Humberston chalet and caravan parks to the south of Cleethorpes, 2002. In the top left is North Sea Lane and the Beacholme Caravan Park. At the top centre is the Pleasure Island Theme Park. The long-standing Humberston Fitties Chalet Park is on the extreme right; the extensive static caravan area in the centre and to the right comprise Thorpe Park. The large open area to the south is the Thorpe Park golf course.*

genteel, bathing place into a rumbustious working-class pleasure venue. The feelings of those residents and visitors who were not happy at this change are shown in the disputes over liquor licensing and Sunday observance. But although such rows sprang out of genuine beliefs and concerns, they were also symptomatic of the wider tension between the changing nature of the resort and a nostalgic wish to revert to what were seen as earlier 'halcyon' days. The aspiration to recapture the trade of the gentility and middle classes and make the resort more attractive to 'respectable' visitors is a recurring theme in the resort's later history. The development of the Thrunscoe seafront carried the prospect that it might be the means of effecting this aspiration, whilst the pleasure-seeking 'hoi polloi' would hopefully be drawn and held by the magnet of the North Promenade's more earthy amusements.

The development of the Thrunscoe seafront also marked the rise of another major influence on the resort, namely the local authority. For many years the authority was inadequately financed and had few powers, but its influence grew as its income increased and it gained confidence and new powers. It worked to improve the public health of the town and maintain its reputation as a 'health resort'. The authority's desire to improve the resort led to tension between it and the railway company as it strived to acquire control of the seafront. This aim was achieved in the 1930s when the local authority took over as the dominant figure in resort development. However, the high days of municipal enterprise have been replaced nationally by a much more constrained economic role for local government. This, coupled with the high cost of major new development, brought in a phase during which the local authority has had to step back and adopt a policy of encouraging large-scale investment in the resort by private enterprise. The simile of a wheel completing its full circle may be seen in the similarity of this turn of events to the position of the resort in the 1870s and 1880s, when the Local Board of Health courted large-scale investment by the MS&LR.

It is also essential to acknowledge the influence of Grimsby. This is especially noteworthy in view of the amalgamation of the two towns in 1996—which must have set many an early 'thorper' spinning in his or her grave. Although the port was regarded by many residents of Cleethorpes as a persistent thorn in their municipal flesh, its proximity, historical relationship to Cleethorpes and greater size meant it had unavoidable effects on the resort. It was, for example, the demand for housing for Grimsby workers which led to the building of New Cleethorpes, which physically joined the two towns together, so that it is not apparent now where one ends and the other begins. But it may also be argued that, because Grimsby has been a major source of employment and services for Cleethorpes residents, it has had a tendency to undermine the resort's self-reliance, thus leading some to question whether Cleethorpes viewed itself essentially as a resort or, alternatively, as a residential adjunct to Grimsby. On the other hand, the determination of Cleethorpes not to be absorbed into Grimsby encouraged a combative and competitive spirit which worked to prove that the town could stand alone both as a holiday resort and as a healthy and attractive residential area.

Recent years have seen the arrival of new outside influences. One of these is the nationwide tendency for towns to see service and tourism industries as important parts of their economic survival. Another is the national awareness of the importance of the country's seaside resorts, both from an economic standpoint and viewed as part of the nation's heritage. Within such a context it may be seen that Cleethorpes has a crucial part to play in North East Lincolnshire's social and economic strategy and well-being: a positive note on which to end this account of the resort as it enters the new century.

Appendix

Cleethorpes Population and Houses[1]
1801-2001

Year	Population	Houses
1801	284	60
1811	375	70
1821	406	112
1831	497	129
1841	803 [2]	159
1851	839	198
1861	1,230	287
1871	1,768	427
1881	2,840	655
1891	4,306	968
1901	12,578	2,926
1911	21,417	5,145
1921	28,155	5,711
1931	28,621	7,108
1941	No census [3]	
1951	29,557	8,670
1961	32,700	10,421 [4]
1971	35,837	12,170 [4]
1981	35,637	12,770 [4]
1991	34,722	13,888 [4]
2001	34,907	14,817 [4]

Notes

1. Sources: *Victoria County History of Lincolnshire Vol.II* (1906) p.366 and the decennial census volumes (GCL Local History Library).
2. The 1841 census was taken late in the year (on 7 June 1841) and, accordingly, the population increase since 1831 was partly attributed by the census takers to 186 visitors to the resort for 'sea bathing and the annual Clee Feast'.
3. No census was taken in 1941 but the National Registration figure for Cleethorpes in 1939 gives a total of 27,142 people.
4. The figures given for houses refer to 'Dwellings Occupied' in the 1971 census and to 'Households' in the 1961, 1981, 1991 and 2001 censuses.

References

See page xiii for Abbreviation list

Chapter 1: Cleethorpes Before the Resort

1. C.W. Foster and T. Longley, *The Lincolnshire Domesday and the Lindsey Survey* (1924), pp.26, 41, 45, 79, 140, 169 and 248.
2. E. Gillett, *A History of Grimsby* (1970), p.4; S.H. Rigby, *Medieval Grimsby: growth and decline* (1993), p.81.
3. Gillett, *Grimsby*, p.45; Rigby, *Medieval Grimsby*, p.62; Calendar of Charter Rolls, Vol. V, 1341-1417, p.170.
4. R.E. Glasscock, 'The Lay Subsidy of 1334 for Lincolnshire', Lincolnshire Architectural and Archaeological Society Reports and Papers, X(1), 1963, pp.115-33; G.A.J. Hodgett, *Tudor Lincolnshire* (1975), p.196.
5. R.W. Ambler and B. and L. Watkinson, *Farmers and Fishermen: the probate inventories of the ancient parish of Clee, South Humberside, 1536-1742* (1987), passim.
6. R.W. Ambler and A. Dowling, 'The Growth of Cleethorpes and the Prosperity of Sidney, 1616-1968' in D.E.D. Beales and H.B. Nisbet, *Sidney Sussex College: historical essays in commemoration of the quatercentenary* (1996), pp.177 and 179.
7. Ambler and Watkinson, *Farmers and Fishermen*, pp.4-6.
8. Gillett, *Grimsby*, p.139; R.E.G. Cole (ed.), *Speculum Dioeceseos Lincolniensis, 1705-1723* (1913), p.33.
9. Ambler and Watkinson, *Farmers and Fishermen*, p.22; *The Methodist Magazine*, Vol. XXXIII, June 1815, p.403.
10. F. Baker, *The Story of Cleethorpes and the Contribution of Methodism through two hundred years* (1953), pp.24-6, 39 and 116-19.
11. Baker, *Cleethorpes*, p.31.
12. Baker, *Cleethorpes*, p.39.
13. E. Drury, *The Old Clee Story* (n.d.), p.23; W. White, *History, Gazetteer and Directory of Lincolnshire* (1856), pp.559 and 566; A. Bates, *A Gossip About Old Grimsby* (1893), pp.115-6; A.R. Maddison, *Lincolnshire Pedigrees*, Vol. 3 (1904), pp.976-7.

Chapter 2: The Bathing Place: 1700s-1840s

1. E. Dobson, *A Guide and Directory to Cleethorpes with an historical account of the place* (1850), p.7.
2. D.N. Robinson, *The Book of the Lincolnshire Seaside: the story of the coastline from the Humber to the Wash* (1981), p.54.
3. E. Dobson, *A New Guide and Directory to Cleethorpes with an historical account of the place* 2nd ed. (1858), p.14.
4. Dobson, *Cleethorpes* (1858), p.14.
5. Dobson, *Cleethorpes* (1850), p.18.
6. Dobson, *Cleethorpes* (1858), p.14.
7. F. Baker, *The story of Cleethorpes and the contribution to Methodism through two hundred years* (1953), p.37.
8. J. Byng, *The Torrington Diaries, a selection from the tours of the Hon. John Byng between the years 1781 and 1794,* edited by C. Bruyn Andrews (1954), pp.366-7.
9. G.A. Cooke, *Topographical and Statistical Description of the County of Lincoln* (c.1802-10?), p.107.
10. J. Dugdale, *The New British Traveller*, Vol. III (1819), p.608; Baker, *Cleethorpes*, p.56.
11. G.L. Gomme (ed.), *Topographical History of Leicestershire, Lincolnshire, Middlesex, Monmouthshire: a classified collection of the chief contents of 'The Gentleman's Magazine' from 1731-1868* (1896), p.117.
12. LRSM, 14 September 1832.

13. I.S. Beckwith, 'The River Trade of Gainsborough, 1500-1850', *Lincolnshire History and Archaeology*, No. 2, 1967, pp.13-14.
14. NA, 30/46/1/8, Travel Diary of John Eyre.
15. LRSM, 17 August 1832.
16. LRSM, 10 July 1844.
17. GCL, *Skelton Papers*, 1831, Vol.1, No. 88; 1832/3, Vol. 3, Nos 285 and 306; 1834, Vol. 1, No. 91.
18. LRSM, 20 June 1844.
19. LRSM, 30 May 1845 and 4 July 1845.
20. M. Smith (ed.), *The Letters of Charlotte Bronte: with a selection of letters by family and friends*, Vol. 1, 1829-1847 (1995), pp.195-6.
21. Byng, *The Torrington Diaries*, pp.366-7.
22. Baker, *Cleethorpes*, pp.44-5.
23. NA, 30/46/1/8, Travel Diary of John Eyre.
24. C. Tennyson and H. Dyson, *The Tennysons: background to genius* (1974), pp.56-7.
25. GCL, *Skelton Papers*, 1832/3, Vol. 3, Nos 285-306; 1834, Vol. 1, No. 91; 1832/3, Vol. 3, No. 293.
26. W. White, *Lincolnshire Directory* (1826), pp.102-3; LRSM, 18 July 1834 and 20 July 1838.
27. GCL, *Skelton Papers*, 1834, Vol. 1, p.86; NA, 30/46/1/8, Travel Diary of John Eyre.
28. Baker, *Cleethorpes*, p.60.
29. GCL, *Skelton Papers*, 1832/3, Vol. 3, Nos. 285 and 306; 1834, Vol. 1, No. 91.
30. GCL, *Skelton Papers*, 1824, Vol. 1, No. 64.
31. Baker, *Cleethorpes*, frontispiece; E. and R.C. Russell, *Landscape Changes in South Humberside: the enclosure of thirty-seven parishes* (1982), p.73; GCL, *Skelton Papers*, 1830, Vol. 1, No. 70.
32. GCL, *Skelton Papers*, 1832/3, Vol. 1, No. 116; 1832/3, Vol. 1, No. 110.
33. Baker, *Cleethorpes*, pp.97-101; White, *Lincolnshire*, pp. 102-3.
34. Baker, *Cleethorpes*, pp.70 and 72.
35. Baker, *Cleethorpes*, pp.48, 66, 118 and 125-6.
36. Baker, *Cleethorpes*, p.129.
37. Baker, *Cleethorpes*, p.111.
38. Baker, *Cleethorpes*, p.vi.
39. GCL, *Skelton Papers*, 1834.
40. Baker, *Cleethorpes*, pp.71 and 76.
41. Russell, *Landscape Changes*, p.72.
42. R.W. Ambler and A. Dowling, 'The Growth of Cleethorpes and the Prosperity of Sidney, 1616-1968' in D.E.D. Beales and H.B. Nisbet, *Sidney Sussex College: historical essays in commemoration of the quatercentenary* (1996) p.180; Russell, *Landscape Changes*, p.72.
43. E. Gillett, *A History of Grimsby* (1970), pp.188-9.
44. A. Bates, *A Gossip about Old Grimsby* (1893), p.11.
45. NELA, 1/80/1, 5 & 6 Vict. cap.1, An Act for Inclosing Lands in the Parish of Clee in the County of Lincoln, 1842.
46. LRSM, 5 August 1842 in Russell, *Landscape Changes*, p.72.
47. NELA, 1/190/2, Clee Enclosure Award 1846.

Chapter 3: The Coming of the Railway: 1840s-1860s

1. LRSM, 6 May 1831; NELA, 1/102/16, Grimsby Mayor's Court Book, 20 September 1831.
2. NA, RAIL 228/1, GG&SJR Provisional Committee and Directors' Meetings Minutes, 1845 ; NELA, 1/110/1, Grimsby Corporation Minutes, 29 October 1844, 22 March 1845 and 2 March 1846; 8 & 9 Vict. cap.l, GG&SJR Act, 1845.
3. NA, RAIL 1110/304, Reports & Accounts of Railway Companies, 1846-68.
4. 9 & 10 Vict. cap. cclxviii, An Act to Amalgamate the Sheffield, Ashton under Lyne and Manchester Railway Company, the Sheffield and Lincolnshire Junction, the Sheffield and Lincolnshire Extension and the Great Grimsby and Sheffield Railway Companies, and the Grimsby Docks Company, 1846; NA, RAIL 228/2, GG&SJR Minutes of Shareholders' Meetings, 1845-6.
5. NA, RAIL 1110/304, Report of Directors of MS&LR to the Proprietors and First General Meeting, 17 February 1847.
6. 9 & 10 Vict. cap. lxxxviii, East Lincolnshire Railway Act, 1846; Leleux, *The Railways of Great Britain, Vol. IX: The East Midlands* (1976), pp.212-3.
7. LRSM, 28 June 1850 and 27 June 1851.
8. LA, Exley 27/77, The Cleethorpes List of Visitors, No.4, 29 July 1854.
9. LRSM, 10 August 1849.
10. A. Kaye, *Aspects of Cleethorpes in the Nineteenth Century and Resort Development* (1987) No.17C.
11. E. Dobson, *A Guide and Directory to Cleethorpes* (1850), p.9.
12. E. Dobson, *A New Guide and Directory to Cleethorpes* (1858), pp.10 and 15.
13. GGG, 20 July 1855, p.4.

14. GGG, 31 August 1855, p.3, 2 July 1858, p.2 and 23 July 1858, p.2; GI, 23 July 1858 p.3.
15. NA, RAIL 463/2, 14 July 1854 and 18 September 1854, and 463/3, MS&LR Proceedings of the Board of Directors, 31 August 1855; SMR, Minutes of College Meetings, 31 May 1854; P.K. King and D.R. Hewins, *The Railways Around Grimsby, Cleethorpes, Immingham and North-East Lincolnshire* (1988), p.17; GCL, *Skelton Papers*, 1854, Vol.2, No.95, 1855-5, Vol.2, No.132; GGG, 13 March 1857, p.2 and 9 November 1855.
16. NA, RAIL 463/3, MS&LR Proceedings of the Board of Directors, 1 October 1856 and 3 April 1857; GGG, 13 March 1857, p.2, 24 April 1857, p.2 and 8 May 1857, p.2.
17. GFP, 22 June 1860, p.2.
18. NA, RAIL 463/5, MS&LR Proceedings of the Board of Directors, 25 July 1860.
19. 24 & 25 Vict. cap.lxxxvi. Manchester, Sheffield and Lincolnshire Railway (Additional Works) Act, 1861; GFP, 5 July 1861, p.2 and 25 April 1862, p.2.
20. GFP, 10 April 1863, p.2 and 25 January 1861, p.2.
21. F. Baker, *The Story of Cleethorpes and the Contribution to Methodism through two hundred years* (1953), pp.97-101.
22. Dobson, *Cleethorpes* (1858), p.12.
23. NA, CRES 58/309, letter 31 May 1860 from R. Thorold.
24. NA, CRES 58/309, letter 11 August 1860 from H. Watson.
25. NA, CRES 58/309, letter 29 August 1860 from John Clutton.
26. NA, CRES 58/309, letter 29 August 1860 from John Clutton.
27. 16 & 17 Vict. *c.*1. Sidney Sussex College Estate Act, 1853.
28. Dobson, *Cleethorpes* (1850), pp.13,14.
29. GGG, 2 May 1854, p.1, 14 March 1856, p.2, 17 April 1857, p.1, 14 March 1856, p.2 and 2 June 1858, p.2.
30 GN, 7 July 1882, p.4; Dobson, *Cleethorpes* (1858), p.11.
31. LRSM, 23 June 1854.
32. GO, 25 October 1871.
33 NELA, 51/1/1, Clee Parish Vestry Minutes.
34. GGG, 8 September 1854, p.2.
35. Baker, *Cleethorpes*, pp.94-5.
36. NELA, 51/1/1, Clee Parish Vestry Minutes, 17 April 1868, 24 April 1868 and 17 June 1869; A. Gait, *Directory of Great Grimsby and Cleethorpes* … (1871), p.6 of Cleethorpes section.
37. NELA, 51/1/1, Clee Parish Vestry Minutes, 21 November 1865, 7 December 1865 and 21 March 1873.
38. Baker, *Cleethorpes*, pp.108-9; B. Herbert, *Lifeboats of the Humber* (1991), pp.16-18.
39. Baker, *Cleethorpes*, pp.114-15.
40. Baker, *Cleethorpes*, pp.115-16.
41. Baker, *Cleethorpes*, pp.128-9.
42 Baker, *Cleethorpes*, pp.102-3.
43. Baker, *Cleethorpes*, p.93.

Chapter 4: Pier and Cliff: the 1870s

1. J. Fowler, *Richard Waldo Sibthorp: a biography, told chiefly in his own correspondence* (1880), p.208.
2. GO, 3 April 1872.
3. GO, 3 April 1872.
4. Fowler, *Sibthorp*, pp.208, 328.
5. GO, 3 April 1872, 9 October 1872 and 16 April 1873.
6. NA, MT 10/137, Cleethorpes Pier.
7. NA, MT 10/137; 30 & 31 Vict. cap lxi, Pier and Harbour Orders Confirmation Act, 1867 (No.3).
8. A. Gait, *Directory of Great Grimsby and Cleethorpes* … (1871), p.6 of Cleethorpes section.
9. SMR, Correspondence Files, letter from W. Ayre to R. Phelps, 29 February 1872.
10. GO, 3 April 1872, pp.1 and 4.
11. NA, MT 10/137, Cleethorpes Pier.
12. NA, MT 10/137, Cleethorpes Pier.
13. GO, 26 June 1872, p.4; 36 Vict., ch.lx, Cleethorpes Pier Act, 1873.
14. GO, 6 August 1873.
15. GO, 1 October 1873.
16. GO, 14 July 1875, p.2 and 24 April 1878.
17. Spalding Free Press reprinted in GO, 7 August 1878, p.4.
18. P.J. Aspinall, 'Speculative Builders and the Development of Cleethorpes, 1850-1900' in *Lincolnshire History and Archaeology*, Vol.11 (1976), pp.47, 49; 51; GO, 30 December 1874, p.2, 17 January 1872, p.4 and 1 July 1874, p.3.
19. F. Baker, *The story of Cleethorpes and the Contribution of Methodism through two hundred years* (1953), pp.134-5; NELA 51/1/1, Clee Parish Vestry Minutes, 13 May 1873.
20. GO, 24 December 1873, p.4.
21. GO, 31 December 1873, p.4.

22. Baker, *Cleethorpes*, pp.125, 154-7 and 160.

23. GO, 7 February 1877, p.2, 21 March 1877, p.3, 30 May 1877, p.3; NELA 51/1/5, CLB Minutes, 20 December 1883.

24. GO, 18 August 1875, pp.2-3; 30 May 1877, p.3 and 3 April 1878, p.3; NELA, 51/90/1, Bye Laws made by the Local Board for the District of Cleethorpes with Thrunscoe, 1875.

25. NELA, 51/1/1, Clee Parish Vestry Minutes, 25 March 1875, 5 May 1875, 9 October 1875, 13 November 1875 and 6 June 1878; SMR, Minutes of College Meetings, 4 November 1875; GO, 26 January 1876, p.3.

26. E. Gillett, *A History of Grimsby* (1970), p.139.

27. E. and R.C. Russell, *Landscape changes in South Humberside: the enclosure of thirty-seven parishes*, pp.72-6; NELA, 1/80/1, Clee Inclosure Act, paragraph 53; NELA, 1/920/2, Clee Inclosure Award; GO, 3 January 1872, 3 April 1872 and 4 June 1872.

28. SMR, Cleethorpes Correspondences File, 1875-1909, letter from W. Ayre to R. Phelps, 8 February 1872.

29. NA, RAIL 463/13, MS&LR Proceedings of the Board of Directors, 23 May 1873; GO, 4 June 1873, pp.1 and 4 and 3 December 1873, p.4.

30. GO, 18 August 1875, p.3, 29 March 1876, p.2, 14 February 1877, p.2, 21 February 1877, p.2; NELA, 51/1/4, CLB Minutes, 1 February 1877.

31. GO, 29 August 1877, p.2; NELA, 51/1/4, CLB Minutes, 20 September 1877.

32. GO, 3 October 1877, p.3, 10 October 1877, p.3; NELA, 51/1/4, CLB Minutes, 4 October 1877 and 18 October 1877.

Chapter 5: The Railway to the Rescue: the 1880s

1. GO, 7 January 1880, p.2.

2. S. Lee (ed.), *Dictionary of National Biography*, second supplement, 1901-11, pp. 601-3; NA, RAIL 1007/348, Papers on Sir Edward Watkin; C.F.D. Marshall, *A History of the Southern Railway*, Vol. I (1963), p.307.

3. NA, RAIL 463/17, MS&LR Proceedings of the Board of Directors, 9 April 1880; GO, 21 July 1880, p.2; NA, RAIL 226/341, letter 27 July 1880 from F.A. Peck to E. Ross.

4. NA, RAIL 463/17, MS&LR Proceedings of the Board of Directors, 13 August 1880; GO, 15 September 1880.

5. NA, RAIL 463/17, MS&LR Proceedings of the Board of Directors, 27 August 1880; GO, 15 September 1880.

6. NELA 51/1/4, CLB Minutes, 8 September 1880; NA, RAIL 226/341, Preservation of the Cliff at Cleethorpes, 9 September 1880 and 10 September 1880.

7. GO, 15 September 1880; NA, RAIL 226/341, Preservation of the Cliff at Cleethorpes, 13 September 1880.

8. NA, RAIL 463/17, MS&LR Proceedings of the Board of Directors, 10 September 1880.

9. NA, RAIL 226/341, Preservation of the Cliff at Cleethorpes, letter 1 March 1881 from F.A. Peck to E. Ross.

10. 44 & 45 Vict., Ch. cxxxvi. Manchester, Sheffield and Lincolnshire Railway (New Works Act), 1881.

11. NA, RAIL 463/18, MS&LR Proceedings of the Board of Directors, 21 April 1882.

12. GN, 23 June 1882, 21 July 1882, p.5 and 28 July 1882, p.5; NA, CRES 58/301, Foreshore; NA, RAIL 463/18, MS&LR Proceedings of the Board of Directors, 16 June 1882, 17 November 1882, 1 December 1882 and 15 December 1882.

13. NA, RAIL 463/126, Indenture of 6 April 1883 between MS&LR and Arthur Fuller James.

14. NA, RAIL 463/18, MS&LR Proceedings of the Board of Directors, 21 September 1883; RAIL 463/19, MS&LR Proceedings of the Board of Directors, 19 October 1883; GN, 14 September 1883, p.6.

15. NA, RAIL 463/18, MS&LR Proceedings of the Board of Directors, 21 September 1883; RAIL 463/19, MS&LR Proceedings of the Board of Directors, 19 October 1883.

16. NA, RAIL 463/19, MS&LR Proceedings of the Board of Directors, 30 November 1883, 14 December 1883, 11 January 1884 and 23 January 1884; 47 & 48 Vict., ch. cxlvi., The Manchester, Sheffield and Lincolnshire Railway (Additional Powers) Act, 1884.

17. NA, RAIL 463/18, MS&LR Proceedings of the Board of Directors, 21 September 1883; RAIL 463/19, MS&LR Proceedings of the Board of Directors, 11 January 1884.

18. NA, RAIL 463/77, MS&LR Proprietors' Half-Yearly Meeting, 23 January 1884.

19. NA, RAIL 463/19, MS&LR Proceedings of the Board of Directors, 4 April 1884 and 12 December 1884; GO, 27 August 1884, p.2.

20. GO, 27 August 1884, p.2.

21. GO, 1 April 1885, p.2.

22. NA, RAIL 463/19, MS&LR Proceedings of the Board of Directors, 21 January 1885.

23. NA, RAIL 1151/1, George Dow Collection.

24. The Official Programme of [the] Opening of [the] Promenade and Cliff Gardens, Cleethorpes with an account of the improvements etc. (1885)

25. The Official Programme of [the] Opening of [the] Promenade and Cliff Gardens, Cleethorpes with and account of the improvements etc. (1885)

26. NA, RAIL 463/20, MS&LR Proceedings of the Board of Directors, 22 July 1885, 4 September 1885, 18

September 1885, 16 October 1885, 5 February 1886, 19 February 1886 and 19 March 1886.

27. NA, RAIL 463/22, MS&LR Proceedings of the Board of Directors, 16 March 1888 and 10 May 1889; GO, 3 October 1888, p.2; RAIL 463/21, MS&LR Proceedings of the Board of Directors, 25 January 1888; GO, 24 April 1889, p.2.

28. GO, 4 July 1888; G. Dow, *Great Central*, Vol. II (1962) p.172.

29. NA, RAIL 463/20, MS&LR Proceedings of the Board of Directors, 22 July 1885, 7 August 1885 and 4 September 1885; GO, 9 September 1885, p.2; RAIL 463/22, MS&LR Proceedings of the Board of Directors, 16 March 1888.

30. GN, 18 May 1888.

31. GN, 6 July 1888, 13 July 1888, 3 August 1888 and 28 September 1888.

32. Playbill, Pier Concert Hall, 15 July 1889.

33. GCL, Moore cuttings, 20 June 1890.

34. *Ward's Cleethorpes Guide*, 1900.

35. NA, RAIL 463/24, MS&LR Proceedings of the Board of Directors, 7 November 1890; RAIL 463/29, MS&LR Proceedings of the Board of Directors, 21 February 1896; *Ward's Cleethorpes Guide*, 1900.

36. GO, 16 April 1873.

37. GCL, Skelton Papers, 1851, Nos. 46a and 82a; Baker, Cleethorpes, pp.128-9, 166.

38. GO, 26 May 1875 p.2; 3 April 1872 p.4; 28 August 1878 p.3.

39. GO, 12 August 1885.

40. GN 20 July 1888.

41. GN, 31 August 1888.

42. GN 7 September 1888.

43. F. Baker, *The Story of Cleethorpes and the Contribution of Methodism through two hundred years* (1953), pp.154-7.

44. GO, 11 August 1886, p.3; NELA, 51/1/5, CLB Minutes, 5 August 1886.

45. NA, CRES 58/311, letter 7 August 1889 from B. Greaves to CWF.

46. NA, CRES 58/311, letter 5 September 1889 from E. Ross to CWF.

47. NA, CRES 58/311, letter 24 September 1889 from CWF to B. Greaves.

48. NELA 51/1/6, CLB Minutes, 15 November 1890.

49. NA, RAIL 463/77, MS&LR Proprietors Half-Yearly Meeting, 23 January 1884.

50. *Cleethorpes Gazette*, 6 September 1887; GO, 29 March 1888.

51. *Lincolnshire Life*, 4 July 1977, p.35.

52. Cleethorpes Public Hall Company prospectus, 1895.

Chapter 6: New and Old Cleethorpes: 1880s–1890s

1. A. Dowling, 'The Corporate Landowner in Town Development: with particular reference to Grimsby and Cleethorpes, *c.*1800-*c.*1900' (PhD thesis, Hull University, 1997), p.218.

2. J.H. Price, *The Tramways of Grimsby, Immingham and Cleethorpes* (n.d.), p.17.

3. Dowling, 'The Corporate Landowner', p.206.

4. SMR, Cleethorpes Correspondence 1875-1909, letter 13 October 1885 from W.H. Daubney to R. Phelps.

5. Dowling, 'The Corporate Landowner', p.224.

6. L. Triggs, D. Hepton and S. Woodhead, *Grimsby Town: a complete record, 1878-1989*, pp.41-3; GN, 5 September 1899, p.4 and 8 September 1899, p.6.

7. GO, 11 March 1885, p.2, 15 July 1885, p.3, 12 August 1885, p.3, and 13 July 1887, p.2; NELA, 51/1/6, CLB Minutes, 6 October 1892.

8. NELA, 51/1/5, CLB Minutes, 11 October 1883.

9. GO, 19 May 1886, p.3

10. GO, 26 August 1885, p.3.

11. GO, 13 January 1886, p.3; NELA, 51/20/3, UDC General Orders, Forms and Agendas, Vol. III, 1908-9.

12. NA, RAIL 463/22, MS&LR Proceedings of the Board of Directors, 11 May 1888; GO, 13 May 1891, p.3.

13. GO 6 September 1893, p.3, 13 September 1893, p.3 and 20 September 1893, p.2.

14. GO, 20 September 1893, p.2 and 11 October 1893, p.3.

15. GO, 6 November 1892, p.2.

16. GO, 15 February 1893, p.2.

17. GO, 15 March 1893, p.3, 22 March 1893, pp.2-3, 14 June 1893, p.2 and 19 July 1893, p.2.

18. GO, 23 May 1894, p.2.

19. GO, 2 May 1894, p.2 and 9 May 1894, p.2; GN 15 February 1895, p.3.

20. NELA, 51/1/8, UDC Minutes, 8 May 1895 and 12 June 1895.

21. GO, 15 December 1897, p.3; GN, 5 August 1904, p.5.

22. GN, 14 November 1899, p.8, 17 November 1899, p.3 and 4 December 1900, p.6.

23. SMR, Cleethorpes Correspondence File, 1875-1909, letter 21 September 1896 from A. Bates to F.H. Neville.

24. GN, 1 July 1898, p.6 and 24 June 1904, p.6; SMR, Minutes of College Meetings, 10 October 1898.

Chapter 7: Changing Times: 1900–1914

1. GN, 17 February 1897, p.3 and 30 October 1914; NELA, 51/1/9, UDC Minutes, 27 January 1897 and 10 February 1897.
2. NELA, 51/1/9, UDC Minutes, 16 June 1897 and 51/1/11, UDC Minutes, 14 January 1903; GN, 1 December 1897, p.3 and 25 February 1898, p.6.
3. NELA, 51/1/9, UDC Minutes, 9 March 1898; GN, 11 March 1898, p.7.
4. NELA, 51/1/9, UDC Minutes,16 March 1898; GN, 18 March 1898, p.5 and 27 May 1898, p.8.
5. SMR, Cleethorpes Correspondence File, 1875-1909, 28 April 1898; GN, 6 May 1898, p.7 and 10 June 1898, p.5; NELA, 51/1/9, UDC Minutes, 4 May 1898.
6. GO, 21 September 1898, p.8 and 16 November 1898, p.8; NELA, 51/1/9, UDC Minutes, 12 October 1898 and 9 November 1898; SMR, Cleethorpes Correspondence File, 1875-1909, 31 October 1898.
7. GN, 6 January 1899, p.6.
8. SMR, Cleethorpes Correspondence File, 1875-1909, Report of Meeting, 20 February 1901.
9. GN, 7 May 1901, p.6 and 15 November 1901, p.7; NELA, 51/1/10, UDC Minutes, 14 May 1901; 2 Edw. 7, Ch.cliv, Cleethorpes Improvement Act, 1902, Part VI and Third Schedule.
10. GO, 14 September 1898, p.5, 12 October 1898, p.5 and 16 November 1898, p.8; NELA 51/1/9, UDC Minutes, 14 September 1898.
11. GN, 30 July 1901, p.7 and 13 August 1901, p.7.
12. 2 Edw. 7, Ch.cliv, Cleethorpes Improvement Act, 1902, Sections 73-8; NELA, 51/1/11, UDC Minutes, 3 June 1903.
13. GN, 10 October 1901, 15 November 1901 and 22 November 1901.
14. GGG, 13 December 1901; NELA, 51/1/10, UDC Minutes, 18 December 1901 and 8 January 1902.
15. GN, 11 April 1902, p.7 and 8 May 1903, p.7.
16. 2 Edw. 7, Ch.cliv, Cleethorpes Improvement Act, 1902, Sections 73-78; NELA, 51/1/11, UDC Minutes, 3 June 1903.
17. GN, 28 October 1902, p.5 and 9 January 1903, p.7.
18. NELA, 51/1/11, UDC Minutes, 14 January 1903 and 11 February 1903; GN, 20 March 1903, p.3.
19. GN, Immingham and Kingsway Supplement, 13 July 1906.
20. GN, 23 February 1906, p.6 and 27 February 1906, p.3; NELA, 51/20/8, UDC General Orders, Forms and Agendas, Vol.VIII, 1914.
21. NELA, 51/1/12, UDC Minutes, 25 October 1905 and 51/20/1, UDC General Orders Forms and Agendas, Vol. I, 1896-1905, 18 May 1905; GN, 18 May 1906, p.6, 1 June 1906, p.6 and 22 June 1906.
22. GN, 4 May 1906; GT, 15 May 1906; SMR, Minutes of College Meetings, 22 May 1906.
23. GN, 13 July 1906.
24. GN, 4 January 1907, pp.7-8.
25. GN, 5 January 1906, p.3.
26. GN, 29 September 1905, p.6.
27. NELA, 53/D/220, UDC Medical Officer's Report for 1914, p.5.
28. GN, 21 Feb 1908, p.6.
29. GN, 22 May 1908, p.6, 5 June 1908, p.6 and 12 June 1908, p.6.
30. NA, BT 31/19254/107748, Cleethorpes Switchback Co. Ltd, 1910.
31. NA, BT 31/7706/55047, Warwick Revolving Towers Co. Ltd and RAIL 226/1, GCR Board Minutes, 13 July 1898; GN, 29 July 1898, p.5.
32. GN, 6 March 1900, p.8 and 24 June 1902, p.8; A. McEwen, 'Revolving Observation Towers' in Yarmouth Archaeology, (1995), p.33; L.F. Pearson, The People's Palaces: the story of the Seaside Pleasure Buildings of 1870-1914 (1991), p.66.
33. GN, 10 October 1902, p.6, 21 October 1902, p.4, 11 September 1903 and 18 September 1903, p.3.
34. GN, 6 November 1906.
35. GN, 4 August 1908, p.5.
36. GN, 30 June 1903, p.5 and 3 July 1903, p.3.
37. GN, 3 July 1903.
38. NA, RAIL 226/5, GCR Board Minutes, 9 October 1903 and 11 February 1904.
39. NA, RAIL 226/5, GCR Board Minutes, 7 October 1904 and RAIL 226/6, GCR Board Minutes, 1 June 1906; GN, 9 June 1905, p.6 and 13 June 1905, p.6.
40. GN, 18 December 1908, p.6 and 22 October 1909, p.7; Grimsby Daily Telegraph, 21 October 1909, p.4.
41. GN, 21 October 1904, p.2.
42. NELA, 51/1/13, UDC Minutes, 28 September 1910; GN, ; 21 January 1910, 19 October 1910 and 21 March 1911.
43. GN, 8 April 1904, p.6.
44. GN, 13 July 1906, pp.5 and 7.
45. GN, 9 April 1903, p.4.
46. GN, 14 April 1903, p.5.
47. GN, 29 April 1910.

48. GO, 28 August 1878, p.3.

49. GN, 27 June 1905, p.4.

50. NELA 51/1/12, UDC Minutes, 8 March 1906; NA, RAIL 463/5, MS&LR Proceedings of the Board of Directors, 26 August 1859 and 463/8, MS&LR Proceedings of the Board of Directors, 2 June 1865; GI, 6 August 1858, p.2.

51. LRSM, 20 July 1894.

52. GO, 9 September 1896, p.2, 16 September 1896, p.2 and 23 September 1896, p.2.

53. GN, 2 August 1907, p.7.

54. GN, 12 June 1908, p.6.

55. GN, 23 June 1908, p.6.

56. NELA, 51/710/1, UDC News Clippings; GT, July 1910; *Sheffield Daily Telegraph*, 18 August 1910; *Grimsby Daily Telegraph*, 18 August 1910.

57. GN, 19 August 1904, p.6; NELA, 51/20/4, UDC General Orders, Forms and Agendas, Vol. IV, 1910, paper by E.H. Turner.

58. NELA, 51/111/55/5, Conveyance of the Cleethorpes Golf Links together with the estate and interest of the College in five acres of foreshore adjoining, 16 March 1903; Agreement dated 9 April 1902 between Sidney Sussex College and the Cleethorpes UDC, incorporated as the Third Schedule in 2 Edw. 7, Ch.cliv, Cleethorpes Improvement Act, 1902.

59. SMR, Minutes of College Meetings, 14 October 1905; NELA, 51/1/12, UDC Minutes, 20 December 1905.

60. GN, 18 October 1907, 22 May 1908 and 20 November 1908; NELA, 51/1/13, UDC Minutes, 20 May 1908 and 16 June 1909; 51/5/2, UDC Highways etc. Committee, 8 June 1909, 11 April 1911 and 9 December 1913.

61. NELA, 51/111/5/1, letter 19 May 1914 from Bates & Mountain to UDC.

62. GN, 8 October 1901, p.8; 11 October 1901, p.7; 15 November 1901; 17 February 1905, p.3; 5 June 1903, p.6.

63. NELA, 51/111/55/5, Conveyance of Cleethorpes Golf Links.

64. NELA, 51/20/3, UDC General Orders, Forms and Agendas, Vol. III, 1908-9 and 51/1/12, UDC Minutes, 16 October 1907.

65. NELA, 51/11, UDC Sewerage Committee Minutes, 30 January 1908 and 11 November 1909; GN, 11 November 1910 and 13 November 1908, p.6.

66 NELA, 53/D/220, UDC Medical Officer's Report for 1914.

67. NA, ZLIB 19/383, *John Heywood's Illustrated Guide to Grimsby and Cleethorpes* (1890), p.5.

68. GO, 15 November 1893, p.3, 22 November 1893, p.2 and 6 December 1893, p.2; GN, 20 May 1895, p.8.

69. GO, 12 May 1897, p.3, 19 May 1897, p.2 and 27 October 1897, p.3.

70. NA, PC 8/482, Cleethorpes Incorporation Petition, 1897.

71. SMR, Minutes of College Meetings, 18 June 1900.

72. GN, 13 August 1901, p.7.

73. GN, 5 August 1904, p.5.

74. GN, 2 August 1907, pp.4-5, 6 August 1907, p.4 and 9 August 1907, p.6.

75. GN, 10 September 1907, p.6 and 20 September 1907, p.6.

76. NELA, 51/1/12, UDC Minutes, 30 October 1907; SMR, Minutes of College Meetings, 11 October 1907; GN, 29 October 1907, p.4 and 3 December 1907, p.4.

77. GN, 20 September 1907, p.6, 18 October 1907, p.4, 22 October 1907, pp.4-5 and 4 February 1908 p.8.

78. A. Dowling, 'The Corporate Landowner in Town Development: with particular reference to Grimsby and Cleethorpes, *c*. 1800-*c*.1900' (PhD thesis, Hull University, 1997), p.239.

79. GCL, County Borough of Grimsby. Incorporation Scheme 1908. Local Government Board Inquiry Proceedings.

Chapter 8: War and Expansion: 1914-1929

1. NELA, 51/199/7, UDC Medical Officer's Report for 1915, pp.3-4.

2. C. M. Thorneycroft, 'The 3rd Battalion (Militia) The Manchester Regiment: its origin and services with special reference to its work during the Great War 1914-1918' (Typescript, n.d.), p.30. (Tameside Local Studies Library and Archives, MR1/3/1/25).

3. NELA, 51/1/15, UDC Minutes, 6 September 1914.

4. Thorneycroft, *Manchester Regiment*, pp.29-33, 92; NELA 51/199/7, UDC Medical Officer's Report for 1915, p.26.

5. Thorneycroft, Manchester Regiment, p.41.

6. Thorneycroft, Manchester Regiment, pp.40, 53-8.

7. Thorneycroft, Manchester Regiment, pp.59-60.

8. Thorneycroft, Manchester Regiment, p.60.

9. T. Crossley, The Cleethorpes National School, 1815-1933 (Typescript, 1963), p.111.

10. Thorneycroft, Manchester Regiment, p.92.

11. Thorneycroft, Manchester Regiment, p.93; plaque in St Aidan's Church, Cleethorpes.
12. Thorneycroft, Manchester Regiment, pp.73-4; *Lincolnshire Echo*, 18 July 1917.
13. J.E. Dorman, *Guardians of the Humber: a history of the Humber Defences, 1856-1956* (1990), pp.75-94.
14. GCL, Grimsby Register of Electors, 1918: Absent Voters.
15. NELA, 51/1/18, UDC Minutes, 5 March 1918.
16. NELA, 51/1/19, UDC Pleasure Grounds Committee Minutes, 8 May 1918, 11 June 1918 and 10 September 1918.
17. GN, 7 June 1918, p.7.
18. GN, 25 May 1918.
19. GN, 15 November 1918.
20. GN, 21 March 1919, p.7.
21. GN, 17 August 1923, p.7; 24 August 1923, p.7; GT, 3 July 1923.
22. Thorneycroft, Manchester Regiment, p.89; NELA, 51/1/19, UDC Minutes, 10 March 1919.
23. NELA, 51/1/19, UDC Minutes, 3 September 1919 and 8 July 1920; 51/1/21, UDC Minutes, 10 February 1921 and 5 March 1921; 51/1/22, UDC Minutes, 11 July 1921.
24. NELA, 51/1/20, UDC Minutes, 10 November 1919; 51/1/22, UDC Minutes, 1 October 1921; 27 March 1922; 51/1/23, UDC Minutes, 12 March 1923.
25. NELA, 51/1/24, UDC Finance Committee Minutes, 12 July 1923; 51/1/24, UDC Pleasure Grounds Committee Minutes, 10 September 1923.
26. NELA, 51/1/24, UDC Pleasure Grounds Committee Minutes, 30 July 1923; UDC Minutes, 31 July 1923.
27. GN, 10 August 1923, p.7; 17 August 1923, p.7.
28. NELA, 51/1/25, UDC Pleasure Grounds Committee Minutes, 17 June 1924 and 22 July 1924.
29. NELA, 51/1/26, UDC Pleasure Grounds Committee Minutes, 17 June 1925 and 13 October 1925.
30. NELA, 51/1/26 UDC Minutes, 18 November 1925; 51/1/27, UDC Pleasure Grounds Committee Minutes, 7 December 1926.
31. NELA, 51/1/29, UDC Pleasure Grounds Committee Minutes, 31 May 1928, 6 June 1928 and 3 July 1928.
32. NELA, 51/1/29, UDC Pleasure Grounds Committee Minutes, 17 December 1928 and 6 March 1929; 51/1/30, UDC Pleasure Grounds Committee Minutes, 1 May 1929.
33. NELA, 51/1/30, UDC Pleasure Grounds Committee Minutes, 3 July 1929 and 2 October 1929.
34. NELA, 51/1/26, UDC Finance Committee Minutes, 10 September 1925; 51/1/27, UDC Finance Committee Minutes, 10 March 1927.
35. NELA, 51/1/29, UDC Pleasure Grounds Committee Minutes, 6 June 1928; Finance Committee Minutes, 12 July 1928.
36. GN, 9 September 1921; NELA, 51/1/22, UDC Finance Committee Minutes, 10 November 1921.
37. NELA 51/1/27, UDC Finance Committee Minutes, 10 June 1926; GN, 24 September 1926.
38. GN, 17 December 1926.
39. GCL, UDC, Official Opening of the Marine Embankment by Lord Heneage on 6th September, 1930.
40. NELA, 51/1/29, UDC Pleasure Grounds Committee Minutes, 6 March 1929.
41. GCL, UDC, Official Opening of the Marine Embankment by Lord Heneage on 6th September, 1930.
42. NELA, 51/1/31, UDC Pleasure Grounds Committee Minutes, 3 September 1930 and 7 January 1931; 51/1/32, UDC Pleasure Grounds Committee Minutes, 6 May 1931 and 7 October 1931.
43. NA, RAIL 390/984, LNER Memorandum to Traffic & Property Committees, 21 June 1926.
44. NA, RAIL 390/984, LNER, extract from minutes of Traffic Committee, 3 July 1926.
45. GT, 9 December 1927.
46. GN, 20 January 1928.
47. 18 & 19 Geo 5, Ch. lxxvi, Cleethorpes Urban District Council Act, 1928.
48. J.H. Price, *The Tramways of Grimsby, Immingham and Cleethorpes* (n.d.), p.42; NELA, 51/1/36, UDC Highways Committee Minutes, 2 May 1935.
49. NELA, 51/1/21, UDC Highways Committee Minutes, 8 March 1921; 51/1/26, UDC Highways Committee Minutes, 7 September 1925.
50. O.A. Hartley, 'Housing Policy in Four Lincolnshire Towns, 1919-1959' (PhD thesis, Oxford University, 1969), p.92.
51. A. Dowling, *Humberston Fitties: the story of a Lincolnshire Plotland* (2001), p.121.
52. Dowling, *Humberston Fitties*, p.122.
53. NELA, 51/199/7, UDC Medical Officer's report for 1923, p.19; 51/1/22, UDC Housing Committee Minutes, 6 April 1922.
54. NELA, 51/1/20, UDC Pleasure Grounds Committee Minutes, 10 November 1919 and 12 January 1920.
55. *Cleethorpes Guide* (1927).

Chapter 9: Coming of Age: 1930-1939

1. NA, RAIL 390/984, LNER Memorandum to Traffic & Property Committees, 25 April 1935; GET, 19 September 1935; NELA, 51/1/36, UDC Parliamentary Committee Minutes, 14 October 1935; UDC Minutes, 10 January 1936; UDC Finance Committee Minutes, 13 February 1936.

2. GET, 30 October 1935 and 3 December 1935, GN, 29 November 1935.

3. GET, 16 April 1936.

4. GET, 16 April 1936; J.H. Price, *The Tramways of Grimsby, Immingham and Cleethorpes* (n.d.), pp.54-6.

5. GET, 6 July 1933.

6. GET, 17 November 1933, 30 October 1934, 9 November 1934 and 10 November 1934; GN, 16 November 1934; *Hull Daily Mail*, 15 October 1934.

7. GET, 14 November 1933 and 1 November 1934.

8. GN, 16 November 1934.

9. GCL, Borough of Cleethorpes Charter Day 23rd September 1936 Souvenir, p.21.

10. GCL, Borough of Cleethorpes Charter Day Souvenir, pp.21, 23 and 25.

11. NELA, 51/1/37, CBC Pier Committee Minutes, 16 October 1936; 51/1/38, CBC Minutes, 12 November 1936; *Lincolnshire Life*, August 2001, p.38; GT *Bygones*, 13 March 1999, p.6.

12. NELA, 51/1/38, CBC Pier Committee Minutes, 30 August 1937.

13. NELA, 1001/4, Borough of Cleethorpes. Application to Ministry of Health for sanction to the borrowing of £12,000 for the layout of Pier Gardens and Works in connection therewith. Inquiry to be held 14 January 1938; 51/1/39, CBC Pier Committee Minutes, 18 January 1938.

14. NELA, 51/1/39, CBC Pier Committee Minutes, 30 May 1938 and 4 July 1938.

15. NELA, 51/1/40, CBC Pier Committee Minutes, 2 January 1939, 3 April 1939, 1 May 1939, 5 June 1939 and 3 July 1939; CBC Finance Committee Minutes, 6 June 1939.

16. NELA, 51/1/36, CBC Pier Committee Minutes, 16 March 1936; 51/1/40, CBC Pier Committee Minutes, 15 November 1938 and 3 April 1939.

17. NELA, 51/1/40, CBC Finance Committee Minutes, 31 May 1939 and 13 July 1939; CBC Pier Committee Minutes 1 May 1939 and 4 September 1939.

18. NELA, 51/1/38, CBC Pier Committee Minutes, 27 March 1937; 51/1/39, CBC Pier Committee Minutes, 31 January 1938 and 27 September 1938.

19. *Cleethorpes Holiday Annual* (1939), pp.64-5 and 81.

20. GET, 31 July 1931; GN, 6 August 1937.

21. GET, *Carnival Supplement*, 11 August 1932; GET, 17 August 1933.

22. NELA, 51/1/32, UDC Sands Committee Minutes, 2 December 1931; 51/1/33, UDC Minutes, 6 July 1932; UDC Finance Committee Minutes, 10 November 1932; 51/1/34, UDC Sands Committee Minutes, 5 July 1933, 6 September 1933 and 7 March 1934.

23. NELA, 51/1/35, UDC Sands Committee Minutes, 6 June 1934, 2 July 1934 and 16 July 1934.

24. NELA, 51/1/35, UDC Minutes, 17 October 1934; UDC Sands Committee Minutes, 2 January 1935.

25. NELA, 51/1/35, UDC Sands Committee Minutes, 6 February 1935.

26. NELA, 51/1/40, CBC Sands Committee Minutes, 7 June 1939; 51/1/36, UDC Pleasure Grounds Minutes, 1 May 1935.

27. NELA, 51/1/40, CBC Finance Committee Minutes, 9 February 1939.

28. O.A. Hartley, 'Housing Policy in Four Lincolnshire Towns, 1919-1959' (PhD Thesis, Oxford University, 1969), pp.92-3.

29. Hartley, 'Housing Policy', pp.72 and 93.

30. Souvenir of the Official Opening of the Cleethorpes Electricity Showrooms 10 May 1937, p.9.

Chapter 10: War and Recovery: 1939-1974

1. NELA, 51/1/40, CBC Minutes, 18 October 1939; The *Telegraph*, 1 January 1926; GET, 22 July 1938, 25 September 1939 and 26 September 1939; GN, 29 September 1939.

2. NELA, 51/1/40, UDC Air Raid Precautions Committee Minutes, 4 May 1939, 6 June 1939, 4 July 1939 and 5 September 1939.

3. NA, CRES 64/17, Foreshore Leases, 1929-48, letter 15 July 1946; J.E. Dorman, *Guardians of the Humber: A History of the Humber Defences, 1856-1956* (1990), pp.75-94.

4. NA, WO 199/87, Messages Nos.12 and 13 from Admiral Dreyer, 11 June 1940 and 13 June 1940; Memorandum from the Royal Naval Base, Immingham, 28 September 1941.

5. S. H. Adamson, *Seaside Piers* (1977), p.101; C. Bainbridge, *Pavilions on the Sea: a history of the seaside pleasure pier* (1986), p.165; C.S. Dobinson, *Twentieth Century Fortifications in England, Vol.I: Anti-Invasion Defences of World War II* (1996), p.109; M. Hart, *Cleethorpes and the Meggies* (1981), p.41.

6. GET, 3 August 1954; Hart, Cleethorpes, pp.41 and 43.

7. M. Smith, *Blitz on Grimsby* (1983), pp.1, 3, 10-12, 20-2, 25 and 31-4; O.A. Hartley, 'Housing Policy in Four Lincolnshire Towns, 1919-1959' (PhD Thesis, Oxford University, 1969), p.77.

8. GET, 30 November 1989.

9. SMR, Leases, etc. 1939-60; GET 19 February 1960 and 30 November 1989.

10. NA, CRES 64/17, Foreshore Leases, 1929-48, letter 27 July 1946.

11. Dorman, *Guardians of the Humber*, pp.75-94.

12. GET, 3 August 1954; Hart, *Cleethorpes*, pp.39 and 43-4; GN, 2 January 1948.

13. F. Baker, *The story of Cleethorpes and the Contribution of Methodism through two hundred years* (1953), p.152; GET,

        16 September 1948, reprinted in GT 16 September 2002 and 16 September 2003.
14. GET, 27 January 1949 and 14 April 1949.
15. GET, 4 May 1946.
16. GT, 24 June 2003 p.15.
17. GET, 2 February 1953, p. 4 and 3 February 1953, p.6.
18. GET, 11 August 1953.
19. GET, 11 August 1953, p.5.
20. D.N. Robinson, 'The Changing Coastline' in D.R. Mills (ed.), *Twentieth Century Lincolnshire* (1989), p.175.
21. A. Dowling, *Humberside Fitties: the story of a Lincolnshire Plotland* (2001), p.70.
22. GET, 29 June 1956, p.5.
23. *Cleethorpes Guide* (1959).
24. P.R. White, 'Roads Replace Railways', in D.R. Mills (ed.), *Twentieth Century Lincolnshire* (1989), p.127.
25. GT, 17 May 2003; White, 'Roads Replace Railways', pp.120 and 123.
26. GCL, North Promenade sale catalogue, 17 September 1965; GET, 27 July 1965.
27. GET, 16 September 2004; I. Shannon, 'Cleethorpes: a Special Survey' in *Lincolnshire Life*, February/March 1965, pp.31-9.
28 Hartley, *Housing Policy*, pp.86 and 88.
29. Hartley, *Housing Policy*, p.93.
30. R.W. Ambler and A. Dowling, '*The Growth of Cleethorpes and the Prosperity of Sidney, 1616-1968*' in D.E.D. Beales and H.B. Nisbet, *Sidney Sussex College: historical essays in commemoration of the quatercentenary* (1996), pp.192-3.

Chapter 11: Recent Times

1. GET *Bygones*, 10 February 2001, pp.16-7; GET, 6 January 1988, p.6; GT, 7 April 2003; C. Ekberg, *The Book of Cleethorpes* (1986), p.75.
2. G.D. Powell, *A Leisure Park Feasibility Study* (1985), p.4.
3. Powell, *A Leisure Park Feasibility Study*; GET, May 1985, *passim*.
4. *A Sense of Purpose: a business plan for Cleethorpes BC* (May 1992), p.7.
5. GET, August 1992, Grimsby BC 'Better Together' advertising supplement.
6. GET, 27 August 1993; Cleethorpes BC, The Case for Unitary Status (December 1992); Radford Marketing Ltd, *Cleethorpes BC Unitary Status Survey* (September 1992)
7. GET, 21 July 1993, pp.1-2.
8. GET Special Supplement, 25 March 1996.
9. F. Baker, *The story of Cleethorpes and the Contribution of Methodism through two hundred years* (1953), *passim*.

Bibliography

Repositories

Grimsby Central Library, Local History Collection, Town Hall Square, Grimsby, DN31 1HG

Lincolnshire Archives, St Rumbold Street, Lincoln, LN2 5AB

National Archives, Kew, Surrey, TW9 4DU

North East Lincolnshire Archives Office, Town Hall Square, Grimsby, DN31 1HX

Sidney Sussex College, Muniment Room, Sidney Sussex College, Cambridge, CB2 3HU

Tameside Local Studies Library, Stalybridge Library, Trinity Street, Stalybridge, SK15 2BN

Printed Sources and Further Reading

Adamson, S.H., *Seaside Piers* (1977)

Ambler, R.W. and Dowling, A., 'The Growth of Cleethorpes and the Prosperity of Sidney, 1616-1968' in D.E.D. Beales and H.B. Nisbet, *Sidney Sussex College: historical essays in commemoration of the quatercentenary* (1996)

Ambler, R.W. and Watkinson, B. and L., *Farmers and Fishermen: the probate inventories of the ancient parish of Clee, South Humberside, 1536-1742* (1987)

Aspinall, P.J., 'Speculative Builders and the Development of Cleethorpes, 1850-1900' in *Lincolnshire History and Archaeology, Vol. 11* (1976), pp.43-52

Bainbridge, C., *Pavilions on the Sea: a history of the seaside pleasure pier* (1986)

Baker, F., *The Story of Cleethorpes and the Contribution of Methodism through two hundred years* (1953)

Bates, A., *A Gossip About Old Grimsby* (1893)

Beckwith, I.S., in 'The River Trade of Gainsborough, 1500-1850', *Lincolnshire History and Archaeology, No. 2* (1967), pp.3-20

Borough of Cleethorpes Charter Day 23rd September 1936 Souvenir (1936)

Byng, J., *The Torrington Diaries: a selection from the Tours of the Hon. John Byng between the years 1781 and 1794*, edited by C. Bruyn Andrews (1954)

Calendar of Charter Rolls, Vol. V, 1341-1417

Cleethorpes Holiday Annual (1939)

Cleethorpes UDC, Official Opening of the Marine Embankment by Lord Heneage on 6th September, 1930

Cole, R.E.G. (ed.), *Speculum Dioeceseos Lincolniensis sub episcopis Gul. Wake et Edm. Gibson, A.D. 1705-1723* (1913)

Cooke, G.A., *Topographical and Statistical Description of the County of Lincoln* [1802-10?]

Crossley, T., 'The Cleethorpes National School, 1815-1933' (Typescript, 1963)

Dobinson, C.S., *Twentieth Century Fortifications in England, Vol.I: Anti-Invasion Defences of World War II* (1996)

Dobson, E.A., *Guide and Directory to Cleethorpes with an historical account of the place* (1850)

Dobson, E.A., *New Guide and Directory to Cleethorpes with an historical account of the place* (1858)

Dorman, J.E., *Guardians of the Humber: a history of the Humber Defences, 1856-1956* (1990)

Dow, G. *Great Central* 3v. (1959-65)

Dowling, A., 'The Corporate Landowner in Town Development: with particular reference to Grimsby and Cleethorpes, *c.*1800-*c.*1900' (PhD thesis, Hull University, 1997)

Dowling, A., *Humberston Fitties, the story of a Lincolnshire Plotland* (2001)

Drury, E., *The Old Clee Story* (n.d.)

Dugdale, J., *The New British Traveller, or a modern panorama of England and Wales,* Vol. III (1819)

Ekberg, C., *The Book of Cleethorpes* (1986)

Foster, C.W. and Longley, T., *The Lincolnshire Domesday and the Lindsey Survey* (1924)

Fowler, J., *Richard Waldo Sibthorp: a biography, told chiefly in his own correspondence* (1880)

Gait, A., *Directory of Great Grimsby and Cleethorpes* (1871)

Gillett, E., *A History of Grimsby* (1970)

Glasscock, R.E., 'The Lay Subsidy of 1334 for Lincolnshire' in *Lincolnshire Architectural and Archaeological Society Reports and Papers, X(1)* (1963), pp.115-33

Gomme, G. L. (ed.), *Topographical History of Leicestershire, Lincolnshire, Middlesex, Monmouthshire: a classified collection of the chief contents of 'The Gentleman's Magazine' from 1731-1868* (1896)

Hart, M., *Cleethorpes and the Meggies* (1981)

Hartley, O. A., 'Housing Policy in Four Lincolnshire Towns, 1919-1959' (PhD thesis, Oxford University, 1969)

Herbert, B., *Lifeboats of the Humber* (1991)

Heywood's Illustrated Guide to Grimsby and Cleethorpes (1890)

Hodgett, G.A.J., *Tudor Lincolnshire* (1975)

Kaye, A., *Aspects of Cleethorpes in the Nineteenth Century and Resort Development* (1987)

King, P.K. and Hewins, D.R., *The Railways Around Grimsby, Cleethorpes, Immingham and North-East Lincolnshire* (1988)

Lee, S. (ed.), *Dictionary of National Biography*, second supplement 1901-11 (1912)

Leleux, R., *The Railways of Great Britain, Vol. IX: The East Midlands* (1976)

McEwen, A., 'Revolving Observation Towers' in *Yarmouth Archaeology* (1995)

Maddison, A.R., *Lincolnshire Pedigrees, Vol. 3* (1904)

Marshall, C.F.D., *A History of the Southern Railway,* Vol. I (1963)

Methodist Magazine, vol. XXXIII, June 1815

Official Programme of [the] Opening of [the] Promenade and Cliff Gardens, Cleethorpes with an account of the improvements, etc. (1885)

Pearson, L.F., *The People's Palaces: the story of the Seaside Pleasure Buildings of 1870-1914* (1991)

Pimlott, J.A.R., *The Englishman's Holiday* (1947, 1976)

Powell, G.D., *A Leisure Park Feasibility Study* (Cleethorpes BC report, 1985)

Price, J.H., *The Tramways of Grimsby, Immingham and Cleethorpes* (n.d.)

Rigby, S.H., *Medieval Grimsby: growth and decline* (1993)

Robinson, D.N., *The Book of the Lincolnshire Seaside: the story of the coastline from the Humber to the Wash* (1981)

Robinson, D.N., 'The Changing Coastline' in D.R. Mills (ed.), *Twentieth Century Lincolnshire* (1989)

Russell, E. and R.C., *Landscape Changes in South Humberside: the enclosure of thirty-seven parishes* (1982)

Shannon, I., 'Cleethorpes: a Special Survey' in *Lincolnshire Life*, February/March 1965, pp.31-9

Smith, M., *Blitz on Grimsby* (1983)

Smith, M. (ed.), *The Letters of Charlotte Bronte: with a selection of letters by family and friends* Vol. 1, 1829-1847 (1995)

Tennyson, C. and Dyson, H., *The Tennysons: background to genius* (1974)

Thorneycroft, C.M., 'The 3rd Battalion (Militia) The Manchester Regiment: its origin and services with special reference to its work during the Great War 1914-1918' (Typescript, n.d.) (Tameside Local Studies Library and Archives, MR1/3/1/25)

Triggs, L., Hepton D. and Woodhead, S., *Grimsby Town: a complete record, 1878-1989* (1989)

Walton, J.K., *The English Seaside Resort: a social history 1750-1914* (1983)

Walton, J.K., *The British Seaside: holidays and resorts in the twentieth century* (2000)

Ward's Cleethorpes Guide (1900)

White, P.R., 'Roads Replace Railways' in D.R. Mills (ed.), *Twentieth Century Lincolnshire* (1989)

White, W., *Lincolnshire Directory* (1826)

White, W., *History, Gazetteer and Directory of Lincolnshire* (1856)

Index

References which relate to illustrations only are given in **bold**.